Tenryū-ji

天龍寺

Tenryū-ji

LIFE AND SPIRIT
OF A KYŌTO GARDEN

Norris Brock Johnson

Stone Bridge Press · *Berkeley, California*

Published by
Stone Bridge Press
P.O. Box 8208
Berkeley, CA 94707
TEL 510-524-8732 · sbp@stonebridge.com · www.stonebridge.com

Cover and text design by Linda Ronan.

Photographs by the author unless otherwise indicated. Copyright notices accompany their respective images. Image credits and permissions appear after the Index.

First edition 2012.

Printed in the United States of America.

2017 2016 2015 2014 2013 2012   1 2 3 4 5 6 7 8 9 10

LIBRARY OF CONGRESS CATALOGING-IN-PUBLICATION DATA
Johnson, Norris Brock.
  Tenryuji: life and spirit of a Kyoto garden / Norris Brock Johnson.—1st ed.
     p. cm.
  Includes bibliographical references and index.
   ISBN 978-1-61172-004-4.
   1. Tenryuji (Kyoto, Japan) 2. Zen temples—Japan—Kyoto. 3. Gardens,
Japanese—Japan—Kyoto. 4. Gardens, Japanese—Zen influences. 5. Church
gardens—Japan—Kyoto. I. Title. II. Title: Life and spirit of a Kyoto garden.
  SB458.J64 2012
  712.0952'1864—dc23
                                    2011044825

For my ancestors

Beatrice Brock, 1892–1957
Richard Lawrence Johnson, 1948–86
Alfreda Belle Johnson, 1910–95
Rufus Norris Johnson, 1902–99

CONTENTS

Tenryū-ji

FIGURE 1. *The principal islands of Japan.*

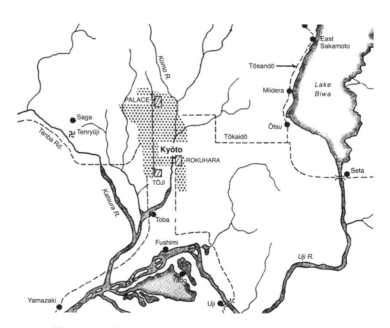

FIGURE 2. *Tenryū-ji and Saga, to the west of central Kyōto.*

THE POND IN THE GARDEN

Myriad stones appear to float on water softened by a shimmering late afternoon haze, caressing the pond. The garden is a mosaic of water and stones, foliage and sky, experienced as . . . tranquillity.

The pond in the garden before us appears sheltered by the deep roof eaves of the temple building within which we will envision ourselves sitting. We sit on *tatami* covering the expansive floor of the Quarters of the Abbot of the Temple, until recently the traditional residence of successive abbots of the temple. *Shōji* have been pulled back along tracks in the floor, opening the rear wall of this large room to the garden. Sitting quietly, we look across the veranda of the Abbot's Quarters to contemplate the pond in the garden of the Temple of the Heavenly Dragon (天龍寺, Tenryū-ji; figs. 3, 4).

This book is a contemplative study of the Temple of the Heavenly Dragon, Tenryū-ji, a Buddhist temple nestled within the mountains of western Kyōto, Japan.[1] Tenryū-ji is the main temple of the Tenryū school of Rinzai Zen Buddhism, and the temple participated in significant historical events in Japan. The temple reminds us that landscape and building architecture were a vital presence in events significant to the history of Japan. We will witness the temple emerge across generations through its designed interrelationship of buildings, nature, human-created landscapes, and the participation of people as well as belief in the participatory presence of deities and venerated ancestors. The temple across generations will stimulate the thoughts and ideas, values, and behaviors of people. Sustained attention to Tenryū-ji reveals the manner in which a distinctive human-created space and place, the temple complex,

FIGURE 3. When experienced from within the rear room of the Abbot's Quarters, the pond in the garden appears as a three-dimensional picture framed by roof eaves, projecting rafters, and the expansive veranda.

FIGURE 4. The west/northwest area of the pond, viewed from within the central rear room of the Abbot's Quarters.

conditioned in people distinct ways of conceptualizing as well as being in the world.

The heart of this book is the pond garden aspect of the temple, as "the design of the garden came to have both pictorial and historical importance, attracting people to Tenryū-ji and impressing them."[2] The venerated pond garden participated in the genesis of several defining moments in pre-modern Japan. Quite apart from conventional conceptions of garden as epiphenomenal to other aspects of human life deemed vital such as, say, political economy, sustained study of the pond garden aspect of Tenryū-ji reveals the manner in which gardens have had an abiding effect on our imaginations as well as a determinative effect on human history.

Shimmering Garments of Silence

By way of introduction, let us walk through the complex to the pond in the garden. Passing under a front entrance gate to the temple, noise is muted quite suddenly. The sensation is that we have passed through a gossamer shroud, imperceptibly closing behind us to drape the temple from the world outside the gates. Sounds outside the entrance gate further are silenced the deeper we move into the temple (figs. 5–10).

Intricately knit footpaths of stone lead us deeper into the complex. In the distance, we see the upper portions and roof of the building presently serving as the public entrance to the pond garden. In the thirteenth century, an early version of this building (*Kuri*) housed kitchen and storage areas; presently, the building primarily houses administrative offices and serves as a public reception area for the temple. The facade of the present-day reception building is a contrast of white stucco walls laced crisply by dark timber framing, embraced by the deep green of surrounding trees of maple and pine.

The avenue between the entrance gate and the reception building, along which people walk to the central area of the temple, is lined with coniferous and deciduous trees. Glancing upward while

FIGURE 5. *A map and aerial view of the present-day central area of the complex. Main entrances into the complex are to the east (toward the lower-center of the photograph). At present, public visitors to the temple use the entrance to the right of the center axis and approach the pond garden by walking around the southern (left) side of the Abbot's Quarters.*

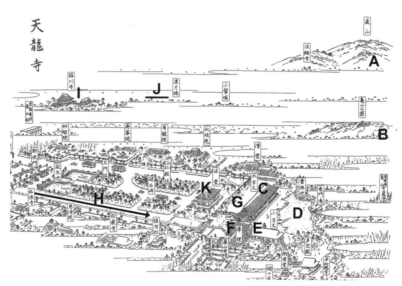

FIGURE 6. *The main buildings and features of nature making up the present-day principal aspects of the complex: (A) Mountain of Storms (Arashiyama); (B) Turtle Mountain (Kameyama); (C) Abbot's Quarters (Dai Hōjō); (D) the pond (Sōgenchi); (E) Guest Quarters (Ko Hōjō); (F) present-day reception building (Kuri); (G) sand garden (karesansui); (H) present-day entrance route, pointing west; (I) Rinsen-ji; (J) present-day location of the Moon-Crossing Bridge; (K) Lecture Hall (Hattō).*

walking within several areas here, we experience the billowing foliage of green under which we pass as a floral nest of sky. We move ever deeper, more intimately, into the verdant silence of the temple.

Through subtlety of architectural design, we experience the landscape aspect of the temple as a sequence of gradually unfolding vistas. The sensate experience is that the landscape aspect of the temple is an exquisite three-dimensional painting, through which we move. The experience is akin to the manner in which we experience a hand-scrolled painting of a landscape, an *emakimono* (絵巻物, picture scroll). *Emakimono* influenced the design of gardens, during the eleventh to thirteenth centuries in particular. *Emakimono*, such as the important *Genji Monogatari Emaki* (*Illustrated Tale of Genji*), combine both characters and images painted on paper or silk, ranging nine to twelve meters in length, furled at the left-end onto a dowel rod. *Emakimono* were experienced by unfurling text and image such that landscapes and commentary flowed scene-by-scene between one's hands. The landscape of an *emakimono* is not experienced all at once; similarly, the landscape aspect of the temple is not experienced all at once. Gates, foliage, and building architecture by design focus awareness on each area through which we pass. By design one is prompted, nonverbally, to pause briefly within defined areas of the temple so as to experience the landscape as though there is nothing else to the temple except this place and this space. This moment. And then . . . we move on.

The walkway opens to broad steps in front of the reception building entrance to the pond garden. Climbing the stone steps, then pausing to glance back along the tree-lined pathway, the world outside the front gates of the temple now cannot be seen or heard. Silence shimmers in the air and hangs in folds, a garment worn by the temple itself (figs. 11–13).[3]

We pass through the reception building, and enter areas preparatory to experience of the pond garden. Now, the walkway under our feet is pebbled stones shifting slightly under our weight, cushioning

FIGURE 7. *The present-day main public entrance to the temple.*

FIGURE 8. *This secondary gateway provides a quiet entrance into the temple, an alternative to the busy entrance near the bus stop (fig. 7). Maps of the complex name early versions of this entrance* Honmon (本門, *Origin Gate; Gate-to-Enlightenment*).

FIGURE 9. *Upon entering the complex, one passes over a bridge-covered stream. The avenue leads from the front gates to the central area of the complex, with the dramatic façade of the present-day reception building in the distance.*

FIGURE 10. *From this vantage the reception building appears embraced within a nest of trees, emphasizing the manner in which nature by design still is experienced as a constituent aspect of the temple.*

FIGURE 11. The approach to and front area of the reception building, through which one passes to experience the pond garden.

our footfalls. A rectangular expanse of gravel (枯山水, *karesansui*, dry-landscape garden) lies to the left of the footpath.[4] The design of the landscape guides our movements, pace, and direction, as the walkway winds around and to the rear of the Abbot's Quarters (figs. 14–16).

The Quarters of the Abbot of the Temple (*Dai Hōjō*) is a magnificent building, elegant in varied hues of aged wood (figs. 16, 26, 29). The deep, sloping eaves of the roof are a haven for shadows and birds that occasionally fly, chirping, through and about the building.

The lines of the footpath and the lines of the Abbot's Quarters visually converge in the distance, pointing our way to the present-day central area of the temple.

Myriad clusters of trees frame the rear of the Abbot's Quarters. Visually, it appears that we will walk into the wooded area ahead but, at its end, the footpath abruptly turns to the right. And, as if

FIGURE 12. *This dramatic arrangement of stones in front of the reception building is intended to evoke the mythic mountain of Meru (figs. 75, 76).*

FIGURE 13. *The roof to the left shelters the east-facing front veranda of the Abbot's Quarters. There are two types of garden within the present-day temple complex. The rectangular bed of gravel and sand (karesansui), to the right, is a recent addition to the temple. In a complementary fashion, this garden bed of gravel and sand was sited on the front eastern-side of the Abbot's Quarters while the rear western-side of the Abbot's Quarters faces the pond garden.*

unfolding into existence upon our approach, the pond in the garden appears quite suddenly before us (figs. 17–21).

An oasis. An initial impression, feeling, about the pond is of an oasis. Stones of varied size and shape are strewn about in the water of the expansive pond, each and every stone long ago having been placed by hand. Large and small, dark as well as light in color, jagged as well as smooth of form and texture, the very presence of the aged stones compels attention. The more one sustains awareness of and contemplates the garden pond, the more one becomes aware of an intricacy of design and complexity of arrangement with respect to the stones in the water (figs. 22–24).

Water shimmers under expansive stands of trees, defining the far shoreline across the pond. The trees lead our eyes upward, directing our awareness to panoramic vistas of mountain and sky.

Visual awareness is complemented by faint sounds stimulating aural awareness of the pond garden:

"Plop"   "Plop"   "Plop"

Myriad fish, *koi*, on the pond's surface leap up briefly into air and sunlight then flip downward into the water (fig. 25). One becomes aware of stillness, and one's breathing.

For many people, as we will see, the experience of the pond garden aspect of the temple continues to impart feelings of renewal (心が洗われた気持ち, *kokoro ga arawareta kimochi*)—emotionally, physically, and spiritually.

Wafting gently through the trees, the wind is the scent of life.

The Life of a Garden

Organized into three parts, this book presents the origin, defining life experiences, and salient present-day aspects of an influential temple and its celebrated pond garden. Earth and stone, water, and human activity (as well as belief in the agency of deities and venerated

FIGURE 14. *The front eastern-side of the Abbot's Quarters. The temple Dharma Drum* (Hokku), *the white circle to the right-side end of the veranda, is sounded as a call for monks to assemble.*

FIGURE 15. *With* shōji *pulled back along their tracks in the floor, glimpses of the pond can be experienced through the Abbot's Quarters as one walks to the western garden.*

ancestors) came together over time in fashioning a still vibrant landscape that continues to touch the feelings, and hearts, of people.

Consider the manner in which contemplative experiences of the pond garden touched Tsutomu Minakami, an award-winning writer who was a priest within the temple during the 1930s. Since 1345, Tenryū-ji has served as a residential arena for the training of priests. Priest Minakami wrote, "When I was young, the shadows of many people did not fall within the temple. There were only mendicant wicker-hatted priests coming into and going out of the temple. As a young priest, I had opportunity to see many gardens in Zen temples but in the Tenryū-ji garden stones, trees, and water are placed in a perfect harmony 〖和, *wa*〗, still alive after hundreds of years."[5]

Priest Minakami personified the garden, and he related animistically to the garden as he would relate to a person. The concept of animism will be of ongoing importance to our study of the temple pond garden. Here, "animists are people who recognize that the world is full of persons, only some of whom are human, and that life is always lived in relationship with others."[6] Conceptualizing animism as a sympathetic relationship rescues a vital existential theory of being from prior dismissals as "primitive mentality." *Anima*, the Breath of Life, is synonymous with spirit as a vital aspect of life; as such, animism challenges conceptions of phenomena labeled "nonanimate." Life lived in relationship with others includes others that perhaps are stones or ancestors or spirit.

As we attend to the pond garden aspect of the Temple of the Heavenly Dragon, animism will be manifest in the manners in which the garden over time is perceived and experienced by people as vital and affecting as well as, importantly, in the interdependent person-to-person manner in which people behave toward the garden and aspects of nature held to be sacred. Priest Minakami, for instance, experienced the garden "in a knowing manner, as hundreds of thoughts appear and disappear; only the garden, the quiet garden, is left before me. The garden remains there, silently."[7] Priest Minakami experienced what we might term the soul (魂, *tamashii*) of the complex, in that "the temple was so quiet, and refreshing. The tranquillity of the Dai Hōjō in the pine trees, and the path paved with stones . . . turning into *something more* than just a view of the garden [my italics]."[8] Something more. Throughout its tumultuous existence, as we will see, the pond garden aspect of the temple was and continues to be experienced animistically by people as vital spirit (精霊, *seirei*)—the "something more," I feel, of which Priest Minakami wrote.[9]

Part I reconstructs the early settlement activity on the land on which the present-day temple buildings and pond garden rest. Tenryū-ji proper was constructed from 1340 to 1345, though the area west of Kyōto within which the temple emerged was the site of what we would term religious (Shintō, principally) activity as early as the tenth century.

Chapters composing Part I recount the manner in which salient events and people of influence defined the character of the region within which the temple and pond garden came into being. In turn, the mountainous region west of Kyōto exercised considerable influence on the character of twelfth- and thirteenth-century Japan. Part

FIGURE 16. *The front eastern-side of the Abbot's Quarters.*

FIGURE 17. *People customarily move rather quietly toward the pond in the garden.*

I is the compelling account of the birth and early life of a landscape continuing as "a powerful domain which includes felt values, dreams . . . and events, to which affect has accrued."[10] In addition to matters of design and construction, emotion also is a vital aspect of the origin and life of landscapes. Compassion and love, as well as fear and guilt, specifically, generated influential activity and historically important events that participated in the genesis of the landscape aspect of the temple.

Part II presents core features of the pond garden aspect of the Temple of the Heavenly Dragon from present-day points of view. Chapters composing Part II are framed by my ongoing experiences with, and interpretations of, the pond garden as well as by a priest with whom I studied while staying periodically within the temple. While teaching at Waseda University and the University of Tōkyō, Komaba, I first came upon Tenryū-ji quite unexpectedly late one spring afternoon in 1985 while exploring the forested regions west of Kyōto. I only had sought to find refreshment within the temple, tea and rice cakes perhaps, and to rest from the day's sojourn.

Initial experiences of the pond garden were deeply affecting for me and I continued to revisit the temple, initially among throngs of visitors (figs. 7, 17). Young couples often entered the temple to stroll hand-in-hand through the park-like wooded upper areas of the complex. School buses, shiny in reflecting midmorning sunlight, would line up in rows in the larger parking area. Quiet and orderly in crisp uniforms, young schoolchildren would file from the buses. Teachers carried poles flying the banner and logo of each school. Students would line up behind the banners then begin their study-excursion through the temple. The pond garden and temple buildings are important historically, as we will see, and are a planned educational experience for many schoolchildren. Many afternoons women, mostly, and a few men would enter the temple to consult with priests, to pray, to copy then recite *sūtra* attributed to Buddha, or to sip green tea (*matcha*) while sitting quietly on the veranda of the Abbot's Quarters overlooking the pond in the garden.

FIGURE 18. *A glimpse of the pond and a view toward the south/southwest, from in front of the rear of the Abbot's Quarters.*

FIGURE 19. *The pond in the garden. The view is toward the south/southwest.*

FIGURE 20. The pond in the garden. The view is toward the west with the piedmont of Turtle Mountain, blanketed with trees, as background.

FIGURE 21. The pond in the garden. The view is toward the northwest.

FIGURE 22. Moss and foliage contribute an organic quality to aged stones, stones appearing to rest on the water of the pond. The faint line of a spider's web reveals a subtle, unintended though engaging manner in which several stones in the pond are interlinked.

FIGURE 23. Variegated light and shadow delineate the faceted intricacies of stones in the pond.

My explorations of the temple complex grew more prolonged and intense and, at dusk, as the front gates were closing, monks often had to usher me up and out from sitting before the garden. One morning, I asked the (exclusively Japanese-speaking, at the time) staff if there was anyone who could tell me about the pond garden in particular, with whom I would be permitted to speak. I was introduced to a senior priest known for his knowledge of the pond garden. After a time, "the priest" (as I will refer to him) began to tutor me into "seeing" the life and ways of the landscape by encouraging my prolonged sitting before the pond so as to let the garden reveal itself to me.[11] I was given access to temple documents for study and I began researching, collecting and translating, and interpreting the few extant articles on the pond garden principally gathered at the libraries at Waseda and the University of Tōkyō. Subsequently permitted to move about the grounds, often alone, after visitors had left, I began to draw maps and photographically document the temple and specific features of the pond garden.

Thus I began ongoing experiences with, and intensive study of, the temple and pond garden, research and writing that continued over the next several decades. I began to devote successive years to learning that which the temple buildings and pond garden continued to demand of me. In attempting to "capture" the temple buildings and pond garden with photographic images and written words, friends in Japan often said I did not notice that the pond garden had "captured my heart."

When in Japan I returned regularly to the pond garden, as if to a touchstone. Away from Japan, I remained mindful of and continued to feel the presence, the quietude and serenity, of the pond garden. When in Kyōto I was permitted to stay within the temple periodically where, on a futon on a floor of the Guest Quarters, in the early haze of morning, "in dreams I drift on, waking at the feet of the great stones" in the pond garden.[12] Arising, I would meet with the priest as he sat and shared with me his vision of and experiences with the pond garden.

FIGURE 24. Stones in the pond, peaking above-water, were set carefully, braced by myriad below water-level stabilizing stones.

FIGURE 25. Koi, *sunning in the warm upper waters of the pond.*

While staying within the temple, I often recalled that the garden scholar Kinsaku Nakane also embraced a firsthand lived-experience method of researching temple gardens. Professor Nakane, for instance, "found a house nearby and visited that garden [Kokedera, the "moss garden," within Saihō-ji, the Temple of the Western Fragrance] every day for over a year. Thus even now I know it down to the smallest rocks. If one really throws oneself into it, with much effort the garden's essence suddenly becomes clear. It is essential to devote oneself in this way."[13] Like Nakane-san , over the years I found that the temple pond garden indeed did begin to reveal its life and spirit to me . . . through a relationship of intimate, devoted, and prolonged direct experience.

Chapters in Part II interpret in detail seven especially significant aspects of the garden highlighted by the priest—stones, compositions of stone, as well as the pond itself. The temple landscape and aspects of the present-day pond garden are envisioned by the priest principally as manifestations of the Buddha-Nature (仏所, *Bussho*) of the still-venerated priest Musō Soseki (1275–1351). Soseki was the first abbot of the temple, and, despite scholarly controversy, the priest with whom I studied argued firmly that Soseki "made" the pond garden. Part II looks at associations made by the priest between selected aspects of the pond garden and Rinzai Zen Buddhist states of awareness (見性, *kenshō*, and 悟り, *satori*, in particular).

Part III elaborates upon the pond garden aspect of the Temple of the Heavenly Dragon as a considerable contribution to our understanding of the very idea of "garden." The gardens of Japan continue to capture the attention, stimulate the feelings, and touch the hearts of people not only in Japan but throughout the world. In 1994 the United Nations Educational, Scientific, and Cultural Organization (UNESCO) designated the pond garden aspect of Tenryū-ji a World Heritage Site, "internationally recognized as a place of exceptional and universal value; a cultural-heritage site worthy of preservation for the benefit of mankind."

It is as if the pond garden asks . . . "Why is the making of gardens, as well as our emotional experiences within gardens, a perennial human activity? Why are gardens so prominent in the human imagination, especially our religious imagination? In particular, why is experience of the temple gardens of Japan, for innumerable people from a variety of cultures, so charged with . . . sacredness (神聖, *shinsei*)?" In Mirei Shigemori's translation of and commentary on *The Book of Garden (Sakuteiki)*, he declares, "we do not yet understand the true meaning of garden making . . . I raise a question for everyone to help in addressing it."[14] Part III of this book is my anthropological response to Shigemori's call for investigations into the idea of garden.

Part III concludes that the landscape aspect of the Temple of the Heavenly Dragon embodies and preserves materially a primordial conception of garden, a conception of a garden centered around stones rather than foliage. Mirroring our walk to the pond garden aspect of the temple, we conclude our contemplative experience of Tenryū-ji by continuing *through* the pond garden, conceptually, to venture deep into prehistory to experience primordial conceptions of garden in the Sumerian accounts of the Garden of Inanna and the Garden of the Sun experienced by Gilgamesh. In the Sumerian literature, we find that a primordial conception of "garden" as a garden of stones antedates our conventional conception of "garden" as foliage.

The landscape aspect of the Temple of the Heavenly Dragon, a garden privileging stones, materially preserves an archetypal conception of garden as the animistic embodiment of spirit, deities, and venerated ancestors within which people participate. The primordial idea of garden is what we now would term a sacred space or place.

Acknowledgments

Research for this book was conducted in the New Territories of Hong Kong, in southeastern China, as well as in Japan. I remain indebted to the Japan–United States Educational Commission and the Fulbright Office in Tōkyō.

When in Kyōto I was invited to live in the home of Mr. and Mrs. Kenya Takeichi, in Uji, south of the city. I am indebted to the Takeichi family, who cared for me as family. Dr. Nobou Eguchi, Professor of Anthropology at Ritsumeikan University, also invited me to stay with him and his family in Kyōto. I am grateful for my friend, priest Takanobu Kogawa, then at Daikaku-ji, who, among other research assistance, secured for me permission to access and study first-hand several influential gardens in Buddhist temples whose gates at the time were closed to the public over an ongoing taxation dispute with the city of Kyōto. I always will treasure the collegial friendship shown to me by Professor Teiji Itoh, Department of Architecture at Kōgakuin University in Tōkyō, who devoted considerable energy and time helping me with my then-budding project on Tenryū-ji. For their collegiality and friendship, I also thank Professor Akio Hayashi of Waseda University and Professors Nagayo Homma and Iwao Matsuzaki at the University of Tōkyō. David A. Slawson provided valuable critical commentary early on in my research. Ms. Kei Nagami, Mr. Tatsuya Nakagawa, and Ms. Rumi Yasutake aided me in gathering and translating, along with Mrs. Makiko Humphreys, many of the historical materials on which this book is based. Mrs. Mitsuko Endo,

FIGURE 26. *The Abbot's Quarters* (Dai Hōjō), *to the right, is the larger wing of the central building complex. The smaller wing of the interlinked buildings, to the left, presently serves as Guest Quarters* (Ko Hōjō).

Mrs. Akiko Nomiya, and Professor Daishiro Nomiya are friends dear to me who aided in the translation of difficult source materials, older *kyūjitai* (旧字体, old character form) especially. I alone am responsible for any errors in this book.

Grants from the Japan Center, North Carolina State University and from the Northeast Asia Council of the Association of Asian Studies sustained my research. At the University of North Carolina at Chapel Hill, a Z. Smith Reynolds Award, several Faculty Fellowships, a Chapman Fellowship from the Institute for the Arts and Humanities, and several research grants from the University Research Council supported work on early manuscripts of this book. A fellowship year in residence at Dumbarton Oaks, Washington, D.C., enabled sustained work on completion of this book. I thank Dr. John Dixon Hunt, then Director of Studies in Landscape Architecture at Dumbarton Oaks, for our many conversations on gardens, art, and landscape architecture. Dr. Michel Conan, subse-quent Director of Studies in Landscape Architecture at Dumbarton Oaks, carefully read and offered invaluable insights on the final manuscript of this book. I remain thankful to Keir Davidson, for his fine-grained critical reading of and gracious comments on the final manuscript.

I remain deeply appreciative of my always-welcoming home in the woods, which has provided over thirty years of shelter, respite, and nourishment of body, soul, and spirit as well as a con-stant stimulus for work. Apart from the aforementioned places, all of the work on this book took place at home amid windows filled with soothing vistas of myriad tree leaves of oak and cedar and pine and, at night, luminous sheets of moonlight filtering through the windows, often literally touching my writing. The house and land always require manual labor, fortunately—the physical work, for instance, of designing and planning home repair and renovation projects; working the land; pruning trees . . . and moving rocks and stones. The house and land participated greatly in the writing of this book by demanding, then reinforcing attention to the exquisite microcosm of myriad details of the part-to-part and part-to-whole interdependent relationships comprising the construction processes. Whether working with board or word, the house and land pro-vided a setting and ongoing opportunities for the direct physical experiences of coupling ideas and feelings with materiality.[15] Physi-cal work/effort also is an important aspect of Zen Buddhism, as we will see.

Completion of this book would not have been possible without the encouragement and support of Dr. T. Elaine Prewitt, Ms. Stepha-nie Parrish Taylor, and Reverend William J. Vance. I am grateful to Peter Goodman and the staff at Stone Bridge Press for their sustained attention to and enormous energy involved in the myriad details of preparing the mauscript and images for publication.

This book exists because of the support of many people at Tenryū temple, notably the priest with whom I studied.

ʔ

Tenryū-ji: Life and Spirit of a Kyōto Garden has been composed to engender in the reader a vicarious, felt-experience of a venerated Buddhist temple and pond garden. The temple and pond garden we will experience are not inscrutable, as "the world of affect is common to all people . . . anyone from any culture is bound to experience a basic substratum of rapport with the affecting presence of any culture."[16] Marcel Proust once declared, "I believe each of us has charge of the souls that he particularly loves, has charge of making them known, and loved."[17] The pond garden in the temple continues to affect my life and spirit. I am privileged to have participated in the life and spirit of the temple and in making the pond garden better known and loved through the words and images of this book.[18] Throughout its genesis and tumultuous life history, the pond garden within the Temple of the Heavenly Dragon always has touched a variety of people from a variety of cultures directly, as Rinzai Zen Buddhists would put it, through one's heart (心, *kokoro*).

NORRIS BROCK JOHNSON
Chapel Hill, North Carolina
Season of the Redbuds Blooming (March), 2012

I Land, Landscape, and the Spirit of Place

Even after decades,

if someone digs in the ruins . . .

human bones'll

still come out,

won't they?

YŌKO ŌTA

"Residues of Squalor"[1]

The Temple of the Heavenly Dragon was sited to the west of Kyōto, and is embraced by the three influential prominences:

the Mountain of Storms (*Arashiyama*)
the Mountain of Dusk and Shadow (*Ogurayama*)
Turtle Mountain (*Kameyama*)

The mountainous region west of Kyōto was altered by people numerous times, neglected, abandoned for centuries, only to be subsequently reinhabited and renewed. The land itself remained compelling and continued to capture the transgenerational attention and imaginations of people. The temple came into being within this particular region in large measure because the land on which the buildings and the pond garden presently rest had long been experienced as deeply affecting, emotionally, aethetically, and spiritually (figs. 2, 5, 30).

During our walk through the present-day complex to the pond garden, we experienced salient aspects of nature from which the landscape aspect of the temple was formed: water, stones and rocks, trees and foliage, and the land itself, especially mountains (figs. 27–29). These aspects of nature were not selected as vital features of the landscape aspect of the temple by any one person exclusively, nor all at one time, but selected at various times by people influential enough to define a landscape.[2]

The human-created landscape aspects of the present-day temple were assembled over time. Successive occupants of the region west of Kyōto, for instance, added large-scale waterways and ponds to the landscape within which the temple emerged (the evocative stones placed in and around the present-day pond in the garden, the subject of Part II, are a comparatively recent addition to the landscape of the temple).

Three people of influence in early Japan began to alter aspects of the mountainous area west of Kyōto for their individual purposes. In time, buildings began to appear as aspects of the landscape. In

FIGURE 27. *An expansive view of mountains to the south/southwest.*

FIGURE 28. *The roofs of buildings within the Temple of the Heavenly Dragon nestle within a sea of trees.*

FIGURE 29. *The pond garden customarily is experienced by people from the veranda of the rear western-side of the Abbot's Quarters . . . and "the temple building, with its beautiful roof and delicate railing, seems to grow from its own reflection."*[f29]

the historical overview to follow we will consider the cumulative landscape-defining influences of Tachibana no Kachiko (786–850, Empress Danrin, consort of Emperor Saga, 785–842), Prince Kaneakira (914–87, the eleventh son of Emperor Daigo, 885–930), and Emperor Go-Saga (1220–72).[3]

The landscape aspect of the Temple of the Heavenly Dragon was fashioned over time from the interdependent relationship of people and nature as well as from belief in the intervention of deities and venerated ancestors in the landscape-making affairs of people.

I

MOUNTAINS, WATER, AND FRAGRANT TREES

Prior to the seventh century, it had been the custom to abandon the court of an emperor or empress after their death, as each site was then considered polluted. New sites, purified places, were prepared for each successive emperor or empress. Imperial courts grew in size, and relocations increasingly became cumbersome; in time, imperial coursts became semipermanent, then permanent.

In 710, during the reign of Empress Genmyō (Genmei, 660–721), Nara (Heijō-kyō, Capital of the Peaceful Citadel) became an influential capital city for imperial courts. Rather than defer to concerns over death and pollution, selection of the site for the Capital of the Peaceful Citadel in large part was based on then-favorable aspects of the surrounding area, in particular, the sensory delights afforded to people of privilege through aesthetic experiences of the Yamato Plain.

Nara (Level Land), though, increasingly became subject to periodic flooding as the imperial city had been sited near the Saho and Tomio rivers. Aesthetic enjoyment of the area around Nara did not offset the growing belief that the land itself was failing to influence the well-being of emperors, the city, and its people.

Virtue and the Breath of Life

Changing conceptions of and attitudes toward the land and landscape around Nara influenced temporary relocation of the imperial capital, in 784, to Nagaoka. In 794, Emperor Kanmu (737–806) ordered the imperial capital moved from Nara to a new site that became known as the Capital of Peace and Tranquillity (Kyōto).

The land on which Kyōto was sited had been donated to Emperor Kanmu by the Hata family, wealthy descendants of immigrants from Korea. Kyōto was believed to be free of the malevolent influences causing undesirable environmental changes within areas in and around Nara. At this time, nature (自然, *shizen*) was believed to embody animistic qualities demonstrably affecting people—land and human-created landscapes were auspicious, or not, and favorably influenced well-being, or not. People of influence felt that the site and topography of Nara were not balancing wind and water, but increasingly favored water. They believed that the area north of Nara better balanced wind and water.[1]

Principles and practices for enhancing aspects of nature deemed beneficent were known as Storing Wind/Acquiring Water (蔵風得水, *zōfū tokushi*), which coexisted with imported Chinese *feng shui* principles and practices of Wind/Water.[2]

Feng shui animistically conceived of the earth as an organic body laced with arterial veins through which the Breath of Life (*qi*; 気, *ki* in Japan) flowed. The Breath of Life flowed and circulated more intensely in some spaces and places more than in others. Well-being was enhanced through detecting intensive flows of the Breath of Life embodied as distinctive features of the land itself, then through fashioning habitats congruent with the flow of the Breath of Life. By the ninth century, the rudiments of *feng shui* were present in Japan; indeed, "the senior Ministry of State, the *Nakatsukasa*, included a special department, the *Onmyō-Ryō* (陰陽寮, *Bureau of Yin-Yang*), with a select staff of masters and doctors of divination and astrology."[3] The Chinese Southern Sung Dynasty (1127–1279) was a period of comparatively intense exchange between China and Japan, and "it was not until the rise of the Sung Dynasty that all the elements of *feng shui* gathered into one system."[4] During the later Southern Sung Dynasty, Buddhist priests from China studied in Japan and Buddhist priests from Japan studied in China. The Ajari, for instance, were Japanese Buddhist specialists in Chinese *yin yang* (陰陽, *in yō* in Japan).

Congruent with Chinese *feng shui*, Japanese *zōfū tokushi* emphasized the conjoining of aspects of nature and specific directions. South was considered a beneficent direction while north was the least propitious direction. East was associated with dragons and water while west was associated with tigers and mountains. In an ideal site for human habitation, enhancing well-being, "mountains come from behind, which is to say from the north, and end at this point [the site selected], overlooked a plain ahead. On the left and right, mountain ranges extend southward to protect the area; they are known as the 'undulations of the green dragon' and the 'deferential bowing of the white tiger.' To the south are spreading flatlands or low hills. As a rule, water from the mountains flows down through the area bounded by them. In short, there are mountains behind and a plain with flowing water in front. Such a location is suitable for *zōfū tokushi* conditions."[5] Selection of the site on which Kyōto was constructed acknowledged the influence of nature on the well-being of people, in particular the influence of a favorable balancing of mountains and water.

Favorably open toward the south, Kyōto was laid out on a plain between auspicious aspects of nature to the north, east, and west.[6] With protecting hills and mountains to the north, east, and west, Kyōto was sited within a beneficent space between tiger (west) and the dragon (east) mountains.

Kyōto was sited with respect to the Katsura River and the Kamo River, both of which flowed auspiciously toward the south into low-lying basins fed by numerous springs flowing down from surrounding mountains. Interestingly, "the mountains surrounding the City

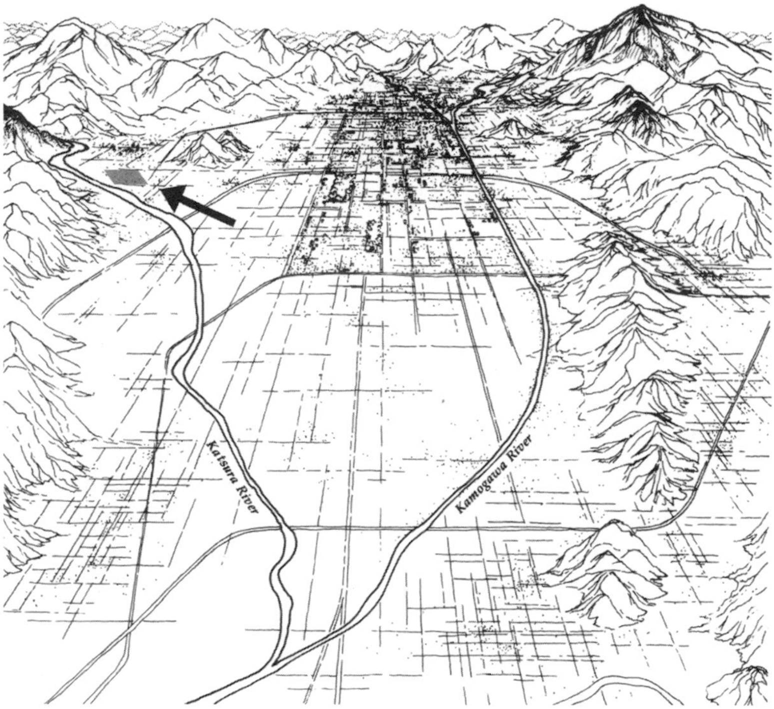

FIGURE 30. *The city of Kyōto was sited within a basin surrounded, and bal-anced, by (tiger) mountains to the weśt and (dragon) mountains to the eaśt. Tenryū-ji (toward where the arrow is pointing), a dragon presence, subse-quently was sited within, and balanced by, the tiger-mountains to the weśt of the city.*

of Purple Mountains and Cryśtal Streams [[Kyōto]] were considered 'male [[in]],' and . . . along the foot of the eaśtern hills flowed the Kamo River, which curved around at the south, again as topographical tra-dition demanded; the Katsura River to the weśt of the city provided the second of the two essential 'female [[yō]]' elements."[7] Kyōto was auspiciously sited within a low-lying basin surrounded on three sides by mountains with the fourth side, the south side, open to the flow-ing waters of rivers, a siting believed to enhance the well-being of the city and its inhabitants (figs. 2, 30).

Kyōto also was known as the City of Purple Hills and Cryśtal

Streams (山紫水明, *Sanshi Suimei*, Place of Great Natural Beauty). This poetic name signified the manner in which the new imperial capital interwove the city proper with aspects of nature, in particular mountains and water. "The capital [Kyōto] itself was situated in beautiful country, encircled on three sides by thickly forested hills and mountains, often delicately wreathed with trails of mist; in the autumn evenings one could hear the deer's cry in the distance, and the desolate call of the wild geese overhead; the landscape abounded in streams and waterfalls and lakes; and into its green slopes and valleys the countless shrines and monasteries blended as if they too had become a part of nature."[8] Here, a human-created landscape was experienced as an intimate aspect of nature, similar to a forthcoming chapter's narratives on people's early experiences of the landscape of the Temple of the Heavenly Dragon as nature.[9] In the section "Revealing the Nature of Buddha-Nature," for instance, we will see that in the fourteeenth century the landscape of the temple included features such as a Dragon-Gate Pavilion, the fabled Moon-Crossing Bridge, and a shrine evocatively renamed Buddha's Light of the World—architectured features placed in nature some distance from the central areas of the temple.

Wind circulates the Breath of Life. Water embraces the Breath of Life. "The *ch'i*, the cosmic breaths which constitute the virtue of a site, are blown about by the wind and held by the waters."[10] A circulating balance of wind and water was believed not only to be auspicious, beneficent, but to be virtuous as well.

The Temple of the Heavenly Dragon, much later, will be sited within a balanced, auspicious confluence of low-lying bodies of water nestled within encircling mountains (fig. 5). Locating the temple amid mountains and water long associated with well-being by contagious contact was believed to enhance the moral character and mission of the complex. The temple was considered a repository of virtue, as we will see, an especially beneficent place for the living as well as for the deceased.

A Most Beautiful Meadow

After the capital had been relocated from Nara to Kyōto, a succession
of emperors and aristocrats began to find favor with Sagano (Saga), a
lush region within the mountains west of Kyōto, for the location of
compounds built as retreats from the city (fig. 2). Sagano was praised
as "the best meadow of all, no doubt because of its beauty as a landscape."[11] Ōigawa (the Abundant-Flowing River), merging with the
Katsura River, flowed through Sagano. The Mountain of Storms lay
to the west/southwest of the river while Turtle Mountain and the
plains of Sagano lay to the north/northeast of the river.

Emperors and aristocrats began to designate Sagano a protected
reserve for hunting, excursions, and retreats from Kyōto. Emperor
Saga, for instance, so loved Sagano that he took his name from that region. His love for the mountains and plains west of Kyōto later will be
shared by Go-Daigo (1288–1339), one of his descendants who will participate directly in the genesis of the Temple of the Heavenly Dragon.

The Sagano region of western Kyōto became important to practitioners of Shintō as well as to the early presence of Buddhism in Japan. In addition to the pleasure retreats of emperors and the nobility,
the human-created landscape in Sagano began to exhibit compounds
physically marking the presence of Buddhism and Shintō.

A Palace-in-the-Field

The *Tale of Genji* (*Genji Monogatari*), most likely written from about
1008 through 1021 by Lady Murasaki Shikibu (ca. 973–1025), provides an early glimpse of the region of Sagano. The *Tale of Genji* contains vivid descriptions of people and events associated with rites of
purification critical to the venerated Grand Shrine at Ise (present-day
Mie Prefecture, southeast of Kyōto).[12]

In the *Tale of Genji*, compounds termed "Palace-in-the-Field"
were built in Sagano as secluded settings for princesses, high priestesses, from the family of an emperor. Prior to representing an emperor

at Ise, a priestess was required to live for a year within a Palace-in-the-Field while undergoing rites of purification.[13] Priestesses were purified in the flowing waters of the Katsura River prior to being escorted to Ise.[14] After a priestess had been escorted to Ise, the compound associated with her purification was dismantled. A new compound was constructed each time a priestess was prepared to represent an emperor by living at Ise.

To our eyes, though, the word "palace" misdescribes the compounds built within Sagano. Consider the manner in which the *Tale of Genji* describes Prince Genji's approach to a Palace-in-the-Field: "They came at last," Lady Murasaki writes, "to a group of very temporary wooden huts surrounded by a flimsy brushwood fence. The archways, built of unstripped wood, stood solemnly against the sky. Within the enclosure a number of priests were walking up and down with a preoccupied air."[15] Prince Genji steals into the compound to secret a love note to Lady Rokujō, of the imperial court, whose daughter (Akikonomu) was being prepared to live within the Grand Shrine at Ise. The area described here was set apart, isolated spatially, and was entered through "archways" (鳥居, *torii*) still signaling spaces and places associated with Shintō.

Prince Genji, we read, then entered an enchanted garden within the Palace-in-the-Field. Having secreted his note to Lady Rokujo, Prince Genji lingers in contemplating how "the garden which surrounded her apartments was laid out in so enchanting a manner that the troops of young courtiers, who in the early days of the retreat had sought in vain to press their attentions upon her, used, even when she had sent them about their business, to linger there regretfully; and on this marvelous night the place seemed consciously to be deploying all its charm."[16] A striking aspect of this garden is its animistic quality and presence. The garden enchants, casts a spell, and the spell of the garden is so compelling as to force the gaze of courtiers away from the handsome Rokujō. As in William Shakespeare's *Midsummer Night's Dream*, the enchantment of the garden weaves its spell most charmingly at night, in moonlight (fig. 125).

FIGURE 31. *Shrine buildings peek through dense groves of tall bamboo-grass, framing the walkway to the central area of the present-day Shrine-in-the-Field (Nonomiya).*

At this time, a garden was a vital component of compounds such as the Palace-in-the-Field in Sagano. The word *niwa* (庭, garden) at the time defined a purified area into which *kami* (神) were invited, venerated, and/or housed. "Garden" was an animistic, spiritual concept as well as aesthetic landscape. The *Tale of Genji* brings Sagano to life as a region saturated with what we would recognize as religious belief and practice. To this day Sagano remains associated with purification, divinity, and spiritual renewal.

The present-day Shintō shrine of Nonomiya (Shrine-in-the-Field) is to the north and within sight of the Temple of the Heavenly Dragon. Nonomiya is descended from the Sagano compounds to which imperial princesses came to be purified (figs. 31, 32).

This contemporary version of the Shrine-in-the-Field often appears in the landscape of contemporary fiction. In *The Makioka*

Sisters, by Jūnichirō Tanizaki, we accompany a newly married couple
to the area around the Temple of the Heavenly Dragon where "a
chilly wind had come up by the time they passed the Nonomiya, the
Shrine-in-the-Field, where in ancient times court maidens retired for
purification before leaving to become Shrine Virgins at Ise."[17] Nonomiya still is considered an especially generative place to petition *kami*
for happy marriages, healthy children, and the like. Nonomiya is
swaddled in lush groves of bamboo and brushwood, similar to the
foliage surrounding the Palace-in-the-Field described within the *Tale
of Genji*. A winding path of gravel cushions the walk to the central
area of the shrine. The surrounding foliage through which one passes
is a tunnel of verdant green, punctuated by golden shafts of light.
Nonomiya is entered through and under *torii*. The shrine still retains
the seclusion and aura of sacredness of the Palace-in-the-Field in the
Tale of Genji.

The Empress and the Priest

In addition to Shintō, the Sagano region west of Kyōto was significant
to the early presence of Buddhism in Japan. In this regard, the present-
day temple of Danrin-ji (Forest Temple) is important historically.

In 836 Tachibana no Kachiko ordered the construction of a small
complex, initially a nunnery with about twelve subtemple buildings,
to be constructed within Sagano. She was keenly interested in the
Buddhism of China. She had sent an invitation to I-k'ung (Gikū Zenshi, as he came to be known in Japan), a Rinzai priest, asking him
to travel to Sagano to instruct her in Chinese Zen Buddhism. Gikū
Zenshi accepted her invitation, and the Forest Temple was built as a
residence and teaching arena for him. In 1191, 355 years later, Myōan
Eisai (Zenkō Kokushi, 1141–1215) would institutionalize the Rinzai
school of Zen Buddhism in Japan.

During the time of Tachibana no Kachiko, though, Chinese
Zen Buddhism was not widely received in Japan. Disillusioned, Gikū
Zenshi subsequently returned to China. The teachings, the way of

FIGURE 32. *The entrance into the central area of the present-day Shrine-in-the-Field (Nonomiya).*

life, of Gikū Zenshi nonetheless profoundly affected Tachibana no Kachiko. She shaved her head, and began living as a Buddhist priest.[18]

Buddhism was present in Japan during the time of Empress Genmyō and Lady Tachibana. The word "Shintō" (神道, Way of the *Kami*) had begun to appear around the seventh century, in large part to name indigenous belief distinct from the growing influence of Buddhism in Japan.

The historical Buddha was born Siddhārtha Gautama in 563 B.C. in Nepal. Siddhārtha ("He Whose Aim Is Accomplished") experienced existence-as-it-is (真如, *shinnyo*; *tathatā*, in Sanskrit), then

FIGURE 33. Sculpture of Siddhārtha Gautama (Shākyamuni). First century A.D., sandstone, Mathura, India. H: 23 cm.

chose to reveal the nature of existence (Dharma), to others. The belief is that "one who really knows truth, lives the life of truth, becomes the truth itself. This was realized in the person of Buddha (literally, "One Who is Enlightened about Ultimate Reality")."[19] Upon his awareness of the Truth of existence, Siddhārtha subsequently became known as Shākyamuni (the Sage of the Shākyas—Shākya being the name of his family of birth; fig. 33).

A principal concern of Buddhism is the suffering of people as well as the suffering of non-human life (Four Noble Truths). The belief continues to be that suffering in large part lives within conceptions of ego-consciousness-as-reality—the belief that "self" is a distinct, autonomous phenomenon. A Truth apprehended by Shākyamuni was that "self," ego-consciousness-as-reality, is an illusion giving life and power to suffering; one has an "Original Face"; every person already has Buddha-Nature, of which Shakyamuni became aware ("enlightenment") while sitting in meditation under the Bodhi tree. Awareness of the fundamental reality of Buddha-Nature is the experience of existence-as-it-is, "enduring, permanent, a secure shelter, unassailable bliss. It is the supreme Truth and Reality . . . a state of neither being nor non-being."[20] Awareness of Buddha-Nature is said to be clouded by fear, pain, desire, and other misery-inducing illusions of life. Upon relinquishment of ego-consciousness-as-reality, "one's ordinary personality is transcended and becomes an embodiment of Truth."[21] The

Truth experienced by Shākyamuni was a way to end, in this life, the cycle of birth and rebirth (*samsara*).

Buddhism arose amid the Vedic system of *varna* in India where low-caste and outcaste persons were considered closer to animals than to people. Shākyamuni on the other hand held that all beings, "animal" as well as "human," inherently possessed Buddha-Nature. "Whether he is tall, average or short . . . , whether he is black, brown, or yellow," a Truth experienced by Shākyamuni was that all persons in their life-times can experience an end to suffering.[22] Shākyamuni presented to people a Middle Way (Eight-Fold Path) between the asceticism he ex-perienced while living among forest and mountain-dwelling *yogi* in In-dia and the indulgences and excesses of daily life he experienced before leaving the gates of his father's extensive palace.

Gikū Zenshi presented Tachibana no Kachiko with a then fairly new practice of Buddhism. He taught her the Way of Zen (禅那, *Ze-nna*), from China.

Buddhism from India melded with the Daoism of China to form Zen Buddhism, which then passed to Japan. In the *Dao de Jing*, at-tributed to Laozi (ca. 500 B.C.), Daoism conceptualized nature as a Way, a way of Being, that humans ought to emulate. Daoists sought to live naturally, to be "supple and pliant like ice about to melt; genuine, like a piece of uncarved wood; open and broad, like a valley."[23] Na-ture thus was a vital aspect of the Zen practice of Buddhism passing from China to Japan.

Zen Buddhism held that experience of Buddha-Nature could occur suddenly in one's lifetime, as "the immediate expression and actualization of the perfection present in every person at every mo-ment."[24] Such awareness was not something for which one ought to strive, for "life is impermanent . . . Do not wait another moment to practice the Way. Strive not to fruitlessly pass this very moment."[25] Emphasis on the unfettered experience of existence-as-it-is meant that, from moment to moment, Zen Buddhism was "an absolutely pure exercise from which nothing is sought and nothing is gained."[26] When experienced, the Truth of Shākyamuni was said often to occur spontaneously as one's moment-to-moment awareness of one's inherent Buddha-Nature.

Tachibana no Kachiko and Gikū Zenshi met together as student and enlightened teacher (*rōshi*). The still-communal nature of Buddhism early on is present in this intimate student-teacher relationship. Tachibana no Kachiko defined a religious landscape in Sagano by constructing a family-temple complex as a *sangha* —an ongoing Buddhist community of believers. A *sangha* was one of the Three Baskets of Shākyamuni to which followers were admonished to adhere.²⁷ A connotation of *sangha* was "the whole universe transformed into a spiritual community of Buddhas and Buddhas-to-be, in terms covering past, present, and future, and in terms of space extending in all directions."²⁸ As a Buddhist community of believers, a temple was both visible (present adherents) and invisible (past and future adherents).

Accompanying her intensive study of Zen Buddhism within Danrin-ji, Tachibana no Kachiko became known as Danrin. By 850, the year of her death, she had established a school at Danrin-ji for successive generations of the Tachibana family who were expected to study Buddhism and Zen within the compound. The Tachibana clan of families, though, eventually was eclipsed in power by a branch of the Fujiwara clan of families. After the passing of the Saga emperorship, Danrin-ji suffered neglect and lapsed into ruin.²⁹

A Grass House and the Shadow of Mountains

In 975, Prince Kaneakira traveled into the region of the Mountain of Storms west of Kyōto to pay homage to the "spirit" of Turtle Mountain. "I wished to retire the bureaucratic world to have a rest," he wrote, "and to end my life at a quiet place at the foot of Kameyama [Turtle Mountain]."³⁰ Descriptions of the habitat constructed by the prince are sparse, but the compound apparently was small in size, what we might term rustic. As the prince wrote, "I had my grass-house built . . . at last."³¹ Mirei Shigemori tells us "the mountain villa and the garden which stood near Mount Kameyama had a gate [*torii*] and bamboo fence and had woods in front and a bamboo grove behind. The mountain villa and the garden were very beautiful in every season."[32] The "house of grass" most likely was constructed from bamboo and thatch. Surrounding stands of bamboo perhaps stimulated Prince Kaneakira to experience poetically the area around Turtle Mountain as beautiful aurally as well as visually. Sound is prominent in the experience of bamboo grass. Amplified by hollow trunks, a variety of tones are produced when stalks move against each other in the wind. Extensive fields of bamboo surrounded the garden in the *Tale of Genji*, within the Shrine-in-the-Field (Nonomiya), and extensive fields of bamboo still are present within the landscape aspect of the Temple of the Heavenly Dragon.

The entrance to the prince's compound was marked by "archways," as they are termed in his writings (recall the "archways"(*torii*) through which Prince Genji passed upon entering the Shrine-in-the-Field in Sagano). Prince Kaneakira also constructed a modest building, the Shrine of Perfect Virtue, within his compound. Prince Kaneakira did not impose himself on nature but instead "asked" if he could cohabit, as it were, with the spirit (霊, *rei*) of Turtle Mountain—a place of felt beauty and tranquillity. The prince honored Turtle Mountain as a distinct animistic presence (存在, *sonzai*) by petitioning to form a relationship with the mountain as he similarly might petition to form a relationship with a person of high status.

Prince Kaneakira's conception of and behavior toward Turtle Mountain was consistent with early Shintō conceptions of and behaviors toward nature. The prince visualized Turtle Mountain as the embodiment, the materialization, of a deity (甘南備山, the mountain as *kannabiyama*).[33]

Kameyama "means Tortoise Hill and, as the name implies, the hill is rather low and in the shape of a tortoise."[34] As a learned man, Prince Kaneakira undoubtedly was aware of isomorphic correspondences between the shape of turtles and the shape of the land, as turtles long had been vital to divination both in early China and Japan (see pp. 197–210). Perhaps Prince Kaneakira in part chose to site his retirement lodge on the piedmont of Turtle Mountain to share in, through the contagious contact of direct participation, the well-being ascribed to turtleness via the distinctive shape of the mountain.

The *kami* of Shintō at the time in part were experienced through affecting, emotional responses to nature-as-*kami*, as *kami* were ascribed authority by virtue of their ability to affect people via their felt presence.[35] Shapes and physical features of nature were believed to be embodiments of *kami*—*kami* were trees and wind . . . and water.[36] We read that Prince Kaneakira beseeched Turtle Mountain to usher forth water, to nourish the human-made garden aspect of the compound and "we learn from his poem in praise of the god of Kame-yama that his garden had a pond fed by water from a spring on the hill."[37] *Kami* were the generativity and vitality of life itself. The *kami* of a site were known and felt through the fecundity of the site and belief in *kami* conditioned one to visualize the land as animated. Vital.

The "grass house" and compound of Prince Kaneakira became well known among aristocrats in Kyōto for the affecting beauty of its landscape and surrounding lands. The prince was privileged by birth, "excelled in scholarship, achieved considerable mastery in literature and calligraphy, and is represented by poems in several extant anthologies."[38] Prince Kaneakira was renowned for his accomplishments in poetry, stimulated no doubt by the land and human-created landscape near Turtle Mountain to which he sought retirement—for peace of mind and heart.

Prince Kaneakira passed away in 987. The buildings and pond in the shadow of Turtle Mountain lay abandoned for several hundred years until Emperor Go-Saga began to incorporate aspects of the then-desiccated compound into his imperial villa.

A Taste Quite Elegant

The Turtle Mountain Villa on the Banks of the Rising River (Kame-yama Dono) was constructed around 1255 under the guidance of Tachibana Tomoshige, a magistrate in the court of Emperor Go-Saga.

FIGURE 34. *An interpretative sketch of a Sleeping-Hall Compound* (shinden zukuri style).

Tachibana Tomoshige no doubt felt kinship with the area west of Kyōto through family ancestry traced to Tachibana no Kachiko. The emperor maintained a primary residence in the Imperial Palace in Kyōto. The Turtle Mountain Villa was a detached palace (*rikyū*) for prolonged retreats, and also was intended as the future retirement residence of the emperor.

Detached palaces were constructed around several interconnected buildings, a style of architecture (*shinden zukuri*; literally, Sleeping Hall Building) patterned after imperial palaces in T'ang Dynasty (618–907) China. Buildings were laid out and interconnected in a U-shape; to protect high-status occupants, buildings were linked by roofed corridors elevated off the ground (figs. 34, 35).

Detached palaces, though, "lacked the most elementary comforts of life. Winter was extremely cold in the basin formed by the plain of Kyōto. For all that, the emperor had nothing to warm himself but a simple brazier [and elaborate, layered clothing] . . . He remained nearly all day seated on a thick straw cushion covered with woven grass, sheltered alike from observations and insidious draughts by screens of wooden lattice . . . The only light he had [apart from

FIGURE 35. *Covered walkways still link several buildings within the present-day Temple of the Heavenly Dragon. The walkways preserve the influence of Heian-period (794–1185) shinden zukuri architecture on the design of the temple.*

natural light] came from lamps. There was little or no furniture—just a few chests. Summer time . . . was more bearable . . . It was quite cool in the palace but it was very dark inside, a place of perpetual twilight."[39] To our eyes, imperial retreats undoubtedly would appear spartan and rustic.

Tachibana Tomoshige and Go-Saga designed and oversaw construction of the landscape aspect of the villa. Emperor Go-Saga possessed a keen aesthetic sensibility, and quite elegant tastes. The villa
was constructed near the Ōi River. The river was to the south, with
mountains in the background—"a place of great scenic beauty . . .
which gave the appearance of a mountain village."[40] Remnants of
Prince Kaneakira's cottage were to the east of the villa.

As will be the case later with the layout of Tenryū-ji, here
Tachibana and Go-Saga incorporated aspects of previous habitats into
the design of the compound. Rather than the spiritual sensibilities
of Tachibana no Kachiko and Prince Kaneakira, though, the human-
constructed landscape of the imperial villa at Turtle Mountain privileged Go-Saga's aesthetic sensitivity to nature.

Eternity, and a Palace Pond

There was an extensive pond garden within Go-Saga's imperial villa
at Turtle Mountain. Despite the careful selection of the site, water
shortages at the time were endemic within the basin where Kyōto
was located (opposite, interestingly, of the flooding in Nara). One account from this period reveals "a terrible drought dried up the earth
. . . where the young green shoots were wont to grow. The fields
overflowed with the bodies of those who starved."[41] Possession of a
well-maintained pond of water must have been a welcome, yet privileged, experience.

Construction of Go-Saga's pond garden required solving several problems, as the emperor's detached palace was sited on ground
somewhat higher than the nearby Ōi River. A waterwheel initially
was fashioned to bring water from the river into the villa. Lower-
caste people forced to live along the banks of nearby rivers were
conscripted to construct the waterwheel but, not being specialists,
the waterwheel was not well engineered and did not function properly. Subsequently, craftsmen from the village of Uji, south of Kyōto,
were conscripted to rebuild the waterwheel, which then functioned

properly. The bed for the garden pond was excavated then lined with clay, to better retain water in the pond (remnants of the clay at the bottom of the pond in the emperor's detached palace are held to still be present at the bottom of the pond within the present-day Temple of the Heavenly Dragon).⁴²

Go-Saga's pond garden "did not adjourn the house, rather did the house form an integral part of the garden . . . the dwelling place begins in the garden."⁴³ Buildings and the pond garden aspect of the detached palace were interrelated architecturally, yet the garden was the privileged aspect of the compound.

Two smaller buildings flanked a larger central building, and long corridors were placed at right angles at each end of the flanking buildings. Pavilions were built at the ends of the corridors, extending out and over the water of the pond, such that one could walk the corridor and remain sheltered yet still be surrounded by water (fig. 34).

The manner in which Go-Saga's detached palace interrelated buildings, nature, and the human-created landscape was quite subtle. A small branching stream (*yarimizu*), fed by higher mountain water, was channeled under the corridors and floors of buildings then into the garden pond and "care was given to such details as the foaming and gurgling of the water as it dashed against the stones . . . lining the small stream."⁴⁴ Wooden planks served as the floor. People could remove the planks, perhaps merely to experience the murmuring of water streaming underneath the buildings.

In 1276, a visitor experiencing the pond garden wrote of experiencing "eternity, and the pine trees on Tortoise Hill [Kameyama] reflected in the clear waters of the palace pond."⁴⁵ At night, boating parties often were held on the pond in the garden. The *Mirror of Increase* (*Masukagami*) says "at that time, they floated a boat on the pond and performed *Bugaku* [a courtly dance, and associated music], and so on."⁴⁶ When retired Emperor Go-Fukakusa (1243–1304) visited the villa on May 10, 1261, "a temporary pavilion was erected on the islet. The emperors sat under the pavilion, enjoying a feeling of being in the pond and on land at the same time."⁴⁷ Musicians performed and people danced. Music wafted in the air, as flowers were strewn on the pond.

Go-Saga was an accomplished poet. Boating parties were settings for "Battle of the Seasons" contests in which guests composed poems extolling the felt qualities of each season. People "called to imperial poetry contests on moonlit nights and snowy mornings" boated on the nearby Ōi River while composing poems by torchlight, an indication that the river at this time was a vital aspect of the villa's garden landscape.[48]

The Fragrant Spirit of Trees

Go-Saga further defined a fairly permanent aspect of the landscape in the area through the planting of myriad cherry trees around the imperial villa beneath Turtle Mountain. Cherry trees were transplanted from the legendary Yoshino region south of Kyōto. The mountain area of Yoshino (Fields of Good Fortune) was known as Fragrant Mountain and Beloved Fields. Yoshino remains a venerated, sacred mountain area.

Cherry trees are wonderfully fragrant, and visually arresting. In bloom, the cherry trees of Yoshino sprout fragrant blossoms primarily in subtle shades of pink. Shortly after vibrantly bursting forth in the spring, blossoms fade to white then drop, swirling, to blanket the ground. People still graft feelings of transience and impermanence (無常, mujō) onto the fleeting life of blossoms falling from cherry trees, and "the sad fleeting quality of the moment [物の哀れ, mono no aware] is savored just as fully as the moment itself."[49] It is said that veneration of blooming cherry blossoms "derives from the idea of the bud where the divine spirit is closeted until the tip bursts and blossoms."[50] Divine Spirit. Kami.

The Mirror of Increase tells us "in this spring the Emperor came to this Detached Palace [the villa] and enjoyed seeing cherry blossoms."[51] One can only imagine the sight and fragrance of myriad cherry trees in bloom on the slopes of the mountains of Sagano. It was said that the cherry trees transplanted from Yoshino added to the "fragrance of the spirit" of the emperor's villa.[52] After Go-Saga's retirement as emperor in 1246, Go-Uda (1267–1324) ordered the additional planting of several thousand cherry trees from Yoshino onto the slopes of the nearby Mountain of Storms.

Emperors Go-Saga and Go-Uda ordered the transplanting of trees for purposes aesthetic and ornamental, as there is no evidence that the cherry trees were cultivated for their fruit. Alteration of the land surrounding the imperial villa emphasized aesthetics and the sensory, affective pleasure attendant upon a primarily visual experience of the landscape.

※

We have noted the increasing energy invested in the location and construction of buildings, as well as physical alterations of the land west of the City of Purple Hills and Crystal Streams, in the fashioning of an affecting human-created landscape. Three people of influence initially defined the character of the land and landscape west of Kyōto within which the Temple of the Heavenly Dragon will emerge. Tachibana no Kachiko ordered construction of a *sangha*, supporting the early presence of Chinese Zen Buddhism in Japan. Prince Kaneakira subsequently constructed a complex with Shintō-inspired features such as *torii*, waterways, extensive stands of bamboo, and the Shrine of Perfect Virtue. Emperor Go-Saga initiated construction of an elaborate settlement in Sagano, and altered the land through the planting of trees as well as the construction of a comparatively large pond garden. Go-Saga also altered the Ōi River to direct water into his villa and under and through several of its buildings. The affecting presence of cherry trees transplanted from Yoshino in particular was a profound alteration of the land and resulted in a lasting dramatic impact upon the visual landscape.

These alterations of the land, the defining of a human-created landscape, were cumulative in their effects and affects. Each alteration contributed to the character of the later landscape within which the Temple of the Heavenly Dragon will emerge.

The significance (religious significance, for the most part) of the land itself will be ongoing. The sensate colors and textures of the human-created visual landscape also will continue aesthetically and emotionally to touch those privileged to experience the region west of the City of Purple Hills and Crystal Streams.

2

DEATH, DREAM, AND THE GENESIS OF A TEMPLE

The Temple of the Heavenly Dragon was not parented by aesthetic and religious sensibilities, exclusively. Generations of brutal conflict flowed across the mountains and plains west of the City of Purple Hills and Crystal Streams. Fear and violence, betrayal and atonement, and compassion, also were constituent aspects of the birth of the Temple of the Heavenly Dragon and the life of the pond garden.

Nearly half a century had passed since the Saga emperorship. Four people of influence subsequently appeared who will directly influence the birth of Tenryū-ji: Emperor Go-Daigo (1288–1339); the brothers Tadayoshi (1306–52) and Takauji (1305–58) of the Ashikaga, a branch of the Minamoto clan of families; and the venerable priest Musō Soseki (1275–1351). Along with religious belief and aesthetic sensibilities, we will discover sharp shards of suffering strewn about our archaeology of the Temple of the Heavenly Dragon.

Emperor and Shōgun

Emperors continued to claim authority for the divine right to rule imperially, through societal belief in the descent of emperors from the Shintō deity Amaterasu-o-mi-Kami. Yet, imperial rule increasingly

was challenged by aristocratic families and by the appointed adminis-
trators (regents) of lands, provinces, outlying Kyōto.

Revolts in the provinces against imperial authority were frequent. As a repercussion of a decisive revolt in 1185, in 1192 Yoritomo of the Minamoto clan of families declared himself Seii Taishōgun
("Barbarian-Subduing General"). Yoritomo established the seat of his
military regime (*bakufu*) in Kamakura, thereby challenging the authority of the court of emperors in Kyōto. With the death of Yoritomo
in 1199, clans of aristocratic families, the Hōjō especially, and subsequent shōgun, continued to challenge the rule of emperors for the
next several centuries.

In April of 1318, Crown Prince Takaharu ascended to the
throne in Kyōto as Emperor Go-Daigo. In 1326, Hōjō in Kamakura
"requested" that Go-Daigo assume the position of Titular Emperor,
an impotent position without influence, so that an emperor of Hōjō
choosing could be installed on the throne in Kyōto. Go-Daigo wanted
to restore the power of emperors, weakened over the last several hundred years. Go-Daigo rebuffed the direct challenge to imperial rule
and right of succession and began a series of attacks on Kamakura.

In 1331, Takatoki of the Hōjō sent thousands of soldiers to Kyōto
in response to Go-Daigo's continuing attacks on Kamakura. Informed
of the forces riding against him, Go-Daigo and many of his loyalists
fled Kyōto and retreated southward to a monastery on Mount Kasagi.
Soldiers from Kamakura pursued Go-Daigo and, though met with
force by warrior-monks loyal to Go-Daigo, the monastery on Mount
Kasagi was seized then razed. Go-Daigo managed to escape but was
captured in 1332 and exiled to the island of Chiburi (present-day
island of Oki). The military regime in Kamakura then installed young
Prince Kazuhito (Emperor Kōgon, 1313–64) to the imperial throne in
Kyōto.

In 1333, Go-Daigo escaped from the island of Chiburi as loyalists began military campaigns to restore the emperor's rule in Kyōto.
Prince Daito [Morinaga, the eldest son of Go-Daigo], his son Akamatsu Norimura, Nitta Yoshisada, and Takauji of the Ashikaga led

large armies in attacks around Kyōto and in Kamakura on forces loyal
to the Hōjō and the military regime, such that "by afternoon the sky
was full of smoke . . . there was no daylight [in Kamakura]. It was as if
the scene had been rubbed over with ink."[1] Returning to Kyōto as emperor, Go-Daigo initiated the Kenmu Restoration and Era [Kenmu no
Shinsei, 1333–36], a short-lived period meant to solidify imperial rule.

The power of the emperor, though, remained weakened. Go-
Daigo had to depend on military men, such as Takauji and Tadayoshi,
for control of lands under imperial rule.

Takauji of the Ashikaga initially had provided military support
for the Hōjō, to which his family was related by marriage. Takauji led
one of the wealthiest and most influential families in the provinces
east of Kyōto. Hōjō regents named him a constable, placed a sizeable
military force at his command, and ordered him to march against Go-
Daigo, then in Kyōto. Takauji, though, sensed the eventual demise of
the Hōjō and subsequently changed allegiance. He placed his army at
the disposal of loyalists campaigning for restoration of imperial rule
under Go-Daigo.

Go-Daigo then dispatched Takauji to quell a rebellion in Kamakura. Takauji followed the orders of the emperor and marched to
Kamakura where he quelled the forces of rebellion against imperial
rule. Soldiers such as Takauji, though, expected spoils of war rather
than leadership of ceaseless military campaigns as reward for supporting emperors. Takauji desired control of provincial lands to the east
of Kyōto. He coveted the title of shōgun. Takauji initially had asked
Go-Daigo to appoint him shōgun, but Go-Daigo denied his request,
as he did not want to encourage potential challenges to the authority
of emperors.

In 1335–36, Takauji seized control of Kamakura, routed the
last of the Hōjō regents and the *bakufu* and had himself appointed
shōgun. He then began to distribute land to his officers, undermining
Go-Daigo's authority to command imperial lands and soldiers. Go-
Daigo branded him a traitor and sent punitive expeditions to Kamakura to rout Takauji and his army.

At roughly the same time, Nitta Yoshisada also turned against Go-Daigo when he was sent by the emperor to dispatch Takauji from Kamakura. Yoshisada subsequently joined forces with Takauji and their combined forces moved on Go-Daigo in Kyōto, defeated imperial troops, and marched into the city "leaving flames behind them as they destroyed the palace and the mansions of Court nobles and generals, notably those of their enemies."[2] For a second time, Go-Daigo was forced into exile; this time, the emperor fled into the mountains of Yoshino south of Kyōto. Mountainous and difficult to access, "the wild country of Yoshino was like a natural fortress."[3] In early 1336, Kitabatake Akiie, a loyalist to Go-Daigo, forced the troops of Takauji and Yoshisada from Kyōto, and Go-Daigo briefly returned to the city. In response, in late 1336 Takauji again forced Go-Daigo from Kyōto and installed Prince Yutahito (Kōmyō, 1322–80, a brother to Emperor Kōgon) as emperor.

Two emperors thus simultaneously claimed the right to rule: Go-Daigo organized an administrative court (Nanchō, the Southern Court) while in exile in Yoshino; the child-emperor Kōmyō, a puppet of Takauji, held court (Hokuchō, the Northern Court) in Kyōto. Most historians privilege the stronger position of Go-Daigo, as he managed to keep possession of the imperial regalia—the seal of the emperor and perhaps a mythic sword (Kusa-Nagi, "Grass Mower"), one of the Three Treasures of Shintō.[4] Armies of the Northern Court supported Kōmyō and, under the leadership of Takauji, fought armies of the Southern Court, who supported the restoration of Go-Daigo to the throne in Kyōto.

Forests of Suffering

Violence and bloodshed seeped and settled into the land on which the Temple of the Heavenly Dragon will rest. Amid suffering, though, there appeared the influential presence of the venerable Rinzai Zen Buddhist priest Musō Soseki (fig. 36).

Soseki remains indelibly linked to the present-day Temple of the

FIGURE 36. *Musō Soseki (Kokushi).*

Heavenly Dragon, especially so for priests within the temple, as we will see.[5] Soseki was born on November 1, 1275, to an influential family in the province of Ise (present-day Mie Prefecture). His father belonged to the influential House of Genji (Minamoto, descended from the prominent clan of families in the *Tale of the Genji*), and his mother, who died when he was about three years old, belonged to the influential House of Heike, by kinship related to the Taira. When Soseki was nine years old, his father presented him to the venerable priest Kūa Daitoku at the Buddhist temple of Heian-ji.

Soseki initially studied Shingon and Tendai practices of esoteric Buddhism (密教, *Mikkyō*). Esoteric meant hidden and secreted, as *Mikkyō* was intended only for an initiated elite.[6]

The Shingon studied by Soseki at the time conceived of existence as a manifestation of the Supreme Cosmic Buddha, with less emphasis on the historical Buddha. Though esoteric, "we can discern, when free from illusion, the body and life of the Great Illuminator even in a grain of dust or in a drop of water, or in a slight stir of our consciousness."[7] Shingon is attributed to Kūkai (Kōbō Daishi, 774–835). Nature was the nature of the Cosmic Buddha. Kūkai loved mountains, in particular, and he lived much of his life within forests and on mountains. The Ise area within which Soseki was born still is associated with venerated mountain shrines (such as Ise-jingū), natural features venerated as *kami* (such as Meoto Iwa, the "Wedded Rocks" near the village of Futami), and with the mountain *yamabushi*, practitioners of Shugendō. Soseki was deeply and persistently attracted to the love of nature he found associated with practitioners of Shingon, such as Kūkai.

Soseki's studies of Shingon were successful. At the age of seventeen Soseki was given the monk name Chikaku ("Clear Knowledge"). In 1292 his head was shaved and he was ordained a Shingon priest at Tōdai-ji in present-day Nara Prefecture. Here, Soseki studied intensively with the venerated Gyōren (Jikan Rishi). A formative phase in his life began when he witnessed the prolonged death of Gyōren. The beloved teacher appeared to suffer greatly as he died. Esoteric rituals did not ease the priest's death. Nothing Gyōren had been studying so intently all of his life demonstrated efficacy in negating suffering. "He [Gyōren]" Soseki wrote, "studied the sūtras diligently but not one word could help him at his death."[8] In despair over suffering, as well as witnessing that apparently nothing could negate suffering, Soseki ceased his studies of Tendai and began a hundred-day solitary meditative retreat—"effectively 'sitting under a tree' again, his mind roaming in the landscapes that had comforted and calmed him when he felt confused or overwhelmed by the suffering in the world around him."[9] For Soseki, mindful experience of nature provided him with some respite from suffering. Mindful experiences of nature will be a predominant intent of the temple landscapes, compassionate aids to calming the mind and heart, with which Soseki later will be involved.

It was during the later phase of his retreat that, from deep within his meditative experience, Soseki became aware of the thought that led him to the name by which he still is venerated. His Way for some time will be trekking, alone mostly, within nature. Nature will continue to be a mirror for deep, calming, meditative experiences of his own nature—thus "*mu* 〖夢〗, dream, and *sō* 〖窓〗, window."[10] Musō. This name says that Soseki conceived of himself as the vehicle seeing

into and potentially negating his own suffering and perhaps the suffering of others.

Musō (as we now will refer to him) went on to study Tendai, a
school of Buddhism traced to Saichō (Dengyō Daishi, 767–822). Tendai sought to free Buddhism from the dogmatism of esoteric ritual
Musō experienced within Shingon. The Tendai to which he was
exposed accommodated study of the venerated words attributed to
Shākyamuni.

Musō's early life experiences at this point in several respects re-
capitulate early life experiences of Siddhārtha Gautama. Musō's early
confrontations with death and his despair over suffering, for instance,
mirror the confrontation with death and despair over suffering early
experienced by Shākyamuni.

Siddhārtha was the son of Shuddhodana [Pure Rice King], ruler
of the influential Gautama lineage of the Shākya clan of families. The
Shākya were high-caste (Kshatriya) twice-born rulers over hundreds
of thousands of people in Kapilavastu in the southern foothills of the
Himalaya Mountains, the fertile delta area of the river Ganges in the
present-day Terai region of Nepal. It is believed that Siddhārtha's
preordained destiny was to confront suffering directly, and Buddhism
fruited from Siddhārtha's compassionate response to the suffering he
witnessed beyond the privilege within the gates of his father's palace.
There are variant narrative descriptions of a signal incident where
Siddhārtha, one day riding with Channa, his charioteer, initially
bore witness to suffering, first clothed as an old man riddled with
decay. The old man, though, was a deity compassionately taking on
this form so as to stimulate Siddhārtha's "awakening." As they rode
in his chariot, Siddhārtha then spied another old man covered with
boils. He then witnessed a body being carried by untouchables to
the cremation grounds. Finally, Siddhārtha spied a beggar, a wandering priest, who while outwardly poor appeared powerfully calm of
mind. Siddhārtha is reputed to have said that "although brought up
in wealth, I was by nature very sensitive, and it caused me to won-
der why, when all men are destined to suffer old age, sickness, and

death, and none can escape these things, they yet look upon old age, sickness, and the death of other men with fear, loathing, and scorn. This is not right, I thought."[11] Siddhārtha subsequently renounced th privileges of the Shākya, left his family, and began to wander amid forests and mountains. Siddhārtha's renunciation of inherited privilege, and his subsequent compassionate response to suffering, became especially important to Musō.

Musō Soseki and Siddhārtha Gautama both were born into families of relatively high social status. Around 563 B.C., Queen Māyā gave birth to Siddhārtha within the still-celebrated gardens of Lumbini. She died several days later. Both Musō and Siddhārtha early in life experienced the death of their mothers. Siddhārtha "was reared in delightful palaces from whose parks every sign of death, disease and misery was removed."[12] Both Musō and Siddhārtha were attracted to what we would term a religious life in association with similar reactions to death and to the apparent persistent existence of suffering in the world. Finally, gardens were an intimate aspect of the life of Siddhārtha Gautama, who was born in a garden, and of Musō. Musō came to see gardens as a compassionate means to stimulate states of awareness and behavior termed "enlightenment," and he later will influence the design of the pond garden aspect of the Temple of the Heavenly Dragon.

THE BONES OF EMPTINESS

Musō felt that the textual study of esoteric Buddhism, both Shingon and Tendai, did not affect suffering in the world. Musō was led to the Zen school of Buddhism through his conclusion that the truth of suffering could not be experienced through formal study of sūtra or the practice of esoteric ritual.

The pedagogy of Zen Buddhism emphasizes the direct face-to-face relationship of teacher and student, as with Empress Danrin and Gikū Zenshi. Musō thus began his study of the Zen school of Buddhism by seeking an enlightened teacher and a *sangha* in which to study. Musō had thought to study with the venerable priest Hottō Kokushi. A fellow monk, though, advised Musō to develop his practice (of Zen) before approaching so renowned a priest. So, when he was twenty years of age, Musō traveled to Kyōto to study with the venerable priests Mu-in Eban at the temple of Kennin, with Tokeitokugo at the temple of Engaku, and, traveling to Kamakura and to the temple of Kenchō-ji, with the venerable priest Chido-oshō.

In 1299, while in Kamakura, Musō studied with the influential Chinese priest Yishan Yining. Ichizan Ichinei, as Yishan Yining was known in Japan, had become abbot of Kenchō-ji. Musō desired an-swers concerning suffering, but Ichizan Ichinei only replied calmly to Musō that within Zen Buddhism there were no "answers" to "ques-tions." Frustrated with this pedagogy, Musō ceased his studies with Ichizan Ichinei.

Kōhō Kennichi, a descendant of Go-Saga, subsequently be-came Musō's influential teacher during this phase of his life. Kōhō's priest name was Bukkoku Zenji (later, Kokushi), and Bukkoku was renowned for having studied Zen Buddhism under the venerable Chinese priests Wu-an P'u-ning and Wu-hsueh Tsu-yuan. Musō also approached Bukkoku expecting to receive direct answers to his direct questions, but was met with the same reply he received from Ichizan Ichinei. Bukkoku sternly told Musō that he must not expect others to provide the awareness he sought.

Musō then returned to live on mountains and within forests, this time traveling to the far north of Honshū. He built shelters, within which he lived. He sat within nature, often on what he termed "meditation rocks" (see Chapter 8, "Sitting in the Garden").[13] Musō vowed not to return to speak with Bukkoku until he had experienced the awareness he had sought from his teachers.

WANDERINGS OF LIGHT AND DARK

For more than twenty years, Musō lived mostly amid forests and mountains.[14] During this time, he wrote of several initial experiences of awareness of Buddha-Nature. It was said that "once a person awakens to the field of Original Nature, he sees that Buddha-Nature, mind, 'thusness' [shinnyo] . . . as well as . . . the great earth, mountains, rivers, grass, tiles, or stones, are all the field of Original Nature."[15] During this phase of his life, Musō's teachers, his examples of enlightenment, were trees and water and mountains.

He became aware of the subtle manner in which sunlight and shadow flowed as the surface of bamboo, ebbing to and fro with the wind. One evening, sitting at fireside near the Okita River, Musō contemplated flames flickering in the darkness. At moments, it would appear as if there was no distinction between wood and flame. Between light and dark.

Musō began to experience everyday existence as Buddha-Nature in that "living in this way . . . everything right and left, everywhere, was full of existence. And he heard the voice of existence itself."[16] Musō, though, felt that he had not yet experienced the awareness experienced by Shākyamuni under the Bodhi tree. Musō wrote of one experience where he fell asleep during a long session of zazen and, upon waking, became ashamed of having fallen asleep. Yet at that moment also, he began to question distinctions such as sleeping and waking, remembering and forgetting. He felt that if he had truly not made a distinction between wakefulness and sleeping, he would not have experienced the suffering of shame at having fallen asleep.

Musō began to watch the ebb and flow of his thoughts. He felt that he still was making distinctions that did not exist, except within his clouded mind. Distraught, he thought of returning to Bukkoku Kokushi to announce his defeat when, unexpectedly, he experienced a signal Zen Buddhist state of awareness.

The year was 1305. One night, while staying with friends, he rose from a long session of zazen "and stepped out *into the garden* of the house in which he was staying [my italics]."[17] He sat for some time under a tree in the garden (again, reminiscent of Shākyamuni sitting under the Bodhi tree). Rising from his meditation, Musō moved to retire to the house. Darkness obscured his way, and he tripped over a piece of the roof that had fallen to the ground and . . . he fell to the ground.

A simple, ordinary act. Yet, Musō's response was to . . . laugh, in surprise. In this sudden, spontaneous laughter Musō perhaps felt he had experienced the state of awareness Zen Buddhists term *satori*. Importantly for us, if so, he had experienced *satori* within a garden.

Satori is held to be awareness of "pure existence," existence experienced directly and not filtered through ego-consciousness. "Original Nature [Buddha-Nature] is pure existence," and experience of pure existence often is associated with overwhelming calmness, joy, and peace of heart and mind.[18]

And laughter. Buddhists often say, "laughter is the cancellation of ego."[19] In Zen Buddhism, "a smile or laugh . . . cancels the world of opposition . . . laughter rescues the mind."[20] Musō "fell through" his walls of expectation and illusion, and awoke to existence-as-it-is (*shinnyo*). He experienced existence-as-it-is without texts or ritual. He experienced existence-as-it-is . . . within nature.

It was the custom at the time to compose a poem upon the initial experience of what was believed to be *satori*, and Musō wrote:

> Year after year
>> I dug in the earth
>>> looking for the blue of heaven
> only to feel
>> the pile of dirt
>>> choking me
> until once in the dead of night
>> I tripped on a broken brick
>>> and kicked it into the air
> and saw that without a thought
>> I had smashed the bones
>>> of the empty sky[21]

Musō had been preoccupied with what we would term dual-isms: "earth"/ "sky," for instance. Existence was experienced as ob-stacle, as suffering, until a chance stumbling shattered illusion such that "the activity of consciousness is stopped and one ceases to be aware of time, space, and causation."[22] Musō's experience spontane-ously shattered "bones," the conventional manner in which he had been experiencing illusion-as-reality. In a garden, Musō initially ex-perienced "this state that we call pure existence."[23] We read, "you can appreciate . . . the beauties of nature with greatly increased un-derstanding and delight. Therefore, it may be, the sound of a stone striking a bamboo trunk, or the sight of blossoms, makes a vivid im-pression on your mind . . . This impression is so overwhelming that the whole universe comes tumbling down."[24] Often, in laughter.

Musō journeyed back to Kamakura to relate his experience to Bukkoku Kokushi. Bukkoku acknowledged that Musō's experience in the garden indeed had been *satori* and, in the traditional rite of succession, Bukkoku presented Musō with his *Inka* (印可, Seal of Enlightenment), one of his robes, and a portrait of himself.

GREEN MOUNTAINS BECOME YELLOW

After having received a seal of succession from the venerable Buk-koku Kokushi, Musō's fame spread widely and people increasingly petitioned to study with him. Yet he continued to feel that "the great earth, mountains, rivers, grass . . . stones, are all the field of Original [Buddha] nature."[25] In 1312, Musō and several fellow priests went to live within forests and to practice sitting amid mountains. Dur-ing this period, Musō founded Eihō-ji in 1314. Mostly alone now, throughout 1315 he lived around the Tōki River area.

Word reached Musō that Bukkoku Kokushi had died on Decem-ber 20, 1316. Upon hearing of his teacher's death, Musō wrote "green mountains have turned yellow so many times . . . When the mind is still the floor where I sit is endless space."[26] Musō's Buddha-Mind appears now to be able to peacefully attend to what conventionally

is conceived of as death in a manner quite different from his prior tur-
moil over the death of the venerable priest Gyōren. Musō lived the
next several years within mountains and forests.

In 1325, at the request of Go-Daigo, Musō temporarily came
down from the forest mountains to became abbot of Nanzen-ji in
Kyōto. Returning to Kamakura in 1327, he was appointed abbot of
Zuisen-ji. In 1329, monks petitioned Musō to become abbot of the
influential temple of Engaku-ji. Recall that in 1333 Go-Daigo returned
to Kyōto from exile in Chiburi. At this time, as well, the emperor
presented himself to Musō as a pupil desirous of studying Zen Buddhism.[27] Go-Daigo subsequently installed Musō as first abbot of
Rinsen-ji, a small Buddhist complex near the present-day Temple of
the Heavenly Dragon.

Musō was three times honored as Kokushi (国師, National
Master). He received the honored title of Kokushi from Go-Daigo,
as well as the title of Supreme Enlightened Teacher (正覚心宗国
師, Shōgaku Shinshū Kokushi) from emperors Kōgon and Kōmyō.
Musō also became known as Teacher to Seven Emperors (七朝帝師,
Nanchō Teishi).

Vengeful Spirits and a Sky of Dream

The Temple of the Heavenly Dragon will be born amid violence and
betrayal, suffering and death, as well as from the devotion of people
to aesthetics, nature, and spirituality. In addition, interestingly, the
temple will be conceived amid belief in the reality of dreams as a tangible presence affecting the sensibilities and decisions of people of
influence.

In early 1339, Musō told fellow priests that he had had a startling
dream about Emperor Go-Daigo, then in exile in Yoshino. Strangely,
the emperor appeared in his imperial carriage amid the clouds then
glided into the old compound of Go-Saga's imperial villa near Turtle
Mountain.[28] Musō had dreamed of Go-Daigo seated within his imperial carriage as he glided into the compound; yet, rather than draped

in his imperial regalia, in the dream Go-Daigo wore the clothing of a Buddhist monk! Go-Daigo died suddenly (August 16, 1339), in Yoshino, shortly after Musō's pregnant dream. The dream was taken as a sign that the spirit of the emperor longed for the peaceful place important in his childhood.

Takauji of the Ashikaga especially was troubled by the death of Go-Daigo, because of his behavior toward the emperor. Takauji was preoccupied with his fate, with the still-present danger that the spirit of Go-Daigo posed to him.

People believed in ghosts (幽霊, yūrei) and in vengeful "hungry" spirits (餓鬼, gaki). The Record of Ancient Matters "reveals strong traces of a belief that certain deities and the spirits of the dead could lay a curse upon living men . . . The idea of possession by a vengeful spirit . . . was very prevalent."[29] In particular, a ghost abiding in the dwelling and habitat of its former life could be tormented by unease. It was desirable to try to put at ease spirits believed abiding in their former residences.

Takauji subsequently beseeched the spirit of Go-Daigo to find peace, and not seek revenge upon him for his treacherous behavior. "He [Takauji] knew that his conduct was reprehensible . . . He prayed for the mercy of Kannon [a Bodhisattva, a deity of compassion], asking that he should not be forced to suffer in the next world for his offenses in this. Life on earth was a dream."[30] In addition, Takauji thought to make an offering to compensate for his turning against the deceased emperor, conscripting his lands, and appointing himself shōgun. With the dream of Musō, and the solace-seeking behavior of Takauji, people of influence once again turned awareness toward the legendary regions west of Kyōto.

In an initial gesture of atonement, Takauji ordered the release of a number of prisoners, captives in war, as well as the release of a number of his political enemies. Further, Takauji ordered that cherry trees from Yoshino, where Emperor Go-Daigo had lived in exile, be replanted around the ruins of Go-Saga's old villa at Turtle Mountain where Go-Daigo had lived as a child. Subsequently, the Bodhisattva

Jizō (deity protecting travelers, especially children and pregnant females, through the realms of existence as well as saving souls from
the torments of hell) came to Takauji in a dream. The Bodhisattva instructed that "thousands of small images [of Jizō] be cast," intending
that each statue "express his compassion for the soul of one man whose
death in battle he had caused."[31] At the very least, sixty thousand
people were slain during the war between the Northern and Southern Courts. In what we can interpret as an act of compassion, Takauji
ordered the casting of a Jizō in commemoration of each life lost.

Still not yet at peace, Takauji sought out the venerable Musō
Kokushi at Rinsen-ji, where Musō subsequently counseled Takauji to
offer more substantive amends to the spirit of Go-Daigo. There was
discussion of Musō's dream of Go-Daigo entering into Go-Saga's old
imperial villa at Turtle Mountain as well as discussion of Takauji's
dream of Jizō.

Musō and Takauji increasingly became aware of their connection
to each other. Both men, through dreams, indeed were connected to
the land and landscape around the Mountain of Storms, with the old
site of the imperial villa at the piedmont of Turtle Mountain, as well
as with (the deceased emperor) Go-Daigo. Both men subsequently
were struck by the idea, revealed through dreams, of resurrecting the
deserted villa into an offering to Go-Daigo, a temple perhaps, "where
the spirit of the emperor could be venerated and laid to rest."[32] Go-
Daigo had loved nature, and he had spent much of his childhood
on the grounds of the imperial villa at Turtle Mountain. After the
reign of Go-Saga, the villa lay in mossy ruin. Buildings sagged with
inattention and the grounds were deep brown and green, saturated
with shades of neglect. Until the appearance of Ashikaga Takauji and
Musō Kokushi, no one had attended to nor cared for the site west of
the City of Purple Mountains and Crystal Streams.

In October of 1339, Emperor Kōmyō issued permission for
Takauji to begin construction of a temple on the site of the old imperial villa at Turtle Mountain. By imperial decree, the future temple
was a *chokugan* (a temple dedicated to an emperor) to the spirit of

Go-Daigo as well as to the spirits of those who died during the war between the Northern and Southern Courts.

Deeply affecting landscapes often are constructed on a foundation of powerful emotions such as anger and love.[33] Both Takauji and Musō felt connected to the old imperial villa at Turtle Mountain through a desire for peace, harmony, and compassion. "If one just forgets this self," Musō wrote, "and rouses the intention to benefit all living beings, a great compassion arises within and imperceptibly unites with Buddha-Mind."[34] Musō felt compassion not only for the spirit of Go-Daigo but also for all those who died in the fighting between the Northern and Southern Courts; indeed, for all forms of being. Placing emphasis on compassion, Musō also sought to honor the spirits of the many animals, horses and oxen mostly, that suffered violent deaths during the war. Takauji, as well, sought peace of mind.

Services commemorating initial construction of the temple were held on January 5, 1339. At this time, a service also was held for Musō to honor his counsel to Takauji and to serve notice that Musō was to become the first abbot of the Buddhist temple. Musō reminded the assembled that, "everything the world contains—grass and trees, bricks and tile, all creatures, all actions and activities — are nothing but manifestations of the Law [the Dharma experienced by Buddha]."[35] Musō declared that the temple initially would be a family temple for the Ashikaga, promote the Rinzai school of Zen Buddhism, and function as a place within which Buddhist priests would be trained.

It was the custom at the time for a newly constructed Buddhist temple to have an honorary name (山号, *sangō*) referencing a venerated mountain to which it was linked. *Reikizan* (霊亀山, Mountain of the Spirit of the Turtle) was the mountain-name of the new complex, with respect to the long-standing veneration of Kameyama (as well as Ogurayama to the northwest). The formal name (寺号, *jigō*) of the temple was considered carefully as the name also would embody and participate in the spirit of the temple. The complex initially was named Precious Zen Temple of the Spirit of the Ryakuō

Period (霊亀山暦応資聖禅寺, *Reikizan Ryakuō Shisei Zenji*). Shortly thereafter, though, the name of the complex was changed to Precious Zen Temple of the Heavenly Dragon (天龍資聖禅寺, *Tenryū Shisei Zenji*). The slight change in name was meant also to commemorate the temple as embodiment of the spirit of a dragon.

The Dragons of Dream

People at the time believed in the reality of dragons. People saw dragons. Dragons had long been associated with growth and fecundity as well as with benevolence and protection. The bones, teeth, and horns of dragons were apothecary treasures. The blood of a dragon was believed to congeal to amber, and the saliva of a dragon was the most potent of perfumes. Dragons were believed capable of transformation in form, and a dragon could be as large or as small as it wished. The appearance of a dragon, either in the life of dreams or in waking life, was a harbinger of good fortune.

The name "Temple of the Heavenly Dragon" accommodated the portentous appearance of dragons appearing in the dreams of Go-Daigo as well as Tadayoshi of the Ashikaga. Before his death, Go-Daigo had a portentous dream of a dragon that came to protect his life. Tadayoshi's dreams were frequented by benevolent dragons of sky and water.

During the time of violent challenges to his rule, a dragon had appeared to Go-Daigo in a memorable dream: "In 1335, Emperor Go-Daigo had been invited to the house of Dainagon Saionji Kimmune, one of the Fujiwara. This invitation was given with the intention to kill His Majesty, who would have stepped upon a loose board of the floor and dropped down upon a row of swords. Fortunately, the Emperor was saved by the dragon of the pond in the park [Shinsen-in, Sacred Spring Park, a precinct of the Imperial Palace in Kyōto], who, in the night before he intended to go to the fatal house, appeared to him in a dream in the shape of a woman. She said to him: 'Before you are tigers and wolves, behind you brown and spotted bears. Do not go tomorrow.' At his question as to who she was, she answered that she lived for many years in the Sacred Spring Park."[36] The narrative further notes that Go-Daigo went to Sacred Spring Park for further guidance and to "pray to the Dragon-god. And lo! All of a sudden the water of the pond was disturbed, and the waves struck violently at the bank, although there was no wind. This agreed so strikingly with his dream that he did not proceed upon his way. So Go-Daigo returned to the Palace, and Saionji was banished to Izumo, which he never reached because he was killed on the road."[37] Lore and legend thus linked emperors to dragons. Dragons safeguarded emperors.

Emperor Jinmu (ca. 771–585 B.C.), the first emperor of Japan, was believed to be the grandson of the daughter of a *kami* of the sea— manifested in the guise of a dragon. *The Record of Ancient Matters* declares that "In the august reign of the Heavenly Sovereign who governed the Eight Great Islands from the Great Plain of Kiyomihara at Asuka, the Hidden Dragon [[Jinmu Tennō]] put on perfection, the Reiterated Thunder came at the appointed moment [[of emperorship in 660 B.C.]]."[38] Emperor Ōjin (270–310) was said to have a dragon's tail extending from his body, which he carefully kept hidden. A dragon was sighted at the beginning of the reign of Emperor Go-Uda (1267–1324).

And so, the spirit of Emperor Go-Daigo became synonymous with a dragon. The emerging temple was linked to Go-Daigo such that the complex demonstrably was a dragon temple.

Tadayoshi had been under the counsel of Musō, and their conversations on Zen Buddhism and on the recent civil war were recorded as *Dream Conversations* (*Muchū Mondōshū*).[39] Like his brother Takauji, Tadayoshi felt abiding remorse with his own du- plicit behavior toward the deceased Emperor Go-Daigo. At one point in their conversations, Musō underscored Tadayoshi's connection to the emerging temple complex: "You are now respected by all of the people because of the good things you have done in your former life," Musō tells Tadayoshi, "but you also have enemies . . . think about all the enemies you killed and all the soldiers who died fighting with you. Think about all their families and numerous descendants. If you honor their memories, you will comfort many people."[40] And the way to further honor memories of the dead as well as comfort the living was through the engagement of Tadayoshi in the birth of the emerging Buddhist temple complex.

In the dream of Tadayoshi, a mighty dragon of gold and silver rose from the waters of the Ōi River skirting the Mountain of Storms. Instead of flying off into the sky, the dragon glided into the garden pond of the old imperial villa at Turtle Mountain. The dragon living in the dream of Tadayoshi made its presence known during the genesis of the new temple complex. In the dream, the dragon surfaced within an area near a river and human-made pond of prior religious significance.

River dragons were believed to dwell within treasure-laden palaces (*ryugu*) beneath the water, and veneration of the deities of the sea and rivers in time became associated with veneration of dragons. "Dragons were kami gods who lived in rivers and seas, valleys and mountains [in rivulets, lakes, and ponds]."[41] A dragon rising from water became associated with rain, literal generativity.[42] The rising of a dragon initiated a cycle of ascent and descent associated with what we would term the vast hydrologic cycle of nature itself—water rising in mist from the earth only to fall again, as rain. Witnessing a dragon rising from a river, even in the life of a dream, was an omen of emerging beneficence (fig. 37).

In the dream of Tadayoshi, a dragon rose from the river to fly off into the sky. Flying dragons were recorded as early as the sixth century. According to the *Chronicles of Japan* (*Nihongi*), at the beginning of the rein of Empress Saimei (ruled 655–61) a dragon appeared in the sky above the western peaks of the Katsuragi Mountains.[43] The Katsuragi Mountains were the site of an early Buddhist complex (The High Temple of Katsuragi), and the subsequent sighting of dragons in the sky became associated with the appearance of Buddhism in Japan.

The snake-like form of the dragon in Japan is related to Nāga, the

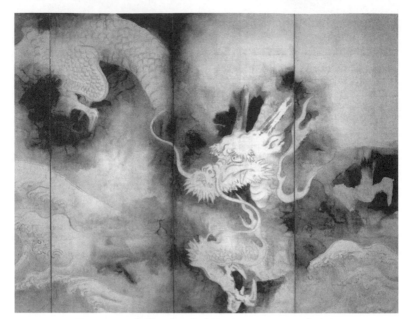

FIGURE 37. *"Dragons and Clouds." Detail of a six-panel folding screen, by Tawaraya Sotatsu (ca. 1600–1643). 1630, ink on paper, 171.5 x 374.6 cm.*

water-serpent deities of India. Nāga were believed to live on Mount Meru, the mythic mountain around which creation had formed. Nāga lived within golden palaces vibrating with ethereal music, ambrosia, and wish-fulfilling jewels and flowers. Nāga lived surrounded by a garden with "the dragon-haunted tree at its center being hung with jewels in which the life of the Golden Embryō is hidden."[44] Through Nāga, dragons in Japan came to be associated with gardens as well as with Buddhism.

Early Buddhism conceived of Nāga as the guardians of Buddha. Indeed, Buddha was believed to have been incarnated as a Nāga king before incarnation as Siddhārtha Gautama. He was "bathed, as soon as born, by the Nāga king and queen, who later created a lotus leaf on which he might reveal himself."[45] Legend has it that, after his awareness of Buddha-Mind while sitting under the Bodhi tree, Shākyamuni traveled to Lake Mucilinda where he sat in meditation for seven days. Mucilinda, the seven-headed Nāga after whom the lake was named, "saw the Buddha's light and rose to the surface, where he was so

FIGURE 38. *"Buddha Protected by Naga."* *Ninth century* A.D., *sandstone, 111 x 52 x 29 cm. Cambodia.*

delighted that he caused it to rain for the whole seven days and pro-tected the sage by curling his seven hoods, or heads, over him."[46] Disciples of Buddha subsequently "converted them to the faith and indeed made them its guardians."[47] The promise of the Nāga was that "until the dawn when Maitreya [["The Loving One," a Buddhist de-ity embodying all-encompassing love]] comes to preach the three ser-mons under the dragon flower tree, even so long I will guard this land and govern the workings of Buddhist law."[48] The hooded cobra-like visage of a Nāga/dragon sheltering and protecting Buddha remains a common, dramatic image (fig. 38).

With respect to the association of dragons with Buddha and Buddhism, it was not uncommon for the name of a Buddhist temple to be "called after a dragon which was said to live there or to have appeared at the time the temple was built."[49] The sighting of a dragon in association with the consecration of a Buddhist temple, again, was considered a favorable omen. In 596, a Buddhist temple in Nara was being dedicated when a "purple cloud descended from the sky and covered the pagoda as well as the Buddha Hall; then the cloud . . . assumed the shape of a dragon . . . After awhile it vanished in a westerly direction."[50] In 1697, a Buddhist temple in Mino Province was being dedicated when "a dragon appeared with a pearl in its mouth, a very good sign indeed."[51] Until quite recently, people continued not only to believe in dragons but also to experience dragons. In the dream of Tadayoshi, therefore, it was a harbinger of good fortune that a dragon had descended into the old villa of Go-Saga, also associated with Emperor Go-Daigo.

The extent to which people deferred to dreams in renaming the emerging temple complex further reveals the power and influence of belief in the animistic reality of dream.[52] The naming of the emerging complex accommodated long-standing belief in the beneficent appearance of dragons in association with commemoration of Buddhist temples as well as with the conception of dragons as the guardians of both Buddha and Buddhism.

Dragons and dreams were influential animistic presences in the final naming of temple. Dreams and dragons were fortuitous omens of the favored future life and significance of the temple.

$$\text{?}$$

Construction of the Temple of the Heavenly Dragon began in late 1339, initially with the labor of one master carpenter and twelve assistants. Six years, though, were required for completion of the complex. We will meet dragons again as a vital aspect of the ongoing life of the temple.

3

CLOUDS OF FLOWERS PRESERVE THE WAY

Construction of buildings intensified in the spring of 1340. To provide initial funds for the construction of the temple, Emperor Kōgon ordered the collection of estate taxes on provincial lands under control of the Ashikaga. As the scope of the project became apparent, the Ashikaga realized that they did not command the capital necessary to complete construction of the complex. Tadayoshi then proposed sending ships to China to engage in trade, hoping to finance completion of the temple. The proposal was bold and ambitious, as formal missions to China had not occurred for nearly five hundred years (it is worth noting that somewhat earlier Musō and Go-Daigo sent a ship to China in 1325 to help fund construction of Kenchō-ji).

With the support of the Ashikaga, and with the urging of Musō, in 1341 Emperor Kōgon commissioned two ships, the Ships of Tenryū Temple [Tenryū-ji Bune], to sail to China. Shihon, a merchant and skilled sailor from Hakata in northern Kyūshū, was appointed captain of the ships and Shūryō Sakugen, a priest, served as navigator. Shihon sailed from Hakata in 1342 and returned from China the following year with pottery, furniture, and other items the significant commercial value of which financed completion of the complex. The temple's trade contact with China continued for the next hundred years or so, sustaining formal Japanese trade with China.

"Opening the Mountain"

Akin to the influences of China on the layout of the city of Kyōto, the ground plan for the layout of principal buildings within the emerging temple was Chinese in inspiration. The spatial layout and architectured features of the temple were modeled after the Sung Dynasty Zen Buddhist temples of Ching-shan, T'ien-t'ung-shan, Pei-shan, and A-yu-wang-shan.[1] As we continue to see, importations into Japan rarely were appropriated without modification. Sung Dynasty Chinese Buddhist temples, for instance, were sited on a north/south axis while the Temple of the Heavenly Dragon would be sited on an east/west axis.

About one hundred and fifty buildings initially were constructed: subtemples, bathhouses and toilets, a kitchen, buildings for the storage of icons and relics, and buildings supporting maintenance of the temple. Temple buildings were constructed on both sides of the Ōi River.

Modeled after Chinese prototypes, a core group of seven structures (禅宗七堂伽藍, *zenshū shichidō garan*) defined the central area of the complex (fig. 40).[2] Three of the four structures were aligned on a primary east/west axis while four buildings were sited two on each side of the east/west axis. Upon entering the temple the three structures on the primary axis would be experienced in sequence, an east-to-west pattern of movement toward the central area of the complex (fig. 41).

A multilevel gate marking the eastern entrance of the complex was the first of the seven core structures to be experienced on the main east/west axis. The name of the gate (三門, *sanmon*, triple gate, with the connotation of a mountain) defined the temple-as-a-mountain.[3] The phrase "opening a mountain" often was used in the ceremonial inauguration of a temple; entering the temple, then, literally would be entering the "mountain" of Buddha and Buddhism. At this time, there also was a small pond and bridge over which people would pass upon entering the complex (fig. 9).[4]

FIGURE 39. *The present-day Dharma Hall* (Hattō).

Continuing into the complex, several buildings specifically associated with Buddha and Buddhism were placed on the main east/
west axis along with the Mountain Gate. West of the Mountain Gate
there was a Buddha Hall (*Butsuden*) for the storage and display of images and icons of Buddha. The Dharma Hall (*Hattō*), primarily a place
where senior priests (*rōshi*) delivered lectures to monks in training,
was sited to the west of the Buddha Hall (fig. 39). Proceeding west-
ward through the complex along the central axis, by design people
first encountered a building associated with the images and relics of
Buddha then a building where residents of the temple would gather
to hear words attributed to Buddha.

   Flanking either side of the central east/west axis, four buildings were constructed primarily for monks. Sited to the south of the
lecture hall, the Monk's Hall (*Sōdō*) marked the complex as a *sangha*
in that "all monks should live a communal life in a single open hall."[5]
At this time, the *Sōdō* could accommodate a thousand monks. Also
included as primary buildings within the core of the complex were a
communal bathhouse (*Yokushitsu*) and toilet (*Tōsu*), and a building for
the storage of foodstuffs and the preparation and communal taking of

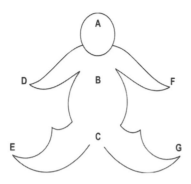

FIGURE 40. *The traditional body:temple correspondence, after a drawing by Mujaku Dōchū: (A) "Head" = Lecture Hall (Hattō); (B) "Heart" = Buddha Hall (Butsu-den); (C) "Groin" = Mountain Gate (Sanmon); (D) "Left Arm" = Monk's Hall (Sōdō); (E) "Left Leg" = Latrine (Tōsu); (F) "Right Arm" = Dining Hall (Kuin); (G) "Right Leg" = Bathhouse (Yokushitsu).*

meals (*Kuri*). Legend has it that "the lay sage Bhadrapala, . . . with 16 followers, attained enlightenment and was granted Bodhisattva-hood through contemplation of water while bathing."[6] Eating, sleeping, eliminating, and bathing were Buddha-Nature and, often spontaneously, could be experienced as such.

A Golden Body, Shining Through

The prototypical form of the layout and spatial interrelationship of the seven core buildings of Rinzai Zen Buddhist temples in China and Japan, by convention, corresponded to the form of a body; the temple-as-a-body, as illustrated via the layout of Tenryū-ji (figs. 40, 41). The temple-body correspondence was detailed in the writings of Ichijō Kanera (1402–81), though he did not associate the seven core buildings of Zen Buddhist temples with an imaged spatial pattern of anthropomorphic interrelationship corresponding to the form of a body. Several centuries later, Mujaku Dōchū (1653–1744) imaged an anthropomorphic design for the layout of core buildings specifically within Rinzai Zen Buddhist temples.[7] In a diagram by Mujaku Dōchū, the position of the "head" in spatial relationship to the "arm" of a body, for instance, corresponded anthropomorphically to the spatial positioning of the Dharma Hall (*Hattō* = "head") and the Dining Hall/Storehouse (*Kuin* = "arm") in the spatial layout of the core area of the "body" of a temple. And so forth.

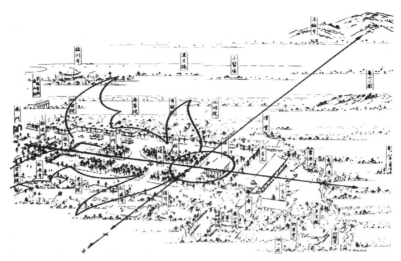

FIGURE 41. A diagram by Mujaku Dōchū, superimposed on the present-day central area of the temple, illustrating the principle of body:temple correspondence.

Importantly, temple-as-body can be conceptualized standing on its "feet" as well as in a supine position from a topographic point of view. Envisioning the temple-as-a-body vertically on its feet, the higher or lower physically placed positioning of each building then can be conceptualized as corresponding anthropomorphically to "higher" occurring or "lower" occurring aspects of an erect bipedal body. From this conceptual point of view, figures 40 and 41 depict the temple complex literally being supported by "lower" aspects of body—the toilet and the bath equal the "feet" of the temple-as-a-body, etc.

Conventional horizontal movement through the temple, as in our introductory walk to the pond garden, thus can be conceptualized as corresponding to vertical ascent. From this perspective, people would have entered the complex through a "lower" area corresponding to the "groin" of the body-temple. Likewise, leaving the temple again would place one in association with "lower" aspects of the body-temple.

Conceptualizing the temple as a vertically positioned body highlights the traditional status-ranked organization of Rinzai Zen

Buddhist temples.[8] The Buddha Hall and Dharma Hall (and Abbot's Quarters and garden pond, for priests), the "higher" realms of the complex associated with *rōshi*, were sited "above" the torso of the temple-body as "[enlightenment] experience is regarded as the primary measure of rank."[9] Figure 40 reveals the Buddha Hall as the center, the "heart," of the temple-body. Indeed, "this plan [the body-temple layout] follows the nature of entering and walking the Buddha path or discipline itself. Moving from profane into sacred space through the entrance . . . the monastery/temple complex becomes an iconographic form . . . of Buddhism itself."[10] To this day, monks still gather periodically in the "heart-area" of the temple, the Dharma Hall, to attend to Dharma being delivered by *rōshi*.

The temple-body motif has been deemed the "'Bliss Body' of Buddha, the 'golden body' shining forth for all to see."[11] A manifestation of the Bliss Body of Buddha also is one's own body.[12] If the temple can be conceived of as a body then, *ipso facto*, the body can be conceived of as a temple.[13] Synonymous with the temple, in Rinzai Zen Buddhism one's own body is conceptualized as the space and place within which experiences of Buddha-Nature occur.

Buddha-Nature often is spoken of as formless, existence-as-it-is prior to distinctions such as "form" and "no form." As "Buddha, he is both formless and form . . . he reveals all this and preaches Dharma [Truth] for all to hear."[14] Rinzai Zen Buddhists often caution people to not mistake the moon reflected in water (here, a temple complex corresponding to a body) for the unseen moon itself (Buddha-Nature). The danger is idolatry, "stopping" at form and image rather than contemplating form and image as embodiment—the compassionate taking on of form by that which is formless. Compelling in its beauty, the Temple of the Heavenly Dragon indeed can be experienced as "good form, but the essence of Zen is to use form to go beyond form, to go beyond all discriminations."[15] Plato of Athens (428–348 B.C.), influenced by Pythagoras of Samos (570–500 B.C.), also understood the idolatry danger of "stopping" at forms themselves—here, arresting forms such as an elegant temple or pond garden experienced as a deeply affecting presence. In Book VII of *The Republic*, Plato fashioned an allegory of people living deep within a cave, mesmerized by compelling forms and images cast as shadows of "reality" on the walls of the cave such that "the prisoners would in every way believe that the truth is nothing other than the shadows."[16] For Buddhists similarly, existence is Buddha-Nature . . . clouded by illusion. "Suchness [*shinnyo*] transcends forms," it is said, "but without depending on forms it cannot be realized . . . The Buddha's teachings [Dharma] which guide people are limitless."[17] Mindful experiences of architectured forms such as a beautifully arresting temples and temple gardens do capture attention, so as to (hopefully) stimulate contemplative awareness of one's Buddha-Nature.

The subtle anthropomorphism of the spatial layout of the Temple of the Heavenly Dragon thus can be experienced as linking the complex to the "suchness" of one's own heart, for "bodymind as the ground of experience is the condition for the spatial character of experience."[18] Compelling forms such as the temple and pond garden, as we further will see, can be experienced as compassionate pointers to the Buddha-Nature of one's own heart (*kokoro*).

Ten Realms of Being

The siting and layout of buildings were accompanied by the fashioning of a landscape aspect of the complex. Here, Musō Kokushi directly begins to influence the character of the temple complex. He defined ten specific spaces and places of singular import. The Ten Favored Views of Tenryū-ji (天龍寺十景, *Tenryū-ji jukkei*) became primary aspects and intended experiences of the landscape aspect of the temple.

Musō's Ten Favored Views, each a realm for favored experiences, were :

One. a branching stream,
  of the nearby Ōi River.
Two. a waterfall of stones,

surrounding a stream flowing off the Mountain
of Storms.
Three. the Mountain of Storms,
as an aspect of the temple landscape.
Four. a grove of pine trees,
near the Ōi River.
Five. a tea arbor,
on nearby Turtle Mountain.
Six. a nine-story pagoda,
on nearby Turtle Mountain.
Seven. a Shintō shrine,
in the distance.
Eight. the entrance gate,
to the complex.
Nine. a bridge,
spanning the Ōi River.
Ten. the pond in the garden,
as a vital aspect of the complex.

Musō's Ten Realms of the temple were composed of naturally
occurring as well as human-made spaces and places. Several of Musō's
Realms lay within the temple complex proper; most lay without, by
design incorporating affecting features of nature into what would
become primarily visual experiences of distant aspects, especially, of
the landscape of the temple. Musō wrote poems on each of these ten
places, that appear in *Sun at Midnight*, a fine translation of his writings.[19] Each of these ten spaces and places was considered a salient
aspect of the complex, the experience of which Musō felt revealed
what we would term the soul (*rei*) of the complex.

Most of Musō's Ten Realms have been lost to fire, human violence, or to time. Several of his designated spaces and places continue
to exist, though, and remain vital to the life and spirit of the present-
day Temple of the Heavenly Dragon. Contemporary temple priests
revere existing aspects of the landscape favored by Musō and believe

that these features, especially the pond garden, both embody and reveal the heart (*kokoro*) of the temple and of Musō. We will consider each of Musō's Ten Realms in turn, emphasizing their mutual interdependence and ongoing affective significance.

STREAMS IN THE SUN, MOUNTAINS, AND TEN THOUSAND PINES

For Musō, water was a vital aspect of the experience of the emerging temple complex. There are two of Musō's Realms of the temple to consider here (in addition to the pond): a branching stream of the nearby Ōi River, and a waterfall of stones surrounding a stream flowing off the Mountain of Storms.

The Ōi River was considered a vital aspect of the complex. Musō wrote of being especially affected by (Realm #1) a branching stream of the Ōi River, which he named "Deep Voice Sounding Day and Night" (絶唱渓, *Zesshōkei*). He apparently felt that this stream was compelling with respect to its color, a consistently deep indigo blue. This stream appears to have been a site for the out-of-doors *zazen* favored by Musō.

A small waterfall (Realm #2) flowing down the slope of the Mountain of Storms also was incorporated as an experiential aspect of the emerging landscape aspect of the temple. Poetically named "Waterfall with the Burning Tail of Gold" (戸無瀬滝, *Tonasedaki*), the stream faced the central core of the complex. The cascade of water apparently glinted in the sun such that "even in the hottest day in summer, you could feel coolness, pure and divine."[20] "The waterfall looked as though it were inside the palace walls"; that is, water flowing down the face of the Mountain of Storms was considered, and experienced, as a component aspect of the temple.[21] The descriptive name for the waterfall, Three-Step Cliff (三級巌, *Sankyūgan*), derived from the form of the waterfall, in that water apparently cascaded over three discernible rock ledges on its way down the mountainside. This naturally occurring three-step waterfall on the mountain was echoed

FIGURE 42. "Borrowed" scenery (shakkei). The Mountain of Storms, an undu-lation of green in the background, peaks above and to the left-rear of foliage billowing toward the rear of the pond.

by a human-made three-step waterfall of stones placed to the rear of the pond in the temple garden (figs. 145, 146).

Several of Musō's Realms therefore included nearby mountains as vital aspects of the landscape. Musō referred to the present-day (Realm #3) Mountain of Storms as Reizan (ねん花嶺; Nengerei, "Peak of the Held-Up Flower"), referencing Vulture Peak in India, on which Shākyamuni spoke to the assembled.[22]

The Mountain of Storms on the other side of the Ōi River is some distance from the core area of the temple. Yet, at about 375 me-ters in height and with a 30-degree angle of elevation, the mountain still appears close at hand when experienced from within the central area of the temple.

The side of the mountain facing the central area of the temple still can be experienced as a dramatic slope sprinkled with foliage such that "the mountain is like a yellow tie-dyed fabric; it is as though embroidered brocade has been spread on the ground."[23] Yishida Togo (1868–1918), a cultural geographer, described the Mountain of Storms as "skirted on the north by the Ōi [Abundant-Flowing

FIGURE 43. *A view to the southwest, from the rear veranda of the Abbot's Quarters. Dense foliage and mist blanket the Mountain of Storms, hazy in the upper distance*

River], a place that is praised in the spring for its cherry blossoms and in the fall for its colorful leaves. It rises majestically from the white sand, green moss, and clear water below."[24] The metaphor of a brocade, evoking a vibrant tapestry spread on the slope of the mountainside, sensuously prefigures present-day experiences of the Mountain of Storms. The cultural geographer Tadahiko Higuchi observed, "in mountains [such as the Mountain of Storms] with elevation angles of 20 degrees or more, the object of interest is the mountainside rather than the profile of the mountain."[25] Viewed from a sitting position on the present-day veranda of the Abbot's Quarters, according to Tadahiko Higuchi, the distant landscape at the time would have appeared to Musō as a short-distance view of the Mountain of Storms draped in perpetual mist and the blue haze of distant sky (fig. 43).

In the late Edo period (1615–1868) the term *shakkei* (借景, "borrowed" scenery) named this practice of visually incorporating distant features of the land, such as venerated mountains, as a design aspect of human-created landscapes. "And which garden was it that first employed the *shakkei* technique?" asks the garden scholar Teiji Itoh.

"Here, we must recall the garden of Tenryū-ji."[26] *Shakkei* meant to borrow a visual experience—not to take or seize or to permanently conscript aspects of nature. *Shakkei* collapsed space and time; distant aspects of nature were apprehended at a glance, fleetingly, moment to moment with each visual experience. "From their point of view [the designer/s of the landscape], every element of the [garden] design was a living thing: water, distant mountains, trees, and stones."[27] Indeed, the visual incorporation of distant aspects of nature was deemed effective to the extent that the animistic "aliveness" of aspects of nature "borrowed" was felt.

Musō's inclusion of the Mountain of Storms as a Realm of the landscape aspect of the temple tells us that the area around the Abbot's and Guest Quarters was not conceptualized as a garden in a conventional sense of the term; that is, akin to our conception of garden as a two-dimensional rearrangement of earth through the planting of flora and/or cultivated food plants. The landscape aspect of the Temple of the Heavenly Dragon appears to have been experienced as a three-dimensional volumetric space in large part defined by the visual incorporation of distant features of nature such as mountains. More specifically, there is an encompassing tripartite structure to the layout of the temple in its interdependent relationship of human-made and natural features. Indeed, "the layout is based on three stages that step down from the mountain behind the temple [Kameyama, from this point of view]. With the mountain as the first step, the temple sits on the second step with its back to the mountainside and looks down over the garden [the pond, specifically] that slopes away in front of it" as the third step.[28] Interestingly, this encompassing tripartite structure of the complex as a whole will be echoed in the tripartite structure of the Bridge of Stones (Chapter 7) and the Waterfall of Stones (Chapter 10) within the pond.

Water, Mountains, . . . and Trees. Musō incorporated into the emerging temple landscape a particularly dense grove of trees (Realm #4), "where old pine trees were close together such as to make a natural cave."[29] This cave-like nest of ancient pine was said to border the

Ōi River, probably within an area near the temple now dense with commercial establishments and residential quarters. The Cave Beneath Ten Thousand Pines (万松洞, *Banshōdō*) was the name given to a particularly affecting dense, extensive grove of pine trees. The name suggests that Musō undoubtedly sat in *zazen* while nested within this cave-like stand of pine trees, near the river. Musō often sat in *zazen* within caves, whether the caves were formed from the boughs of trees or were formed within the belly of mountains (fig. 113).[30]

Musō designated specific features of nature, such as venerated mountains and water and trees, as Realms, especially affecting spaces and places incorporated as vital aspects of the emerging temple. Nature itself was a predominate aspect of Musō's influence on the temple and, as such, "temple" became much more than buildings.

REVEALING THE NATURE OF BUDDHA-NATURE

Musō felt that Buddha-Nature was the Original Face of nature as well as of people. Musō would have been familiar with the earlier argument of Kōbō Daishi (Kūkai, 774–835) for the Buddha-Nature of trees and rocks. Both people and nature "originated from the same common ground," and both participated in the same nature.[31] Esoteric Shingon and Tendai synthesized Shintō and Buddhism. Shintō conceptions of deities embodied as aspects of nature underlay the idea of Buddha-Nature as the nature of nature as well as the nature of people; indeed, Musō wrote, "*Kami* and *Hotoke* [Buddha] are inseparable as water and wave."[32] Preeminently, nature is Buddha-Nature. Nature does not exhibit an ego-conscious "self," nature simply . . . is. As such, perhaps people, young monks in particular, could more clearly, directly, experience the nature of Buddha-Nature as nature: thus, Musō's compassionate incorporation of nature as a vital aspect of routine experiences of the landscape aspect of the temple.

In addition to the incorporation of affecting features of nature as aspects of the emerging landscape of the temple, Musō conscripted existing human-made landmarks as well as incorporated a few

buildings as aspects of his Ten Realms. The several human-architec-
tured Realms of the landscape functioned to reinforce shared, social
experiences of the complex.

A covered seating area named the Dragon-Gate Pavilion (龍門
亭, *Ryūmontei*), an arbor (Realm #5), was constructed as shelter for
people sitting amid nature; in particular, the arbor sheltered contemplative experiences of the nearby Waterfall-with-the-Burning-Tail-of-
Gold (Realm #2). On October 3, 1467, Yoshimasa of the Ashikaga
visited the then-rebuilt temple and climbed to the arbor on Turtle
Mountain "to enjoy the view of the borrowed scenery of Arashiyama and its scarlet maple trees from the Dragon's Gate Pavilion."[33]
Yoshimasa was moved to write that "maple trees surround the *tei*
⟦the arbor pavilion⟧, and Arashi-yama is a brocade."[34] Musō, we
remember, spent more than twenty years for the most part living
in small shelters on mountains and in forests. Shelters in the woods
and rudimentary arbors on top of mountains long had been a part of
Musō's rustic life in nature. The Dragon-Gate Pavilion, though, was
a refined social area sheltering guests invited to the temple for tea and
aesthetic experiences of nature landscaped.

A nine-storied tower (亀頂塔, *Kichōtō*, Turtle-Top Tower; Realm
#6) was constructed on the summit of Turtle Mountain, and the tower
was considered a Realm of the temple. The design of the pagoda-like
tower mirrored earlier *stūpa* (仏舎利塔, *bussharitō*) in India constructed to enshrine the remains of Shākyamuni. Upon the death of
Shākyamuni, and before cremation of his body, disciples gathered hair
and nail clippings and then, after cremation, collected ash and bones.
Legend has it that King Ashoka (304–232 B.C.) divided the remains
of Shākyamuni into 84,000 portions, and ordered a similar number of
stūpa constructed throughout India to enshrine each portion. Japan
continued the tradition of constructing multistoried towers as memo-
rials to Shākyamuni. The tower atop Turtle Mountain signaled the
literal presence of Shākyamuni, of Buddhism, the "traces of the Truth
physically present as a Realm of the temple."[35] Through its physical presence, the towering spire atop Turtle Mountain functioned

as a visual reminder of the presence of the Dharma of Shākyamuni.

The tower atop Turtle Mountain also was a visible manifestation of internecine political struggles within Buddhism. Earlier in 1337, Musō had proposed to the Ashikaga that memorial towers (利生塔, *Rishōtō*, Pagodas of the Buddha's Favor) be constructed in each of the sixty-six provinces and on two islands (Iki, Tsushima) "in which prayers could be recited for the souls of victims of war."[36] Takauji and Tadayoshi agreed, as they discerned in Musō's proposal a way to employ the memorial towers to consolidate power in the provinces and to aid in the "pacification of the rest of the country."[37] Subsequently, memorial towers were placed within areas served by Tendai and Shingon. In effect, Rinzai Zen Buddhism and the lineage of Musō literally came to "tower" over other schools of Buddhism.

Along with the Dragon-Gate Pavilion, the site atop Turtle Mountain was favored for aesthetic experiences of the land and the human-created landscape below. "To enjoy the garden is the basic idea," we read, "and buildings were constructed with respect to this basic idea. The Buddha-tower was built at the best place to look down upon the pond garden. Whether we stand where the pagoda was or stand on the veranda [of the Abbot's Quarters], we can enjoy the perfect beauty of this garden."[38] At this time, guests invited to the tower could gaze down upon the pond garden of stones.

An already-existing Shintō shrine (*Hachiman-gū*; Realm #7) was conscripted, renamed Hall of the Ancestral Guardian Spirit (霊庇廟, *Reihibyō*), and became a Realm of the temple landscape.[39] The village shrine was located some distance from the compound, yet the shrine was conscripted visually into the emerging temple landscape.

The aforementioned triple-gate entrance to the compound (Realm #8) was renamed Benevolent Light of the World (普明閣, *Fumyōkaku*, referring to Buddha) and was designated by Musō as a Realm of the temple. Again, entering into the temple literally was entering into the Dharma of Buddha.

Musō visually incorporated an existing bridge Realm #9) spanning the Ōi River as a Realm of the temple (fig. 44). The bridge had

FIGURE 44. The present-day Moon-Crossing Bridge.

been named Moon-Crossing Bridge (渡月拠, *Togetsukyō*), as Emperor Kameyama once remarked that the curve of the bridge evoked a bright moon crossing over the river to disappear into the night-shrouded Mountain of Storms.[40]

The bridge was associated with the moon, and was said to be best experienced in moonlight. Experienced in darkness, beneath stars and the milky light of the moon, it was felt that "the Togetsu Bridge rises to the Milky Way."[41] During this time, the bridge functioned to connect the area around the Abbot's Quarters to land on the other side of the Ōi River. At this time, the river and the bridge could be seen from the verandas of the Abbot's Quarters and Guest Quarters. The railings of the bridge apparently were crimson red, echoing the red of the Buddha's Light in the World, the Shintō shrine aspect of the temple in the distance. The colors of these two Realms of the temple, the reds, blues, and greens, must have been quite vivid, even experienced at a distance.

Musō wrote, "Arashiyama, white with snow, almost seems to be engulfed in clouds of flowers. Pine trees, by a magic touch. Transfigured into cherry trees."[42] Musō's poem tells us that the Ten Realms of the temple often were settings for mindful experiences of the seasons. The emerging complex was a setting conducive to contemplation of nature, and of mindful awareness of change and transformation.

In the aforementioned *Makioka Sisters*, we later see Teinosuke and Sachiko, newly married, "arrive at the Bridge of the Passing Moon [by which the bridge more popularly also was known], beyond which, rising from the river [Ōi River], was Storm Hill [Arashiyama] with its cherry blossoms."[43] Over the centuries, the bridge remained a favored place from which to experience cherry trees blooming on Arashiyama in the spring and to experience the varied colors of leaves on the maple trees in the fall.

DRAGON PONDS AND FLOWERING TREES

The (Realm #10) pond garden aspect of the temple landscape remains the most celebrated of the Ten Realms of Musō, as "the water of the pond is lapis [*lapis lazuli*] and the exceedingly beautiful stones in the pond are beyond compare."[44] Yet, when Musō arrived here the area around prior pond(s) lay in neglect and ruin. Conscripted workers under the direction of the Ashikaga found remnants of the desiccated pond within the old imperial villa of Emperor Go-Saga as well as remnants of the even older compounds of Prince Kaneakira and Empress Danrin. The desiccation was extensive, as water had not flowed into or within the area for some time.

The dryness and desolation of the area must have been profound. The withering of the area was taken as a sign that a dragon no longer lived there. The area "was in a deplorable condition on account of war, and this must have been very disagreeable for the Dragon-god, who perhaps left because there was very little water in the pond."[45] During the time of Musō, though, water and dragons once again were invited to flow into the site.

Water brought the site back to life, literally, as moisture once again permeated the earth and the air. Revealing his mindful awareness of dragons and the interrelationship of dragons and water, Musō

FIGURE 45. *The pond in the garden, as foreground, with the Mountain of Storms (Arashiyama) in the distance, as background, peaking above the voluptuous mid-ground arena of trees on Kameyama at the rear of the pond.*

wrote that "today I would not dare to expound the secret of the stream bed, but I can tell you that the blue dragon is curled there."[46] Restoring water, life, to the site was associated with the return of a dragon. Dragons remain a pervasive, ongoing reality in the life of the Temple of the Heavenly Dragon. We will continue to witness various ways in which dragons were and still are believed to be present as a vital aspect of the complex.

Conscripted workers cleared the area of accumulated silt and debris.[47] Mud and earth were piled up into a hillock functioning as a backdrop for the pond area (figs. 79, 98, 147). Mirei Shigemori noted how "artificial hills 〖築山, *tsukiyama*〗 were a characteristic of gardens

in those days. Approximately two-thirds of the pond garden was surrounded by an elaborate artificial hill. The artificial hill tapers to the
south and the north, and was centered around ⟦highest point toward⟧
the west. The purpose of the artificial hill was to evoke a scenic vista
of valleys and mountains."[48] Perhaps remnants of the present-day hillock to the rear of the pond were in place when Musō arrived, as
mud and earth also had been piled up in forming the rear retaining
wall for the pond garden within the imperial villa of Go-Saga. Any
preexisting hillocks in the area of the desiccated pond, though, would
have been substantially eroded by nearly two centuries of wear when
Musō arrived at the site. Mud and earth dredged during the time of
Musō were piled up to the rear of the present-day pond either resulting in or adding to the background hillock (figs. 45, 46).

Presently about five-and-a-half meters in height, the "artificial
hill" peaks toward the top (to the west) of the pond and tapers on
both sides to the far edges of the pond. Elaborating upon the interrelationship of the hillock and the curvilinear shape of the present-day
pond, Shigemori adds, "the garden designer evoked a dry valley at
the center of the artificial hill. Viewed from atop Mount Kameyama
⟦Turtle Mountain⟧, the valley appears to lead into the rock-lined
peninsula of earth jutting into the pond. The designer of this pond
garden very much considered this ⟦visual⟧ connection between the
artificial hill and the pond itself."[49] That is, when viewed, say, from
atop Turtle Mountain, the Buddha-tower, or from above and to the
rear of the pond, rather than the pond appearing directly below their
feet, during the time of Musō people would have looked down and
over the piled-up mound of earth and stone to view the pond in the
background below. Experienced from these elevated points of view,
the artificial hill would have established visual distance between the
viewer and the pond garden, akin to looking down into a distant
water-laden valley from atop a mountain.

A path was woven behind the human-made hillock, further
enabling experiences of the pond garden from a variety of visual
vantages (figs. 47, 48). During the time of Musō, the pond garden

FIGURE 46. *A view to the west/southwest, from the rear veranda of the Guest Quarters. Earth from digging the pond was piled up to form the broadly triangular-shaped hillock* (tsukiyama) *spread across the rear of the pond garden.*

was not intended to be experienced solely from sitting positions on the verandas of subtemple buildings within the central area of the complex. Physically demanding movement, ascending then descending movement, was and still is required to experience the garden in its entirety.[50] The Buddha-tower atop Turtle Mountain, the Moon-Crossing Bridge, pavilions, and the path around the pond all became prominent, physically demanding areas for experiencing the landscape of the complex.

FIGURE 47. At the far northern edge of the hillock of earth behind the pond, a formal path leads to the present-day upper-area of the garden.

A River Journey of Origin and Existence Musō referred to the pond in the garden as *Sōgenchi* (曹源池), and the pond poetically was experienced as "autumn in the middle of the sky."[51] In Rinzai Zen Buddhism at the time, *gen* referenced a (metaphysical) point of origin. The name *Sōgenchi* linked the pond in the garden to the origin, and nature, of existence as-it-is (*shinnyo*). *Sōgenchi* referenced both a space/place and a state of awareness "where ordinary people [[*sō*]], like myriad drops of water, begin a journey revealing a river . . . of which

FIGURE 48. A path, and stream, meanders around the present-day upper-area behind the pond.

people are yet unaware."[52] The name *Sōgenchi* tells us that the pond in the garden was conceptualized as an aid to people in the experience of Buddha-Nature. It is in this manner that Musō compassionately linked referents to Buddhism to a variety of still-vital aspects of the landscape of the temple.

Musō's name for the pond in the garden is telling in yet another respect. Dredging mud and earth from the area of prior pond(s) uncovered a stone on which several faded characters were engraved: *Sōgen itteki* (曹源一滴, Source of Existence; meaning, "at its origin, every river is only a single drop of water").[53] The characters appear to say that Buddha-Nature and the compassion of Buddha are but a single drop of water, the source (*gen*) of which people (*sō*) are not yet aware. Writings on the stone apparently engraved the belief that every person already is Buddha-Nature.

Sōgen itteki, interestingly, also was the name of the dragon pond within Nanzen-in, the detached palace of Emperor Kameyama. A prevailing interpretation of the Sōgen Stone therefore is that Shūshin Gidō, a priest, engraved characters on a stone from the pond in Nanzen-in.[54] The stone possibly was transferred by Kameyama to then ex-Emperor Go-Saga, and priest Gidō was said then to have placed the stone in the pond garden of Go-Saga's villa.

Stones previously placed by human hand thus most likely were present in the desiccated area of prior ponds experienced by Musō. Perhaps Musō did not set the stones presently gracing the pond garden within the Temple of the Heavenly Dragon. If so, then who might have set the stones, especially the dramatic upright stones, within and around the present-day pond? Why? And when?

We do not know which specific stones and compositions of stone in the present-day pond garden at this time were "old" (set during the time, say, of Go-Saga's villa on Turtle Mountain) and which stones and compositions of stones at the time were "new" (set, say, during the time of Musō). What is known is that Sung Dynasty (960–1279) China influenced the placement of the stones and compositions of stones in the pond and around the garden.

There is a distinct Chinese character to the present-day pond garden, as illustrated in Part II. Yet, the stones themselves in and around the pond garden are Japanese in origin. Stones possessing a still-reddish hue most likely are from the region of Kishū, and Ao-ishi stones with a still-bluish hue most likely are from present-day Wakayama and Mie prefectures. Large stones were transported to Kyoto by ship, then to the Ōi River by oxcart, then finally carted or drawn across logs to the site.[55]

Tachibana Tomoshige remains associated with the siting, building, and rebuilding of Go-Saga's villa at Turtle Mountain. As best we know, though, Tachibana did not travel to China and therefore probably did not contribute to the "Chinese-ness" of the manner in which the myriad stones in and around the pond garden were composed. The compositions of stone themselves still extant in the present-day pond garden lead us to the Chinese Zen Buddhist priest Lan-hxi Dao-long (Lan-ch'I Tao-lung, 1213–78). Known in Japan as Rankei Doryū, he most likely set the "old" compositions of stones in the pond garden.

Rankei Doryū was a priest at Cheng-tu temple in China when he arrived in Kyūshū in 1246, and subsequently made his way to

Kamakura and Kyōto. Tokiyori (1227–63) of the Hōjō clan of families invited him to establish the aforementioned temple of Kenchō-ji in Kamakura. Rankei Doryū admitted females to his Zen training sessions at Kenchō-ji, a display of egalitarianism uncommon within the highly ranked, socially stratified society into which he arrived. He went on to distinguish himself in the teaching of Chinese Zen Buddhism, and he still is considered "the first and most prominent of the Chinese Zen masters to work in Japan."[56] Rankei Doryū posthumously was given the title of Zen Master of the Great Enlightenment (Daikakuji Zenji).

From 1261 to 1264, Rankei Doryū was invited to live within the imperial villa on Turtle Mountain, where he instructed Emperor Go-Saga in Chinese Zen Buddhism. Rankei Doryū was *the* influential Chinese presence within the area at the time. He was "a fully trained and experienced monk whose spiritual attainments had been recognized by a leading Chinese master."[57] His very presence as well as firsthand knowledge of gardening rendered him more than capable of designing or overseeing the setting of the Chinese-inspired compositions of Japanese stones within the present-day garden pond.

Musō, and the Work of Gardens Musō Kokushi also was an influential presence during the birth of the pond garden. He participated in the construction of the pond garden, though there is controversy as to the degree and character of his activity during this period in the life of the pond garden.

One area of considered opinion is exemplified by the architectural historian Hirotoro Ota's position that "Musō Kokushi, an enthusiastic nature lover, made excellent gardens at every temple to which he moved, thus influencing the development of other gardens."[58] Matsunosuke Tatsui writes, "the garden of Tenryū-ji has been widely known as one of the great works of Musō Kokushi."[59] Bokuō Seki argues, "Sōgenchi [the pond] belongs to the Hōjō [Abbot's Quarters] and is one of the most successful gardens by Musō Kokushi."[60] On the other hand, Teiji Itoh's slightly different conclusion is that "the pond garden, which now extends out in front of the abbot's quarters at the foot of Kameyama, had been redesigned by Musō Soseki from the pond that existed there in the days of the Kameyama Palace."[61] Mirei Shigemori's stark position is that "when Musō Kokushi came to the Tenryū-ji temple as its founder, he did not make this garden but altered it."[62] In each instance, though, the issue of whether or not Musō "made" the present-day pond garden stems from a static rather than dynamic conception of a garden.

Controversies over the nature of Musō's activity within this period in the life of the garden presume that the present-day pond garden was designed and executed all at one time by one person *in toto*, such that one can speak of the "maker" of the pond garden. As we continue to see, the landscape aspect of the temple is not of one piece. The relevant concern here ought not be who "made" the pond garden but who contributed what aspects of the pond garden and, as best as we can reconstruct, when. And why.

The pond garden is an intricate phenomenon coalescing the intent and will of various people of influence living at various times. No one person "made" the present-day pond garden. The pond garden was not so much "made" during the time of Musō, had its beginning at this time; rather, the pond garden coalesced into its present form during the time of Musō. "Making" a garden was much more than the introduction of physical elements such as stones and water and trees. The "making" of the present-day pond garden embodied affect and heart (*kokoro*), in the Rinzai Zen Buddhist sense of the term. From this perspective, at the very least Musō participated in "making" the pond garden by designating the pond garden as one of the experiential Realms of the Temple of the Heavenly Dragon.

Musō brought a lasting Rinzai Zen Buddhist presence to the pond garden. Temple activity during his time in large part was directed toward defining and constructing environments for the training of monks. Musō contributed immensely to the "making" of the pond garden as a prominent landscape aspect of the temple as a *sangha*.

Musō believed that the character of people was revealed in their motives for making, altering, or aiding in the construction of gardens and he wrote that "there are those who practice the art of gardening out of vanity and a passion for display, with no interest whatever in their own true nature. They are concerned only with having their gardens attract the admiration of others."[63] Musō then narrated an incident in the life of the venerable priest Haku Rakuten (Po Chü-i, in China), who once dug a small pond and planted stands of bamboo to define a garden. Haku Rakuten felt that "the bamboo—its heart is empty [free from desire, greed, worldly thoughts, etc.]. It has become my friend. The water—its heart [kokoro] is pure [free of illusion]. It has become my teacher.'"[64]

Musō felt that the character of people such as Haku Rakuten animistically participated in the gardens associated with them; yet, not necessarily in every instance "made" by them. Musō also wrote that people, "especially priests who love the enka [煙霞, an emotionally affecting panorama, ideally shrouded in mist and smoke] of mountains and waters, are like Haku Rakuten and, like the bamboo with which Haku Rakuten identified, priests must be clean-hearted as well. Such people have a very refined taste. But if people have refined tastes concerning nature but are not of a spiritual mind, then their taste is to no avail. These people are not real priests, because they distinguish the mountains and waters of nature from their own nature. A few priests, though, feel that mountains, rivers, plants, and stones are themselves."[65] Both nature and people participate in Buddha-Nature. It is through mindful awareness, contemplation and meditation, of nature and gardens that we contemplate our own heart.[66]

Nature and gardens, though, were not to be idolized as ends unto themselves. Musō concluded, "if it is so then it may be said that such priests truly love nature. To love nature is not a bad habit, but it is not a good habit either. Nature itself is neither good or bad. There is no merit or demerit about the nature. Nature . . . exists within one's heart."[67] Negating dualism, Musō admonished that nature without is not to be privileged over nature within. Musō once admonished priests that the making of a garden ought not reduce the land available

for vegetable plots. No matter how beautiful and affecting emotionally, gardens for gardens' sake are not to be privileged over people.

For present-day priests within the temple, as we will see, experiences of the pond garden evoke Musō and his awareness "that
the entirety of nature is nothing but the Buddha's expression of the
Dharma; that mountains, rivers, grass, and trees are the very body of
the Buddha."[68] When the priest with whom I studied says that Musō
"made" the garden, he has in mind the making of the character, the
heart, of the pond garden experienced as embodiment of venerated
priests such as Musō as well as the Dharma of Shākyamuni.

Priests and Non-People, Alone in the Garden During the time of
Musō, the physical activity of making a garden was considered a low-
status activity. Working the earth was considered defiling, and lower-
caste groups of people who did so were forced to live along the soggy,
disease-ridden banks principally of the Kamo and Katsura rivers. As
such, these lower-caste people came to possess intimate knowledge of
the earth (what we would term geology and mineralogy) giving them
specialized skills useful in the construction of landscapes. Variously
named River-Things (河原者, *kawaramono*) or River-Bank Gardeners (仙隋河原者, *senzui kawaramono*), they were a caste of Despised
People 〔賤民, *senmin*〕 with a social status immutably linked to specific occupational activities. And to the earth.

The Despised were considered not quite human (非人, *hinin*),
merely "corpse-handlers concerned with the provision 〔to samurai〕
of corpses for the testing on them of new swords and they were the
clearers-up after calamities . . . which might result in the bodies of
victims."[69] They skinned and tanned the animal hides wrapping the
armor of samurai. Nobility passing by them on roads speculated as
to "what kind of animal he was."[70] Ivan T. Morris adds that "this
attitude is graphically reflected in some of the picture scrolls. For example, the thirteenth-century *Illustrated Handscroll of the Legends
of Tenjin Engi* (*Tenjin Engi Emaki*) depicts members of the lower orders as wizened *homuncules*, often engaged in brawls or grotesquely

staggering under loads that are larger than themselves. When 'good people' appear on the same painting, they are usually twice as tall as the plebeians, and their dignified features are in striking contrast to the hideously twisted faces of the workers."[71] Helen Craig McCullough describes The Despised "being carried off as laborers . . . having their wretched huts burned down to make beacon fires or torn apart for use in fortifications, or murdered wantonly by head-seeking warriors."[72] The Despised carried out undesirable, polluting tasks associated with working the earth: slaughtering animals, dredging rivers and streams . . . and laboring to make landscape and temple gardens.

The Despised were needed by higher-caste people designing pond gardens because The Despised possessed intimate knowledge of stones, plants, and the earth. The pond garden aspect of the Temple of the Heavenly Dragon physically was "made" by people not privileged to otherwise routinely experience the complex.[73]

The Despised for some time remained unnamed. "In the past," we read, "outcastes [kawaramono] have been permitted in the Imperial Palace [in Kyōto] to do gardening but since these people are unclean, as of last year such permission is no longer granted."[74] About the fourteenth century, though, descendants of The Despised began to design as well as construct landscapes and occasionally were acknowledged as authors of gardens. The still-celebrated gardener Zen'ami (1386–1482), a descendent of The Despised, for instance, designed as well as oversaw the construction of gardens for Ashikaga Yoshimasa (1436–90)—gardens that still are venerated for their beauty and emotional affect.[75]

Through their association with the dead, and with the earth, The Despised also were thought of, shaman-like, as participating in the realm of the spirits. In this sense, "not quite human" also meant "they were spiritually charged."[76] Being considered *hinin* also suggests that The Despised were thought of as perhaps more spirit than human. The Despised at once were held in awe as quasi-spiritual beings as well as beings so impure as to be "untouchable." Through their very presence when physically constructing gardens, the belief was that the realm of spirits, with the beneficence and protection associated with the spiritual realm, also would through contagious contact participate in the gardens.

During the time of Musō, there were Buddhist priests who were judged as defiling their station by choosing to "set stones," that is, by choosing to work in the earth, work on temple gardens physically, and otherwise engage in the work of The Despised.[77] Stone-Setting Buddhist Priests (石立僧, *Ishitate sō*), as they were named, were familiar with esoteric manuals of garden making and principles of garden design (*Zōen Hiden Sho*).[78] The Despised often were conscripted as labor for the physical construction of gardens for the most part designed by stone-setting Buddhist priests who primarily were from the Tendai and Shingon schools of Buddhism. Sutemi Horiguchi adds that Musō "studied Mikkyo and Tendai, and he probably had many opportunities to witness Ishitate sō. It is not unreasonable to [conjecture] that Musō learned how to erect a stone from Ishitate sō."[79] At the very least, during his early studies Musō was in a position to be exposed to and most likely to have mastered knowledge held by stone-setting esoteric Buddhist priests.

During the birth of the pond garden, both Musō and Takauji of the Ashikaga stepped onto the earth alongside The Despised. "During the work on the garden, Musō . . . dug earth himself and carried it in bamboo baskets to the front of the temple hall as the initial ceremony marking the establishment of the new temple."[80] Also, "when it was under construction, Takauji also actually worked carrying mud."[81] Priest Tsutomu Minakami adds, "I can only imagine Musō Kokushi walking around the pond using kawaramono. That, to me, does not look like a priest shrouding himself in political power."[82] For Musō merely to have associated physically with The Despised, and their work, illustrates his choosing not to exercise ascribed power to discriminate available to him via his social rank and status.

By virtue of participation in the believed impurity of working in the earth and through physical contact with The Despised, stone-setting priests themselves often were despised by fellow priests. A venerated Shingon priest criticized Musō for "engaging in work below his station of birth and achievement."[83] Musō's physical work in the garden for the most part was ritual and ceremonial activity; yet, his behavior nonetheless reveals the character of his Zen. Teiji Itoh explains that "though he [Musō] was despised by some for doing what they considered degrading labor, he undertook this work as a kind of Zen discipline and training."[84] Zen priests of the Rinzai school, in particular, continue to link mindful awareness and physical labor. Awareness of Buddha-Nature, "enlightenment," was and often still is experienced amid physical labor. Musō "insisted that all work in the secular world reveals the Buddha."[85] Priest Kōhō's consciousness of station, status, and circumstance was not consistent with Musō's practice of Zen. However briefly or ceremonial, direct involvement in the work of physically making a garden is an important instance of Musō's practice of Zen.

Physical work on the pond garden was a manifestation of Musō's enlightened awareness, where illusory distinctions of social station and circumstance collapse in the direct experience of the mud literally under everyone's feet. Musō wrote, "the four castes [in Vedic India] differ from one another, but they are all alike in being disciples of the Buddha and should behave accordingly."[86] Like Shākyamuni, Musō believed that every person, regardless of birth and social status, preeminently was Buddha-Nature. Musō's behavior in the garden negated distinctions such as clean and defiled, venerated and despised.

In his *Dream Conversations* (*Muchū Mondōshū*), Musō wrote, "it is delusion to think that the pure world of paradise and the profane world of the present are different. The distinction between holy purity and defilement, too, is delusion. Both are only groundless imaginings that spring into the human mind."[87] Consider this poem Musō wrote (and my bracketed commentary) shortly before his experience of death:

In the real world
　　〖*shinnyo*; Buddha Nature; Original Evil〗
the pure world
　　〖freed from the suffering induced by illusion〗
no separation exists.
　　〖dualist categories are products of illusion〗
Why wait for another time and another meeting.
　　〖emphasis on the existential present〗
The teaching on Vulture Peak is here today.
　　〖the timeless Dharma expounded by Shākyamuni
　　on Vulture Peak, in India〗
Who else are you looking for
　　〖Buddha consciousness is pre-existent and extant〗
to preserve the Way?
　　〖Buddha, keeping in motion the Dharma Wheel of
　　the Law through awareness of Buddha Nature〗[88]

Musō did venture among The Despised, however briefly or ceremonially. In so doing, he established a precedent toward acknowledgment of, and respect for, the laborers who physically "made" most
of the still deeply affecting gardens and temple landscapes of Japan.

No substantive alterations of the pond garden occurred from the
time of Musō to the present, save those alterations imposed by nature
and by time (fig. 49). And by fields of fire.

Fields of Fire, and the Brocade of Spring

A ceremony commemorating completion of the Temple of the Heavenly Dragon was held on August 29, 1345, the anniversary of the
seventh year of the death of Emperor Go-Daigo. Parading through the
streets of Kyōto, "Takauji and Tadayoshi, with their leading generals Yamana Tokiuji and Kō no Moronao headed a procession of many
hundreds of armed warriors to a great celebration feast at Tenryūji
. . . the streets of the city were thronged from early morning with

FIGURE 49. A photograph from 1985, from the south-facing veranda of the Guest Quarters. Distant views of the mist-shrouded Mountain of Storms to the south/southwest, "borrowed" scenery, are an aspect of the architectured visual experience of the pond garden.

townspeople hoping to catch a glimpse of the military pageantry. It was impressed upon the city that the *bakufu* . . . was the military master of Kyoto, and that henceforward Zen was to be the privileged Buddhist school within the capital."[89] The ceremony "opened the mountain," and Tenryū-ji became one of the most influential Zen Buddhist temples in the Kansai region of Japan.

As first abbot, Musō delivered a lecture emphasizing the Buddhist spirit and mission of the temple. It was the mission of believers, he said, to carry the Wheel of the Law (Dharma of Shākyamuni) into the future. "As for myself," Musō said, "appearing before you today on this platform [fig. 114], I have nothing special to offer as my own interpretation of the Law. I merely join myself with all others—from the founder Shākya Tathāgata, the other Buddhas, Bodhisattvas, saints and Arhats, to all those here present, including patrons and officials, the very eaves and columns of this hall, lanterns and posts, as well as all the men, animals, plants and seeds in the boundless ocean of existence—to keep the Wheel of the Law in motion. . . . Look here! Don't you see Shākyamuni here right now walking around the top of my cane . . . ? Today I am born again here with the completion of this new hall. All saints and sages are assembled here to bring man and heaven together."[90] For Musō, the Buddhist past, present, and future were conjoined and embodied as the new temple. The temple was considered a vital means by which the (Dharma) Wheel of the Law would be kept in motion.

Shortly after the commemoration ceremony, the temple sheltered about five hundred monks and priests. For some time the temple was open only to monks of Musō's school of Rinzai Zen Buddhism. The temple otherwise continued to be experienced primarily by visitors of influence such as emperors, aristocrats, and the military.

For instance, on September 16, 1344, as work on the garden neared completion, the retired Emperor Kōgon visited the temple, received an elaborate reception, and was invited to admire the stones in and around the pond. During a later visit in 1346, Musō wrote that "we [Musō and Kōgon] climbed to the *tei* [*Ryūmontei*, Arbor of the Dragon-Gate Waterfall] to contemplate the haze of spring, the brocade of a deep blue mountain stream [*Zesshōkei*, Deep Voice Sounding Day and Night], and to hear the laughter of flowers on the mountain [Arashiyama, Mountain of Storms]."[91] Emperor Kōgon "viewed the cherry blossoms of Arashiyama at the height of their beauty, enjoying the scene from the senior priest's chamber [Musō's Abbot's Quarters]."[92] To gain favors for Tenryū-ji, Musō continued to court emperors and aristocrats while promoting his school of Rinzai Zen Buddhism. Visits by people of influence enhanced the status and prestige of the new temple.

Musō continued to bring clans of influential families other than the Ashikaga into relationship with the Temple of the Heavenly Dragon. On November 23, 1344, Kinkata of the Fujiwara visited the temple and composed poems on his experience of the pond garden in winter, surrounded by snow blanketing the peaks of the Mountain of Storms. The Ashikaga, however, continued to exercise principal influence on the character of the temple.

The year 1351 was of some consequence in the early life of the temple. On August 16, 1351, Takauji rode to the temple to offer prayers to the spirit of Go-Daigo then hung a memorial tablet on one of the subtemple buildings. Characters on the tablet declared that descendants of the Ashikaga would continue to support and be faith-ful to the temple, and that the Ashikaga were obligated not only to honor the spirit of Go-Daigo but also to honor the spirit of all the life lost during the war between the Northern and Southern Courts.

Musō then delivered a memorial lecture commemorating Em-peror Go-Daigo. Reflecting on the war between the Northern and Southern Courts, Musō concluded that anger, one of the Three Bud-dhist Evils, was a vital lesson to be learned, memorialized, from the actions of both Go-Daigo and Takauji. "In the realm of True Purity," he said, "there is no such thing as 'I' or 'He,' nor can 'friend' and 'foe' be found there. . . . Peace and disorder in the world . . . follow upon one another as illusion begets delusion . . . We have reason to believe that the Imperial wrath [of Emperor Go-Daigo] will be appeased. Such a worthy intention [on the part of Takauji] is no trifling thing, and the Buddhas in their profound compassion are certain to bestow their unseen favor and protection upon us. Then may warfare come to an end, the whole country enjoy true peace, and all the people rest secure from disturbances and calamities."[93] This was Musō's final formal lecture, in 1351.

Places and architectured spaces deemed sacred customarily also serve as sanctuaries—places and spaces in which peace (平和, heiwa) dwells. In turn, sacred places and architectured spaces often are sites for the diffusion of peace—not as an ideal, but rather manifested as a tangible space and place. Peace did not reside in dreams, exclusively.

Peace was grounded. Peace was materialized, occupied space and a specific place. Peace was substantive. The peace within and flowing from sacred spaces and architectured places often is clothed in for-giveness, renunciation, and reconciliation.

Musō reminded the assembled that, out of entitlement and self-interest principally, peace had been atrophied both by religious (imperial/Shintō) as well as aristocratic/military claims to authority over people. The absence of peace throughout the provinces largely had been owing to the desires and behaviors of people privileged by birth and social position. The temperaments and designs of privi-leged people affected large numbers of people, from a variety of status positions in society and on a large geographic scale. To foster peace, Musō admonished negation of preoccupation with ego-self and as-cribed social status.

We also note the impact of the lack of peace on nature and the human-created environment. Warfare is a significant force for the hu-man destruction of nature. Peace is not just a desired state of being for people, but also enables the flourishing of nature as well as human-created landscapes. Amid desires for continuing peace, restoration of the land began to occur. In peace, people and other forms of nature began to find . . . quietude.

After the memorial service, Musō fell ill. Refusing treatment, the word of his impending death spread and over two thousand monks and priests came to the temple. Musō Kokushi experienced death on September 30, 1351, and his body was placed within the neighboring temple of Rinsen (Temple Overlooking the River). Musō had given his seal of succession to fifty-two pupils, and during his lifetime had instructed perhaps over thirteen thousand monks.

After the passing of Musō, the character of the temple for a time became more distinctly political. The Five Mountain (五山文 学, *Gozan Bungaku*) System of ranking temples began to influence the character of the temple.

The Five Mountain System was a hierarchical organization of temples modeled after the Five Mountain (*Wu-Shan*) System of Zen

Buddhist monasteries in Sung Dynasty China. In turn, the Chinese system had been modeled after a system of five monasteries and ten pagodas in Buddhist India.[94] In Japan, the Five Mountain hierarchy matured in the twelfth century and was reinforced during the time of Emperor Go-Daigo as the political power of Zen shifted from Kamakura to Kyōto. Upon completion, the Temple of the Heavenly Dragon was placed within the third tier of the Five Mountains. The aforementioned memorial pagodas (*Rishōtō*, Pagodas of the Buddha's Favor) towered throughout the sixty-six provinces, further adding to the prestige and influence of the temple. After the death of Musō, the Five Mountains rendered the temple an even more influential adjunct to the political/military state. In 1386, Yoshimitsu of the Ashikaga placed the temple into the first tier of the Five Mountains. The Temple of the Heavenly Dragon became the only first-tier Five Mountain temple in Kyōto. As a consequence, the temple enjoyed considerable prestige and influence.

Death though, as well as life, continued as a felt presence within the Temple of the Heavenly Dragon. After the death of Musō, the temple itself began to suffer several deaths and rebirths. Nearly all of the original buildings and subtemples at one time or another were destroyed by fires that ravished the compound.

In 1358, a fire in the priest quarters quickly spread to burn the entire complex. Open braziers in the floors of buildings often were the source of fires that began easily then spread quickly as the dry wood of buildings burned hot and long. In the spring of 1367, a fire began then spread throughout the complex; the temple burned, again, this time even before previously burned buildings had been rebuilt. Shun'oku Myōha (1311–88), a disciple of Musō, was instrumental in efforts to rebuild the temple. A major fire occurred in 1373, and buildings were reconstructed largely modeling original buildings. In early December 1380, a fire destroyed most of the buildings in the complex, but again they were reconstructed. Another fire occurred in 1447, and then the temple enjoyed relative physical stability until the Ōnin Wars (1467–77) destroyed most of Kyōto as well as many of the mountain temples surrounding the city. In 1467, a fire burned the temple and much of the complex was not restored for nearly a century. The temple became "a field filled by grass . . . in the wilderness of Saga."[95] Full restoration of the complex did not occur until 1585, when Toyotomi Hideyoshi (1536–98) lent his support to the rebuilding of the temple. Another major rebuilding effort occurred in 1624. Subsequent rebuildings occurred sporadically, and in 1815 the temple again nearly was destroyed by fire.

The last major fire within the temple occurred in 1864. This fire was a consequence of the Battle of Hamaguri Gate during the Kinmon War, a particularly violent feud between military factions contesting for power in the provinces of Satsuma (extreme western Kyūshū) and Chōshū (Nagato, extreme western Honshu).

Aspects of the feud that would involve Tenryū-ji began when troops from Chōshū Province forced the use of the temple as a base for military campaigns. Gekkō Oshō, a temple priest, fortunately kept a diary of salient events. "During the dawn of June 28, 1864," we read, "about 1000 soldiers from Chōshū stormed the temple. The soldiers occupied the temple, and made the Abbot's Quarters into a headquarters and living area for Duke Mōri and Duke Kenmotsu. Another building [Guest Quarters] was converted into their kitchen. Generals from Chōshū ordered the Myochi-in and the Shinjō-in [subtemples within the complex] converted into living quarters. We protested this intrusion . . . but the troops from Chōshū remained in the temple."[96] Soldiers from Chōshū Province were positioned on Turtle Mountain. Soldiers pitched camps around the pond within the temple and were stationed at critical lookout points around paths in the garden, and "not only within several subtemple buildings but also some places along paths and by the lake [pond] . . . they pitched camps and placed . . . soldiers with various arms such as spears, long swords, and arrows . . . they placed cannon by the stone bridge."[97] One cannon was placed between the garden pond and the Abbot's Quarters, aimed toward the approach of any troops from Satsuma Province attempting to storm the temple. A cannon was placed on top of Turtle Mountain, aimed toward the main gate of the temple. Two cannons were placed in the forests to the south of the temple, aimed at the (Moon-Crossing) bridge over which soldiers from Satsuma Province might attempt a crossing. Soldiers were stationed at the gates around the complex to monitor the comings and goings of monks and priests.

At night, the compound and surrounding precincts of Tenryū-ji were ablaze with fire—hundreds of watch fires and cooking fires. Men and animals drank from the pond in the garden.

In the early light of the next morning, soldiers from Satsuma stormed the temple in an attempt to drive off the soldiers from Chōshū. Soldiers from Satsuma found a nearly empty compound, though, as soldiers from Chōshū had decided to retreat and abandon the temple during the dark of night. Soldiers from Satsuma began to loot and sack the compound; they broke into storerooms and piled rice and temple treasures into carts. Priests and monks tried to plead with them to stop, but to no avail, as soldiers pushed them aside in preparing to take their bounty back to Satsuma Province. While making their departure, soldiers turned several cannon on the temple "at around 11 A.M. Suddenly, several cannon were fired and some important buildings were blown to ashes in the twinkling of an eye."[98] Cannon rained down thunderous fire into the heart of the temple, ostensibly as revenge for priests housing Chōshū troops. Fires ensued quickly, destroying scores of buildings and scorching the temple grounds.

During the Edo period (1615–1868), descendants of The Despised, under the direction of temple priests, began to "draw up the mud and leaves accumulated in the pond" and to "drive away birds which come [as they still do; see fig. 85], in the autumn and winter, to pick up the fish in the pond."[99] The majority of the buildings comprising the central area of the temple were rebuilt in their present form during the Meiji (1868–1912) and Taishō (1912–26) periods.[100]

The region around Sagano and the Mountain of Storms continued to be experienced by people as an area of aesthetic and religious significance, by this time with a legendary history in need of protection. In 1742 a count was taken of the cherry trees from Yoshino remaining on the slope, facing the temple, of the Mountain of Storms; at this time, only about five hundred trees remained. Over the centuries, people in the area had cleared land and cut trees for firewood. Subsequently, the temple began tree-replanting activities. Saplings were grown on the temple grounds so that more cherry trees in particular could be replanted on the slopes of nearby mountains. Priests and monks within subtemples of Tenryū-ji gathered cherry trees and pine tree saplings, as donations to the parent temple, to be replanted on Turtle Mountain and the Mountain of Storms. Emerging commercial establishments, lodges and eateries, sprang up to cater to tourists and pilgrims frequenting Sagano and Arashiyama in the spring to view cherry trees in bloom. Priests at Tenryu-ji petitioned these establishments to help fund the additional replanting of cherry trees. In the early eighteenth century, prohibitions were established against people cutting trees in the area.

In 1877, an event occurred that dramatically affected the present-day character of the temple. The imperial government had begun efforts to bring provincial Shintō shrines and Buddhist temples more effectively under the control of emperors. Emperor Meiji (1852–1912) ordered temples to tithe a portion of their holdings to the imperial government. With the demise of the Shogunate in 1597, the Temple of the Heavenly Dragon no longer enjoyed the patronage of the military. Unsponsored, the temple was forced to relinquish claim to about fifty-three *chō* (about 130 acres) of land—land mostly around the Mountain of Storms and Turtle Mountain as well as land and buildings on both sides of the Ōi River. After the imperial edict, the core buildings and central area of the complex and land approaching Turtle Mountain and the Ogura Mountains to the north were all that remained of the original temple complex—about one-tenth of pre-1877 land-size.

Trees on Turtle Mountain over time grew to obscure the view, from within the temple complex, of the Ōi River and the

FIGURE 50. *Early evening. The rear room of the Abbot's Quarters, and the pond garden.*

Moon-Crossing Bridge. In 1934, though, a typhoon leveled many of the trees on Turtle Mountain. During this time, the unobstructed view of the Mountain of Storms in the distance, from in front of the Abbot's Quarters, must have been as the mountains appeared during the time of Emperor Go-Saga. The trees have since grown tall, forcing visual attention once more onto the pond in the garden (figs. 50, 53, 55). Subsequently, the pond in the garden began to receive routine maintenance and became a primary experience, now for a variety of visitors, of the temple complex.

℞

Fire and blood. Sentiment and desire. Death and rebirth. The pond garden aspect of the Temple of the Heavenly Dragon has experienced numerous assaults, natural and human-inspired, during its existence.

Yet, the primary stones in and about the pond garden, though damaged here and there, remain as they were when originally set (fig. 50).[101]

The circumstances of the genesis, birth, and early life of the temple now cradle our awareness as we approach Part II of this book and the intricacies and enchantment of the present-day pond garden. Mindful of the history of the complex, with priest Tsutomo Minakami we now can stand in an informed "knowing manner" before the pond garden. We now are more able to fully experience, mindfully contemplate, nuances of the present-day landscape aspect of the complex as well as attend to the vision and interpretation of the present-day pond garden from the point of view of a senior priest within the temple.[102]

II A Garden in Green Shade

. . . a single drop of water . . .

anything

in the life of a monk

can serve

as an opportunity

for awakening

from delusion

TŌICHI YOSHIOKA[1]

Early morning mist.

Ethereal blue-gray haze dissipates gradually . . . revealing the present-day pond garden, Musō's Tenth Realm of the Temple of the Heavenly Dragon. Aspects of the pond garden slowly come into being . . . together, as the morning mist recedes. The pond in the garden comes into being as the dependent co-arising (緣起, *engi*) of buildings and water, foliage and stones (fig. 51).

> "I have been learning about and seeking to understand the garden with you for some time now. But, do you think that my understanding of the temple is sufficient?"

> "Ah, so," the priest replies after a pause. "Gradually, but precisely, I think your understanding is . . . sufficient."

> Again, a long reflective pause.

> "I think that you are ready . . . to learn."

So, during years of periodic though intense study of and direct experiences with the temple and pond garden with the priest, I was told that I merely was ready to learn.

So . . . I continued to learn. But why?

The priest began to consider me a serious student of this still-venerated pond garden, he once said, as he began to see that I loved the garden—feelings he himself had as he began ongoing experiences with, and intensive study of, the pond garden many years ago.

> "The only reason I have been drawn to the garden," the priest confided, "is that I love 〔愛, *ai*〕 the garden very much. I take a walk in the garden at the end of the day, after all the people visiting the temple have left. Peace of mind once again comes to me. There are gardens in many other temples, as you know, but I love this garden in this temple." [2]

FIGURE 51. *The rear of the Abbot's Quarters where "even today, contemplat-*
ing this masterpiece [Tenryū-ji], one is intrigued by its sunny pool, basking
in the warm morning light. Occasionally, a golden carp, warmed by the rising
sun, leaps, and tranquillity is momentarily shattered. In ever widening circles
ripples spread; among detached, mossy stones, around islands; and at last,
turning upon themselves as the shoreline is reached, subside and disappear.
Trees resume contemplation of their reflections; stones seem to grow in stat-
ure, and the tinkling silence resumes its sovereignty."[f51]

Every priest is not required to carry deep knowledge of the
landscape aspect of the temple, its history and varied interpretations.
The landscape aspect of the temple is available to acolytes and priests
whether they are affected by the temple landscape or not. The pond
garden aspect of the temple is just . . . there, one aspect among many
of the temple, available to contemplative experience.[3]

There is a well-known adage verified by my ongoing experiences
with the pond garden aspect of the Temple of the Heavenly Dragon:
if you love something truly, it will reveal itself to you. Love is an epistemology, a Way of knowing. In love, as in the experience of *satori*,
interestingly, everything is present in and of itself. As we shall see,
the priest says that it is while seated before the pond that he experiences, in the sense of priest Minakami's "knowing manner," not only
the Buddha-Nature of the garden but also the heart/mind of previous
priests associated with the landscape aspect of the temple. The priest

loves the pond garden, as do I. Love is a shared experience providing yet another venue illuminating the manner in which the pond garden can be experienced by people not as a phenomenon, a "thing," but as a deeply affecting animistic presence.[4]

I first become aware of the word "garden" at about age ten, and the recollection now appears in my awareness as feelings attached to the word "garden" rather than of a clear memory attached to garden as a place; all of course long before awareness of the existence of, and love for, the pond garden in the temple. In his poem "Aire and Angels," John Donne professed the metaphysical possibility that "Twice or thrice I loved thee, Before I knew thy face or name."[5] Mysteriously, to love a place *before* one experiences the place, to experience the shock of unexpected loving recognition of a place in which one "finds" oneself, therefore is only to say that no place of loving recognition is foreign. A character in Alice Walker's novel *The Temple of My Familiar* adds: "It's like how you love a certain place. You just do, that's all. And if you're lucky, while you're on this earth you get to visit it. And the place 'knows' about your love, you feel."[6] I emotionally recognized immediately, came to know and love, the pond garden aspect of the temple as this *particular* place both evokes feelings about and enlivens subconscious memories associated with "garden"—still-alive childhood feelings of warmth, peace, and love.

Our farm always will exist for me as a quintessentially quiet place, as I often revisit the collage-like haze of childhood memories of and feelings about the farm. There was an exceptionally large maple tree in the front yard. An oval of deep-set stones, undoubtedly set by my father, encircled the tree. The oval must have been slightly asymmetrical, as my mind's eye sees the tree towering toward the perigee of the arc of the stones while the wide apogee arc of the stones bordered the edge of the walkway to the house. My mother's and grandmother's lush flower garden flourished here, interestingly a garden of both flora and stone, as was the Garden of the Sun experienced by Gilgamesh of Uruk (see Part III) as well as the pond garden aspect of the temple.

There are related, lingering memories of and feelings attached to my earliest recollection of the word "garden," intimate memories and feelings coupling "garden" with what I now term "religion." For the loved ones tending to and nurturing my childhood, and their garden, I recollect that religion invariably was present when the word "garden" was spoken; again, interestingly, this mirrors the Garden of the Sun experienced by Gilgamesh of Uruk as well as the pond garden aspect of the temple. There is an undying memory of and set of feelings about the soft voice of my mother, or grandmother, working in the kitchen, a song wafting to the back porch couch where, after my chores, I lingered through many early evenings of childhood watching patches of sky flicker between the leaves of maple trees. Soon, the voice would ask me to go out to the carpentry shop on the lower floor of the barn and tell my father to come to the table for supper. The voice was a song, sweet and soothing, and arose spontaneously as she worked, most likely while looking out the kitchen window at the garden of flora, tree, and stone:

> I come to the garden alone
> While the dew is still on the roses
> And the voice I hear falling on my ear
> The Son of God discloses.
> And He walks with me.
> And He talks with me.
> And He tells me I am His own;
> And the joy we share
> As we tarry there
> None other has ever known.

As such, there is an implanted primal association of garden with what I now term a sacred place in which (belief in) deities and people commune, reminiscent of early beliefs concerning the pond in the temple garden as habited by kami-dragons. In his imagistic short story "The Black Monk," Anton Chekhov writes, "While they were walking round, the sun rose and shed its brilliant rays over the garden. It became warm. Foreseeing a bright, joyous, and long day, Kovrin remembered it was only the beginning of May, and that the whole summer lay before them, also bright, joyous, and long. And suddenly a gladsome, youthful feeling was aroused in his breast, like he used to have when running about that garden in his childhood."[7] Akin to the monk in Chekhov's narrative, my childhood image of garden remains alive, still, as an affecting presence of warmth and love to which I often return.

There is yet another intimate memory/feeling. Somewhere in time, either my mother or grandmother had propped up in the garden a little metal sun-shaped disk. On the disk, embellished with curlicues of sun rays, is written:

> The Kiss of the Sun for pardon
> The Song of the Birds for mirth
> One is nearer God's Heart in a garden
> Than anywhere else on earth.

Now nested within a bed of tulips in my front yard, the garden sun disk is a perennial reminder of a belief that, in a garden, one is never alone. The garden of my childhood now is associated with my ancestors, as is the pond garden for the priest within the temple with whom I studied.

These several lyrical hymns to gardens, the garden of Chekhov's monk as well as the garden of my ancestors, are frequented by archetypal conceptions of garden. In Part III, by way of conclusion we will see that our earliest species' conception of garden by extension also is of a place/space resonate with compassion, love, and nurturance.

I share these personal memory/feelings to encourage the reader to be aware of one's own memories and feelings attached to the word "garden" that, along the way in the experience of this book, perhaps will appear to consciousness. Such memories and feelings are a vital aspect of that which the reader brings to vicarious experience of the

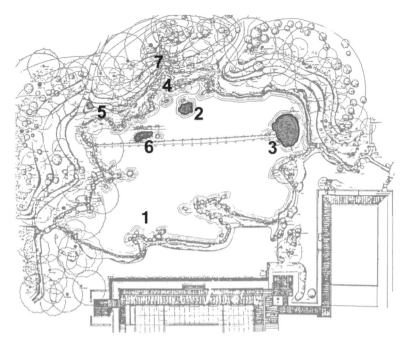

FIGURE 52. A topographic map of the garden, indicating features of interpre-
tive significance: the pond (Sōgenchi); (2) Crane Island (Tsuru Shima); (3)
Turtle Island (Kame Shima); (4) Bridge of Stones (Hashi no Ishi); (5) Zazen
Stone (Zazen Ishi); (6) Night-Mooring Stones (Yodomari Ishi); (7) Dragon-
Gate Waterfall (Ryūmon no Taki).

Temple of the Heavenly Dragon and through which any understanding of the pond garden will come to life. Matters of the heart/mind
(kokoro), as Rinzai Zen Buddhists have it, always are present in experience: here, in the vicarious experience of a venerated garden.

And so now, again, we sit on tatami within the Abbot's Quarters. The priest points to the pond itself then to six specific arrange-
ments of stones within the pond as, for him, especially evocative
aspects of the garden—akin to Musō earlier defining especially evocative core Realms of the landscape aspect of the temple (figs. 52, 53).
Each of the following seven chapters in turn focuses on the priest's
conceptions of each core aspect of the garden.

In the first three chapters to follow, the priest initially discusses
three of his core aspects of the present-day temple garden principally
in association with Buddhism and the historical Buddha: first, the

FIGURE 53. *Early morning. The pond garden. A monk . . . pauses.*

pond (曹源池, *Sōgenchi*) itself, as well as, second, a composition of
stones in the water conventionally referred to as Crane Island (鶴島,
Tsuru Shima) and third, a composition of earth and stones in the water
conventionally referred to as Turtle Island (亀島, *Kame Shima*). In
the next chapters, the priest highlights other of his core aspects of the
pond garden conceptualized principally with respect to Rinzai Zen
and *zazen*: a composition of on-land stones, fourth, conventionally referred to as the Bridge of Stones (橋の石, *Hashi no Ishi*); a single large
on-land stone, fifth, referred to as the Zazen Stone (座禅石, *Zazen
Ishi*); and sixth, a group of stones in the water conventionally named
the Night-Mooring Stones, (夜留まり石, *Yodomari Ishi*). Finally, in
the seventh chapter, the priest points out and discusses a composition
of stones embedded into the earthen embankment at the rear of the
pond, the Dragon-Gate Waterfall (龍門の滝, *Ryūmon no Taki*).

For the priest, the landscape aspect of the temple for the most
part is experienced as a manifestation of Buddha-Nature. The pond
garden, as we shall see, in particular is experienced as manifestation
of the Dharma of Shākyamuni and of Musō Kokushi.[8]

4

A POND OF SHADOW AND SHIMMERING STONES

From within fading shadows and the translucent mist of early morning, myriad stones ethereally begin to appear on the water of the pond within the garden. Reflections on the surface of the water slowly begin to double the visual presence of the emerging stones, suggesting a great depth to the pond (figs. 54, 55, 77, 120).

"Why is it important to notice the water reflecting the stones?"

"It is necessary to give an impression of profundity [[幽玄, yūgen]]," says the priest. "It is not good enough if the pond garden gives an impression of . . . 'flatness [[平ら, taira]].' It is important to give an impression of hidden meaning.

"To [experience] the reverse side or the internal aspect, and not experience [the pond] only from superficial appearance. The same can be said about *haiku*.

"A *haiku* is not just a sequence of words. One cannot say that a person has 'read' a *haiku* unless they feel what the author felt . . . [often hidden]. The same applies to the garden."

The priest cautions us to sustain contemplative awareness of the

FIGURE 54. *Reflections of water on the stones; reflections of stones on the water. Interdependent relationship, evoking the concept of dependent co-arising (縁起, engi), is present in early-morning experiences of the pond in the garden as "mind does not dwell on either form or vacant space but flows freely between both, and includes both."*[f54]

pond garden as-it-is (*shinnyo*). We are encouraged to become aware of our feelings while experiencing the pond garden. As well, the priest links the feelings of people experiencing the pond garden and the feelings of the author(s) of the pond garden. In addition to interpretation then, we are invited to sustain contemplative awareness of the pond garden aspect of the temple as a place and space both embodying and evoking . . . feeling.

Filtered principally through his life amid Rinzai Zen Buddhism, the priest's vision of the pond garden initially focuses on three features and corresponding associations of significance: (1) the curvilinear shape of the pond, and subtle triangular spatial patterns emerging via his visualization of the interdependent relationship of various spatial areas of the pond; (2) the Buddhist legend of Shākyamuni on Vulture Peak, in India, and the pond as evocation of the Dharma experienced

FIGURE 55. Mid-morning. Several of the relatively large stones in the water around which triangular patterns of interdependence, with respect to various spatial arenas of the pond, can be conceptualized.

by Shākyamuni; and (3) the pond as embodiment of the Dharma experienced by Musō Kokushi. We will consider each, in turn.

A Heart Pond

The pond is asymmetrical in form, irregular in shape. Several physically prominent peninsulas of earth, lined with stones of varied size and shape, jut into the water of the pond. Experienced conversely, several peninsulas of water appear to jut dramatically into the surrounding land (figs. 3, 59, 61, 86).

The undulating shape of the foreground of the pond has been compared to a Japanese-style (yamato-e) painting with "peninsulas [evoking] ocean beaches and undulating coastlines."[1] Both the undulating shape of the pond and a painting in the Japanese style stimulate a "quick, sensuous enjoyment of graceful shapes and delicate colors."[2] Also, recall that a dragon had been believed to dwell within prior ponds in the area. People at the time believed that dragons preferred curves, hollows, and undulations as habitats. Associated with this belief was the somewhat later convention of shaping human-made bodies of water to correspond to the curvilinear haunts of dragons, such that "the pond . . . in the Tenryū-ji garden . . . was called Ryū [dragon] Pond."[3]

A prevalent, more contemporary interpretation of the irregular shape of the pond is that, historically, for esoteric reasons, ponds often were shaped to correspond to the form of written characters. The irregular shape of the pond often has been interpreted by scholars as ideographic; that is, the pond often is held to be "heart-shaped" (心字が池, *shinjigaike*), specifically, approximating the shape of the character *kokoro* (心).[4]

"Articles about Tenryū-ji say that the shape of the pond is *kokoro*. Would you please talk about the shape of the pond?"

"The shape of the pond is *not* the Chinese character *kokoro*," says the priest.

"It is true that this pond was called '*shinjigaike*' ['heart-shaped pond'], but it was not because the shape of the pond looks like the Chinese character *kokoro*. It is because the pond embodies [表す, *arawasu*] the heart [*kokoro*] of Buddha, not the Chinese character. Let me tell you how it [embodies] the heart of Buddha.

"The pond does not necessarily have to be this exact shape, insofar as the shoreline is winding. But the shape of the pond cannot be a pure square or pure circle or pure triangle. Buddha's heart is free in its capacity to manifest its being [Buddha-Nature].

"We, the ordinary people, cannot bring our [Buddha-Nature] into full-play because we are bound by something, always. So, for example, let us contrast water and ice. The water contained in a round bowl becomes cubical once it has been moved into a cubical container. It becomes triangle-shaped when it is moved into a triangle-shaped container. Thus, water displays the capacity to become any shape freely.

"You may consider water the heart of Buddha, and ice the heart of ordinary people. Suppose you put the round ice into a square container. Of course, the water won't become square.

Also, if you put the square ice into a round container, the
square ice won't become round.

"Thus, we are bound and restricted in many ways due to
our own worldly desires. That's why we cannot bring our
[Buddha-Nature] into play freely.

"Now, we call this kind of pond with the winding configu-
ration a '*shinjigaike*.' When we speak of the heart of Buddha,
it is important to keep in mind that Buddha's heart is like water and does not stick to one thing. Therefore, it is nonsense
when people talk about the shape of '*shinjigaike*' to claim that
it should be some kind of square, or it should be symmetrical
in its shape, or some kind of circle, or whatever. It can be any
shape."

As we contemplate the pond in the garden, we are accompanied
by the danger of idolatry, of "stopping" at beautiful, compelling forms
of stones, mesmerized, rather than experiencing the pond garden as
an embodiment of that which is prior to dualistic distinctions such
as form/formless. "Suchness [*shinnyo*] transcends forms," in other
words, "but without depending on forms it cannot be realized . . . the
Buddha's teaching [*Dharma*, here envisioned manifested as the pond
in the garden] which guides people is limitless."[5] Form is formless;
formlessness is form.

The priest of course is aware that *kokoro* conventionally is conceptualized as "heart." Myokyo-ni, a contemporary Zen Buddhist
priest, adds that "there is true receptivity for heart touching heart . . .
the liberated heart is so full of warmth that it needs must flow out,
and in so doing touches every heart it comes in contact with, and in-
cites it to become otherwise."[6] Recall Shākyamuni's emphasis on non-
verbal "heart-to-heart" interdependent communication of Dharma.
Priest Myokyo-ni concludes "the Zen School holds itself as the Heart
School."[7] Buddha-Nature also is referred to as "empty heart," the
conception that "form must be strong and firm, but flexible enough
to stand pressure as it builds up, to contain the shift when it occurs

and to accommodate the new structure," as priest Myokyo-ni puts it.[8]

Experience of the pond-as-kokoro thus becomes synonymous with experience of Buddha-Nature prior to dualistic distinctions such as mind ("What does the shape of the pond . . . mean?"), matter, and form ("What is the shape of the pond?"). As "Buddha, he is both formless and form . . . he reveals all this and preaches Dharma for all to hear."[9] Rinzai Zen Buddhist writings often caution people not to mistake the moon reflected in the water (say, the garden pond) for the unseen moon itself (Buddha-Nature). Likewise, priests admonish us not to stop our experience of the pond garden at "things," at shape and form, for "the essence of Zen is to use form to go beyond form, to go beyond all discriminations."[10] Awareness of the arresting shape of the pond in the garden ought not overshadow awareness of that which, for Rinzai Zen Buddhists, is not limited to or by compelling form.

Contemplative experience of the pond-as-it-is thus can stimulate in people awareness of Buddha-Nature as the "heart" of one's be-ing.[11] Throughout the temple and pond garden, as we will see, design and physical form will be envisioned by the priest as compassionate "pointers" stimulating awareness of Buddha-Nature.

Triangles of Form and Formlessness The stones and the arrange-ments of stones in the pond and around the garden do not exist au-tonomously, in isolation. For the priest, the pond in the garden exists as the nonduality of interdependence (縁起, engi).

The priest envisions prominent stones in the water as nodes framing the interdependence of various spatial areas of the pond. The pond garden's interdependence is visualized by the priest as a pat-tern, and the spatial pattern of interdependent relationship for the priest is asymmetrical—triangular.

Taking pen in hand, the priest sketches the manner in which by all appearances spatially distant and distinct areas of the pond exist in interdependent relationship, and that the pattern of interdependent relationship is conceptualized as three encompassing asymmetrical

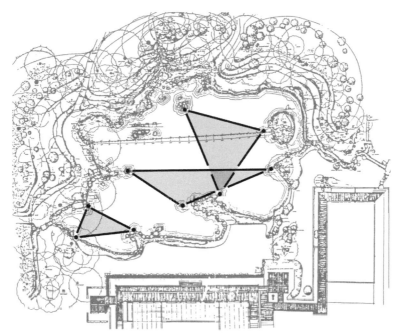

FIGURE 56. *Primary stones and compositions of stones in and around the pond, can be conceptualized in triangular spatial interdependent relationship.*

triangles (fig. 56). The priest invariably mentions triangles in discussing the interdependence of the pond garden and *zazen*:[12]

> "Could you please say more about triangles. You speak of the body, in *zazen*, and triangles. Triangles and stability. Can you say more about why triangles are important?"

> "Yes," the priest replies. "As you mentioned, triangles imply stability. When you look at someone in *zazen* you receive an impression of stability. You might also become aware of the power [力, *chikara*] inside people. You receive an impression that this power is when his body makes a triangle. The same is true of the garden. Like the stones of this part, for instance. Here are three big stones [pointing to several prominent stones in the pond]. There are numerous small stones, too, but let's ignore them for a moment. These three big stones make a triangle. Therefore, they give stability to the pond. At the same

time, it [the pond] gains power. Stability alone is not enough. Power must accompany stability."

Elaborating upon the priest's evocation of triangles, consider the manner in which the form of several basic triangles are isomorphic with the form of *zazen* (as well as the form by which several areas of the pond conceptually are interlinked). Viewed frontally, the form of a person in *zazen* approximates the form of an isosceles triangle (fig. 57). Viewed in profile, the form of a person in *zazen* approximates the form of a right-angled triangle (fig. 58).

The form of a person in *zazen* approximates the form of an isosceles, sublime triangle. By extension, the stable base for the body "is a triangle formed by the buttocks and the two knees."[13] Viewed frontally while in *zazen*, the body appears centered and balanced bilaterally. The body in *zazen* and the pond are isomorphic in their triangularity and, for the priest, the pond and the body in *zazen* each therefore participates interdependently with a formless quieting of heart/mind.

Rotated 90 degrees to a profile view, a person in *zazen* approximates the form of a right-angled triangle in several respects. The straight back of a person in *zazen*, say, seated within the Abbot's or Guest Quarters, from this vantage can be envisioned as the vertical axis of the body as a triangle. The legs correspond to the short baseline of the triangle, while one envisions the longest line of the triangle extending diagonally from the knees to the top of the head (fig. 58). Secondly, the straight back of a person in *zazen*, viewed in profile, from a distant view can be envisioned as the vertical axis of a triangle interlinking the veranda of the temple building as well as the pond garden. The slightly lowered head of the figure in *zazen* then can be envisioned as the node for the long diagonal line of the conceptual triangle as it extends down and out into the distance (envision the base and diagonal lines in figure 58 as extending out into the garden). The three lines of this body-triangle approximate (七五三, *shichigo-san*) proportions of *seven* as the diagonal line, *five* as the base line, and

FIGURES 57, 58. *Drawings of a figure in zazen, viewed frontally and in profile.*

three as the vertical line; here, "the triangle symbolizes [graphically depicts] a method of organization through the joining or mediating of differences."[14]

From this profile perspective, and at an encompassing distance, a person in *zazen* can be envisioned as the vertical node of an encompassing right-angled triangle; envisioned as such provides a means for contemplating the interdependence of (mediating differences between) person, pond garden, and temple buildings.

Garden as Compassion, Sangha, and Spirit of Musō

The felt presence of venerated ancestors, Shākyamuni and Musō in particular, often appears to the priest as he sits quietly, in the late afternoon, before the pond in the garden. For the priest, the pond stimulates awareness of an old Buddhist story about Shākyamuni sitting atop Vulture Peak, in India, a signal moment within Mahāyāna Buddhism. After esoteric conversation, the priest often settles into contemplative awareness of the pond within the garden as the compassion of Musō, embodied as a space and place present to people as an aid in the experience of Buddha-Nature.

After venturing forth from the gates of the family palace, Siddhārtha initially lived a life of aestheticism, fasting (several times close to death), and relative isolation. Siddhārtha subsequently came to understand that extremes of isolation and abuse of the body were not his Way. Siddhārtha then traveled to the village of Senani, where the young girl offered him refreshing milk rice. Sometime later, a grass-cutter offered him kusa grass for a mat; then, Siddhārtha sat under a nearby pipal tree (Pippala tree; *Ficus religiosa*, the Tree of Enlightenment) near present-day Bodhi Gayā.[15] Gathering intention and will, Siddhārtha vowed to himself that he would not rise from this place until he experienced awareness.

Subsequently experiencing the awareness termed "enlighten-ment," Siddhārtha rose from sitting under the Bodhi tree with a re-solve to share that which he had become aware. He journeyed seven days to Vārānasi (Benares), then to Deer Park (Rishipatana Mriga-dava). There, he met with five disciples to share his realization, set-ting in motion the First Turning of the Wheel of Dharma. At Deer Park then, an initial *sangha* was formed. Subsequently, he traveled to Shravasti, where the Third Turning of the Wheel of Dharma prin-cipally revealed to people that Buddha-Nature already was present within all beings.

It was atop Vulture Peak that Siddhārtha, now Shākyamuni, generated the Second Turning of the Wheel of Dharma.[16] The geogra-phy within which the Second Turning of the Wheel was situated, as well as the content of the Second Turning, is of particular importance with respect to a Buddhist legend that came to be linked to the pond garden.

The Mount of Vultures is a prominent outcropping of rock atop Gridhrakuta Hill, just outside the ancient city of Rajgir (Rajagriha). The name "Vulture Peak" flowed from the numerous vultures at one time residing on the hill, from the beak-like shape of rock projections on the hill itself, and from a legendary incident atop the hill where Shākyamuni's meditation once was interrupted by Māra (illusion) in the form of a vulture.

Shākyamuni chose the Mount of Vultures as the place to con-tinue to present to people his experiences while sitting under the Bo-dhi tree. He lived within a now-venerated cave within the mountain and, periodically, he would climb the Mount of Vultures to sit before the assembled. As his Dharma Seat, Shākyamuni sat on a slab of stone on top of the hill (fig. 115).

Words believed spoken by Shākyamuni atop Vulture Peak later were assembled as the *Heart Sūtra* (*Hannya Shin Go*; *Prajñāpāramitā*, in Sanskrit, the Heart of Perfect Wisdom/The Perfection of Insight and Wisdom). The *Heart Sūtra* emphasizes the great assemblies that began to gather from near and far to be present to the Dharma of Shākyamuni—kings and princes, dragons and dragon kings, deities, and non-human beings such as birds and fish (the Dharma was for all beings, not just the human mode of being). Greatly expanded from his few earlier disciples, the assemblies on Vulture Peak in turn expanded the *sangha*, the community of believers and believers-to-be.

The *Heart Sūtra* is centered on an extended conversation between Sāriputra, a disciple of Shākyamuni, and Avalokiteśvara, a Bodhisattva: "Avalokita . . . was moving in the deep course of the Wisdom which has gone beyond."[17] The *Heart Sūtra* does not focus on Shākyamuni so much as on qualities embodied as the historical Buddha and later emphasized by Mahāyāna Buddhists—compassion, insight and wisdom (Mother of all Buddhas), and a gentle heart.

As the priest sits before the pond garden, he speaks of a story, a parable, informed by the *Heart Sūtra*. At some point in history the parable becomes attached to, and associated with, (esoteric) experiences of the pond garden. The priest speaks of the pond garden evoking the legendary *sangha* on Vulture Peak where believers and believers-to-be gathered to be present to the Dharma experienced by Shākyamuni.

Water and vast distance. Boats. A great assembly. The *Heart Sūtra* concludes that "we are on the hither shore, beset with fears and dangers. Security can be found only on the other shore . . . which can be crossed by means of the ship, or raft, of the Dharma."[18] The pond garden, here, is conceptualized and experienced by the priest as evocation of the great *sangha* and the myriad forms of being gathered, *periodically*, before Shākyamuni on Vulture Peak.

FIGURE 59. *Peninsulas of earth extend into the pond, their edges lined with shore-protecting stones (yahaku seki): the priest's "lodging stones."*

FIGURE 60. *The tips of peninsulas extending into the water are a complementary balancing of stones set horizontally as well as vertically. Angular stones are complemented, balanced, by bushes clipped into rounded shapes (karikomi).*

FIGURE 61. *Several peninsulas of earth define an alternating rhythm of water and stones, stones and water.*

The priest's six primary features of the pond garden, to follow, all touch aspects of a Buddhist story (of unknown origin) where, says the priest:

"   the Buddha 〚Dharma〛 is 〚evoked by〛 the Shumisen 〚the Crane Island〛. 〚The story is that〛 the Buddha/Dharma comes down here, along the waterfall 〚the Dragon-Gate Waterfall〛. Here 〚pointing to the edges of the pond〛, there are a lot of big rocks. Every rock 〚evokes〛 a temple. And the people in those temples who we call 'riku' 〚陸; travelers〛 come here in boats to listen to the Buddha's story 〚説, sekkyō〛. When the 'sekkyō' is finished, they go back to the 'yahakuseki' 〚夜泊石, "lodging stones," the prominent stones lining the edges of the pond〛 . . . but, this is only a story."[19]

Only an old story, says the priest; yet, the story tells us that the

FIGURE 62. *A view toward the north/northwest. From this vantage, stones appear to mediate the meeting place of water and foliage.*

pond garden is not a symbol, representation, aesthetics, or "meaning" for him but that he conceptualizes and experiences the pond garden as an evocative manifestation of the Dharma experienced by Shākyamuni (figs. 59–62).

Ongoing experiences of the pond garden for the priest, finally, evoke Musō Kokushi in that Musō "gathered stones," it is believed, "to imitate the color of smoke and gathered the voice of the wild wind through planted trees."[20] The pond garden-as-it-is is experienced by the priest as "pointing to" the enlightened heart/mind of Musō, for "a beautiful mind [heart; kokoro] is essential to the creation of a beautiful garden."[21] Other Buddhist priests, such as Tsutomo Minakami, also feel that "the real self of Musō can be seen in the Tenryū-ji garden . . . the garden is the repose of Musō Kokushi and his noble sentiment."[22] As illustrated in forthcoming chapters, experience of the pond garden is experience, as the priest variously puts it, of the "Mind of Musō Kokushi," "Musō's Zen," or "the compassion of Musō."

§

Let us continue our study, and vicarious experience, of the priest's other selected aspects of the garden aspect of the temple. In addition to the pond, the priest's six selected compositions of stones in the pond and around the garden, to follow, in various fashions all evoke Buddhism in general and Rinzai Zen in particular, the training of monks within the temple, Musō Kokushi, and/or the Mahāyāna legend of assemblies gathering periodically to experience the teachings of Shākyamuni. Each of the following six selected aspects of the pond garden, the following chapters, also are clothed by the culture of Japan via fabric composed of still-enduring threads from India and China.

Tsurukame—Dance of the Crane and the Tortoise

From our seated vantage within the Abbot's Quarters, two distinctive compositions of stones in the pond capture our visual attention. Each composition appears as an island peaking above and surrounded by the water of the pond. Conventionally, one composition of stones is referred to as Crane Island while the other composition of earth and stones is referred to as Turtle Island (figs. 63, 64).

Island-appearing compositions of earth and stone designated "crane" and "turtle" occur quite early in the history of gardens in Japan. Crane and turtle islands were so prevalent that the generic name for these compositions of stone (島, *shima*), early on was synonymous with their garden settings.

Akin to dragons, the turtle and the crane have been long endowed with mythic significance.[23] Pond garden features of significance bear conventional, broadly recognizable names conditioned by well-known sociocultural myth and history.

FIGURE 63. *A view of the pond from a rear veranda of the Guest Quarters, revealing both the Crane Island-Mountain and the Turtle Island. The Crane Island-Mountain is to left-center of the roof-supporting post, and from this distance appears as needles of stone grouped in the water. The "head" of the Turtle Island is a bluish stone just above the bamboo railing, to the lower right side of the post. The view is to the southwest, with the peaks of the Mountain of Storms undulating just below the rain-channeling hoops of the roof eaves. Bushes clipped into rounded shapes* (karikomi) *complement the bulbous shape of trees.*

The two island-appearing compositions of earth and stone set within the pond are distinct spatially, yet interdependent in several respects. Experienced interdependently, these two compositions can be experienced as a complementary-opposed balance of *in* and *yō*. The shape and arrangement of the stones comprising the Crane Island, for instance, emphasize the vertical (*in*, stones primarily upright and

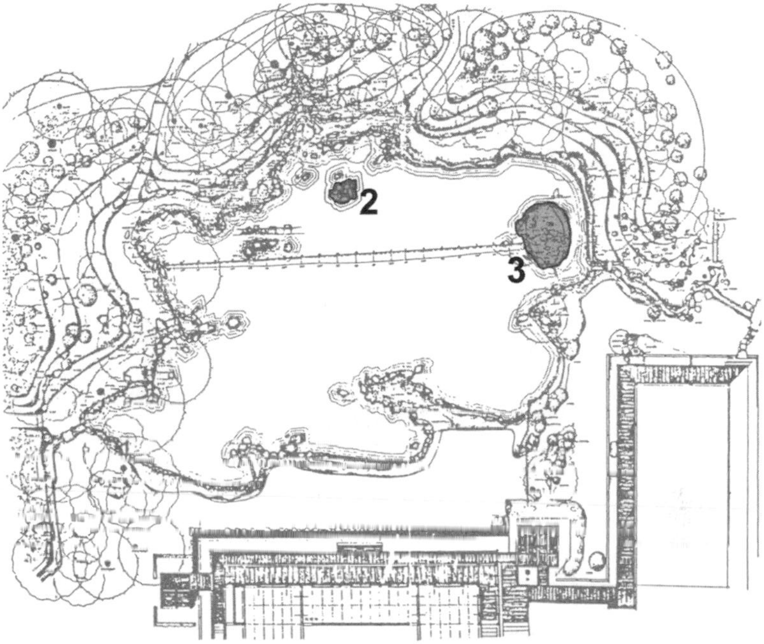

FIGURE 64. *The spatial location of the Crane Island-Mountain (2) and the Turtle Island (3).*

angular of line; "male") while the shape and arrangement of stones comprising the Turtle Island emphasize the horizontal (yō, stones primarily low-lying and curvilinear; "female").[24] An interdependence perhaps more readily perceived by visitors is that the two islands of earth and stone together evoke *Tsurukame* (鶴亀, Crane and Tortoise), a quite familiar duet with a deep historical presence in Japan.

Tsurukame is a melodic narrative recounting mythic aspects of the crane and the tortoise. *Tsurukame* still is performed during festivities marking the New Year, timed to bear witness to the good fortune, longevity, and promise of renewal long ascribed to both the turtle and the crane.[25] The well-known legend is that the crane lives a thousand years (*tsuru sennen*) while the turtle lives ten thousand years (*kame mannen*).[26]

The linkage of the Turtle Island/Crane Island as the Dance of

FIGURE 65. *A view of the pond from in front of the rear west-facing veranda of the Abbot's Quarters. The Crane Island-Mountain is the vertical group of stones in the water, prominent here in the left-center of the photograph. The Turtle Island is hidden in the trees immediately to the extreme left side of the Abbot's Quarters. The view is to the north/northwest, with the peaks of the Mountain of Dusk and Shadow undulating just below the rain-channeling hoops of the roof eaves.*

Tsurukame is quite apt. The Dance of *Tsurukame* concretizes the subtle interdependence between these two by all appearances separate compositions of stones within the pond (fig. 65).

The next two chapters thus are to be experienced as an interrelated whole. In the next chapter, we first consider the Crane Island of stones. We then devote a chapter to consideration of the Turtle Island of earth and stones.

5

FOOTPRINTS IN THE SKY

The Island of the Crane is the tallest composition of stones set within the pond. The stones making up the Crane Island appear to hover delicately on the water of the pond, "very beautiful stones beyond comparison with anything else."[1] This composition in stone has been deemed "one of the finest creations in the whole range of Japanese garden artistry, a masterpiece unsurpassed in any other single arrangement."[2] Experientially, the vertically set stones aesthetically complement water rippling the broad surface of the pond, especially at dusk (figs. 66–68).

Water and stone. Motion and stillness.

At some point in the history of the pond garden, this composition of stones conventionally became associated with the Japanese crane (tancho, Grus japonensis). A poem by Musō envisioned that "the flying birds have left no footprints in the sky."[3] The Ainu of Hokkaido still refer to cranes as "the marsh gods."[4] Considered kami, cranes honorifically are often referred to as "O Tsuru Sama" [Honorable Lord Crane].

Whirling Stones

The Crane Island has been deemed "a group of whirling stones [uzu

FIGURE 66. *The slender silvery peaks of the Crane Island (or properly, Crane Island-Mountain), to the right-center, rise from the water of the pond.*

FIGURE 67 (left). The tall, central stone of the Crane Island-Mountain peaks above flanking secondary and tertiary stones.

FIGURE 68 (above). The Crane Island-Mountain composition of stones, with the rear of the Guest Quarters in the background.

FIGURE 69. *Various stones emerge, disappear, then re-emerge in different combinations and patterns as one moves around the pond in experiencing the composition from various points of view. Moss and foliage presently are encouraged to flourish on the Crane Island-Mountain, contributing an organic quality to the stones. The organic character of the stones in turn evokes the organic character of mythic island-mountains in India, China, and early Japan. The stones themselves generate an experience of sabi (寂)—a patina, the beauty of impermanence, revealed with age. The water between the stones also can be experienced as an aspect of the composition.*

makishiji iwagumi]."[5] The poetic phrase "whirling stones" ascribes movement to the composition itself. Various stones do emerge, disappear, and then re-emerge in different combinations and patterns as one moves around the pond in contemplating the composition from varied points of view (fig. 69). The stones generate perceived combinations and recombinations of patterns in a seemingly infinite manner, as one moves around the composition. In *Stones of the Sky*, Pablo Neruda could be speaking of the Crane Island as he poetically contemplates a vision of stones enlivened as if "they grew wings: the rocks that

FIGURE 70. *Seven primary stones of varied size, shape, and texture (the dot on each primary stone) can be discerned around which the Crane Island-Mountain appears to have been composed. These stones define an oblique angle; as a composition, the Crane Island-Mountain is asymmetrical. The core stones of the composition can be experienced as defining two right-angled planes extending outward, from the tall central stone, at an oblique angle.*

soared."[6] The island of stones can be experienced as a kaleidoscope of continual transformation.

The core stones that make up the Crane Island cannot all be seen at once. No matter one's spatial or visual position while walking around the pond, the core stones of the composition always are present . . . but unseen. The "whole" of the composition only can be experienced, imagined, within one's self and only if effort is invested in sustained contemplation of the stones.

Sustained contemplation reveals that the Crane Island appears to have been composed around seven core stones of varied size, shape, and texture (fig. 70). The three tallest stones of the composition are clustered tightly. Successively lower in height, the remaining core stones surround the tall cluster of three central stones.

Comparatively flat stones appear to float in the water around and

FIGURE 71. *The Crane Island-Mountain, with the Bridge of Stones in the background.*

between what can be termed the core stones. The island is not defined exclusively by the stones themselves. The water between stones is a vital aspect of the design and experience of the Crane Island, as a composition.

Soft afternoon light frames the edges of the island of stones, evoking the aesthetic of *shibui* (渋い, clarity, subtle elegance).[7] The island of stones customarily is experienced from in front of or while sitting within the Abbot's and Guest Quarters. Earlier in the history of the temple, though, the island of stones would have been experienced up close, by priests especially, along the path leading to and across the Bridge of Stones.

As a composition, the Crane Island is asymmetrical. The upright core stones appear to define two right-angled planes extending outward at an oblique angle from the tall central stone (figs. 71–73). The prevalent design principle of asymmetry is manifested in the oblique structure of the Crane Island as a composition. The design

FIGURE 72. The Crane Island-Mountain exists in spatial interrelationship with the Bridge of Stones, in the foreground. The comparatively-large core stones composing the Crane Island-Mountain are stabilized by myriad smaller stones seen just below the water.

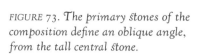

FIGURE 73. The primary stones of the composition define an oblique angle, from the tall central stone.

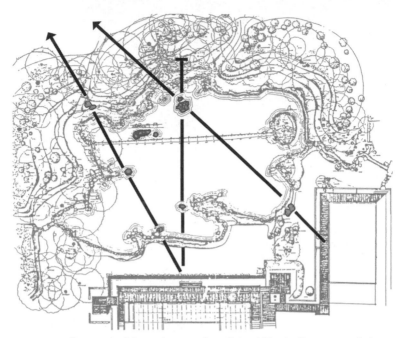

FIGURE 74. *Experienced from the verandas of the Abbot's Quarters and the Guest Quarters, two lines of sight can be formed to intersect visually several compositions of stones within the pond and around the garden. The positioned sight-line view from the Guest Quarters is over the pond and into the mountains in the south/southwest, while dense stands of trees to the west delimit the positioned sight-line view from the Abbot's Quarters to focus awareness on the pond itself. The darkened stone in front of the Guest Quarters, over which a line of sight passes, is the large oblong on-land stone prominent in figures 45 and 107. The darkened dots are stones that can be experienced through positioned sight-lines to visually interrelate spatially distinct areas of the pond (fig. 20). Viewed from the rear veranda of the Abbot's Quarters, the Crane Island-Mountain centers visual experiences of the pond.*

principle of asymmetry also appears in the nearby Bridge of Stones as well as in several other prominent compositions of stones in the pond and around the garden (fig. 74).

When experienced from the verandas of temple buildings, the design of the Crane Island leads our awareness to several more encompassing sight-lines that organize, visually line up, several core aspects of the pond garden. From the Guest Quarters, one's line of sight can be positioned so as to pass over an oblong stone on the shore of the pond, over the Crane Island to intersect the waterfall of stones, and then finally to linger amid the Mountain of Storms in the distance (fig. 45).[8] From the Abbot's Quarters, one's line of sight can be positioned to pass over a primary stone offshore of a foreground peninsula of land extending into the water of the pond, only to linger above the Crane Island nestled under the tree-laden embankment of earth at the far western terminus of the pond (fig. 3). Stones defining core compositions within the pond and about the garden are interrelated visually, and core compositions of stones also are interrelated visually with building architecture—both exemplify the encompassing principle of interdependence, manifested as the structure of the garden.

Viewed while seated on the floor within both the Abbot's Quarters and the Guest Quarters, with *shōji* drawn back, the pond appears as a sliver of water. Sitting on the floor within each building lowers one's plane of vision, and prominent features of the pond and garden settle into each other. Distance collapses, enabling core features of the pond and garden to be visually experienced simultaneously as interrelationship (figs. 3, 128). Awareness of the pond garden as interdependent relationship, again, is dependent upon sustained contemplation.

In addition to visual lines of sight, there is a more subtle manner by which the interdependent relationship of the Crane Island and other core aspects of the pond and garden can be experienced. Mirei Shigemori observed: "This rock islet [the Crane Island] is composed of these seven stones. These *seven* stones, the rock islet composed of *five* stones [the Night-Mooring Stones, *Yodomari Ishi*; fig. 126] and the rock islet composed of *three* stones [the Bridge of Stones, *Hashi no Ishi*; figs. 72, 104] make up a party."[9] Interestingly, the numbers of primary stones comprising the Crane Island (seven stones), the Night-Mooring Stones (five stones), and the Bridge of Stones (three stones) together compose a 7:5:3 (*shichigosan*) proportional interdependent relationship.

Mythic Island Mountains and Cosmic Seas

Imagine the Crane Island simply as an island; an island, though, is not an autonomous mass of earth floating in a surrounding sea. An island is the summit of a mountain mostly submerged within surrounding waters. Envisioned as such, the above-water peaks of the Crane Island visually appear as the tops of an unseen below-water mass of earth. Despite appearances to the contrary, "islands" do not exist within the pond; mounds of earth and stone do not exist autonomously, separated by surrounding water. The "islands" in the pond are the tops of stones and mounds of earth rising mountain-like from the common floor of the pond. Envisioned as such, the Crane Island can be experienced as evoking the peak of an underwater mountain thrusting up from the shared floor of a vast sea. It is in this manner that experience of the Crane Island can evoke archaic cross-cultural legends and myths of an island-mountain in a primal cosmic sea.

The "Crane Island-Mountain," now a more fitting designation, embodies a diverse genealogy. As well as indigenous ancestry, the lineage of this composition of stones in the pond of the garden flows through several cultures. The following section considers the genealogy of the Crane Island-Mountain beginning with the mythic island mountain of Great Meru (Maha Meru, in India), through the Mystic Isles of the Blest in China, to the mythic realm of Shinsentō in Japan.

INDIA, AND THE STONE AT THE CENTER OF THE UNIVERSE

Ancient cosmographies from India envisioned the universe as layered, composed of myriad floating plates, each a distinct World System (Cakkavala). Air and water were spaced, infinitely, between each World System. A cosmic mountain, Meru, was the center of the World System; Meru was an *axis mundi*, a primal pole around which the universe centered its infinite manifestations of being and becoming. Meru often was imaged as a terraced *ziggurat*, roughly triangular in form (fig. 75).

Meru was surrounded by immense seas and was the habitat of Nāga. Nāga favored their gardens, "places of incarnation, dragon-haunted trees at its centre being hung with jewels in which the life

COLOR PLATES CORRESPOND TO SELECTED FIGURES THROUGHOUT THE TEXT.

Tenryū-ji (Temple of the Heavenly Dragon) is located in western Kyōto. Upon entering, the visitor passes over a bridge-covered stream and along an avenue to the central area of the temple grounds (fig. 9). OVERLEAF: *The Abbot's Quarters and Guest Quarters overlook the pond garden, where foliage, rockwork, and building architecture have all been carefully designed and positioned for the expe-*

TOP: *The temple of the Heavenly Dragon is nestled within mountains, hills, and trees (fig. 28).* LEFT: *The pond is typically viewed from the veranda on the rear western-side of the Abbot's Quarters (fig. 29).* TOP RIGHT: *In contrast, the east-facing veranda faces a more recent gravel and sand garden (fig. 13).* RIGHT: *Viewed while seated within the Abbot's Quarters, the pond garden across the veranda is a tranquil composition of water and stone . . . and silence (fig. 128).*

TOP: *Temple building architecture and landscape architecture—the pond garden—are experienced as an integrated whole, each revealing aspects of the other (fig. 50).* LEFT: *The Crane Island-Mountain is one of the most prominent visual aspects of the pond garden (fig. 67).*

TOP: *Priests within the temple say that sustained contemplative experience of the pond garden stimulates awareness of aspects of Buddhism as well as awareness of Buddha and venerated historical priests such as Musō Kokushi (fig. 52).* RIGHT: *The rear of the Abbot's Quarters—"even today . . . one is intrigued by its sunny pool, basking in the warm morning light" (fig. 51).*

TOP AND RIGHT: *The stones and water reflect each other, participate in each other, in an interdependent relationship of matter and space (figs. 54, 23).*

TOP: *Viewed in the distance from the veranda of the Abbot's Quarters, the curved arc of the Night-Mooring Stones is in the water to the left and the vertical Crane-Island Mountain is prominent to the right, with the Bridge of Stones nested horizontally into the rear embankment of earth (fig. 66).* RIGHT: *The Crane-Island Mountain evokes the organic character of mythic island-mountains in India, China, and Japan (fig. 69).*

LEFT: *A bird sits atop the Crane Island-Mountain (fig. 85).*

TOP: *The Turtle Island is another aspect of the pond garden whose presence evokes archaic mythic islands in India and China (fig. 89).*

RIGHT: *The arc of the Bridge of Stones, over-lapping the water to the right, complements the horizontal stones that make up the lower and mid-levels of the Water-fall of Stones on the embankment of earth, upper left (fig. 102).*

arcing Night-Mooring Stones, to the left in the water, are linked to events in the folklore of Japan (fig. 117). OPPOSITE BELOW: The Zazen Stone emphasizes the importance of seated meditation out-of-doors (fig. 109). LEFT: The Waterfall of Stones is experienced as a triangle of stones on the horizontal Bridge of Stones (fig. 130). BELOW: The Bridge of Stones mediates between the verticality of the Waterfall of Stones on the embankment and the Crane Island-Mountain in the water (fig. 104).

OPPOSITE TOP: *A painting of a dragon inside the Abbot's Quarters suggests the historical belief that a dragon lives in the pond garden (fig. 142).* OPPOSITE BELOW: *Opening the shōji of the Abbot's Quarters reveals the verdant pond garden across a quiet expanse of tatami (fig. 15).* TOP: *Covered walkways linking buildings are characteristic of Heian-period building architecture (fig. 35).* LEFT: *Musō Kokushi was a venerated priest, one of the founders and the initial abbot, of the Temple of the Heavenly Dragon (fig. 36).* OVERLEAF: *The temple's pond garden aspect, with its prized koi, continues to attract people from Japan . . . and around the world (fig. 141).*

FIGURE 75. *An image of Meru from a thirteenth-century Jain text* (Trailokyadīpikā). *Meru is imaged as triangular in form, comprising (seven) primary sections of earth and stone (corresponding to the triangular form of the Crane Island-Mountain apparent in figures 67, 69). Meru is depicted as organic, lush with flora and foliage nourishing a rich diversity of beings both human and non-human.*

of the Golden Embryo is hidden."[10] Meru mostly was submerged, and the vast peaks of the cosmic mountain invariably were depicted as but a hint of the enormity of its underwater mass, present but unseen—analogous to envisioning the Crane Island as the above-water peaks of an unseen massive mountain tapering down into the expansive floor of the pond (figs. 70, 77).[11]

The physical form of the Crane Island-Mountain reinforces evocations of Meru. Viewed from various perspectives while walking around the pond, the Crane Island-Mountain invariably appears as a broadly triangular-shaped cluster of stones (figs. 69, 72, 80). Consider the subtle congruence between aspects of the triangular design-form of the Crane Island-Mountain and aspects of archaic images of Meru, also envisioned as triangular in form. In each instance, of particular interest is congruence of number as well as form.

FIGURE 76. *A dramatic contemporary composition of stones, explicitly evoca-tive of Meru, has been placed in front of the entrance to the present-day recep-tion building (fig. 12). With respect to compositional triangularity and oblique angles, there is a similarity of design between this contemporary arrangement of stones and the Crane Island-Mountain composition of stones within the pond (figs. 68, 71).*

As a composition of stones, the Crane Island-Mountain at pres-ent still approximates a (scalene) triangle in the (*shichigosan*) propor-tion of 7:5:3 (figs. 77, 80, 81). The numbers 7, 5, and 3, and approximate 7:5:3 proportions of form also are evident in conceptions and archaic images of Meru.

Meru was believed surrounded by seven smaller mountain-continents of gold, embedded with gems and glinting jewels. Many of the stone placements in the pond of the Temple of the Heavenly Dragon most likely are nearly a thousand years of age. When the stones composing the present-day Crane Island-Mountain were set, their faceted angularity must have been striking. The faceted stones perhaps would have appeared as a cluster of jewels in the water, when caught by the burnished gold of sunlight or the liquid silver of moonlight (similar to the description of the Sumerian Garden of the Sun, in Part III). Meru can be evoked readily through the faceted, still jewel-like form of the interlocking planes of the aged stones com-posing the Crane Island-Mountain (figs. 69, 85).

FIGURE 77. *Reflections in the water enhance the felt-presence of the Crane Island-Mountain of stones.*

Seven underground regions were encountered in descending the slopes of Meru. Seven envelopes of ether were encountered in ascending the slopes of Meru. Congruently, again, the Crane Island-Mountain appears composed around seven principal stones (fig. 70). World Systems were composed of five elements: earth, water, air, fire, and ether/space. The myriad planes and spaces composing the universe coalesced as three primary clusters—the Three Thousand Worlds (Trichiliocosm Nāga, in Sanskrit).

Archaic Indian conceptions of Meru, in sum, envisioned the form of the cosmic mountain as composed of features associated with the numbers 7, 5, and 3. The Crane Island-Mountain, as well, is composed of and around features associated with the numbers 7, 5, and 3.

The King of Mountains was not a lifeless pillar of stone, silent at the center of the universe. Not stopping with compelling number and form, we note that Meru animistically teemed with life.

Culika (Siddha, for Buddhists) was a site at the summit of Meru. Culika was the dwelling place of people released from *samsāra*, who then were welcomed by the guardian deity Taishakuten.[12] Streams and rivers laced the summit and terraced slopes of Meru. As a source of life, rivers on Meru flowed (to the south) to empty into the vast seas of the Great Ocean. Congruently, pond waters winding between the stones of the Crane Island-Mountain readily evoke the vast seas surrounding the stone at the center of the universe (fig. 67). Meru was an organic landscape inhabited by a rich diversity of beings both human and non-human, and "at the foot of the mountain and around each platform are terraces, parks full of trees and flowers."[13] At present, the Crane Island-Mountain is relatively shorn of flora. Recent cleanings removed the moss, small pine, and flowers rooted on the stones; as such, our attention presently is directed to the cubist quality of the stones. Removal of the flora flourishing on the stones, though, deprived the composition of the organic qualities evocative of the organic qualities of Meru. Photographs of the Crane Island-Mountain alive with moss and tiny pine more readily evoke a lush mythic mountain in a vast cosmic sea (fig. 69).

The legend of Meru subsequently passed, with Buddhism, from India to China then to Japan.[14] The Indian legend of Meru in time merged with Chinese legends of the Mystic Isles of the Blest. Both legends influenced the evocation of cosmic mountains, through the setting of stones, within garden landscapes in Japan.

CHINA, AND THE MYSTIC ISLES OF THE BLEST

The Mystic Isles of the Blest were an earthly paradise shrouded within the gossamer mists of vast waters far from the eastern shores of China. The islands were immense in size, and immense also were the distances between the shores of the isles and the shores of China. Five islands composed the Mystic Isles of the Blest: Tai Yu, Yuan Chiao, Fang Hu, Ying Chou, and P'eng-lai. Legend has it that the islands of Tai Yu and Yuan Chiao inexplicably broached their moorings, drifted, and were lost in the mist—along with hundreds of thousands of inhabitants. Three islands remained: Ying Chou, Fang Hu, and P'eng-lai. When the Mystic Isles of the Blest later were evoked, these three islands initially came to stand for the original five islands.

The Mystic Isles of the Blest by legend were inhabited by immortal sages. Immortals inhabiting the Mystic Isles were humans who, primarily through Daoist ascetic practices, had transformed into *xian* (仙, genii). *Xian* had transcended the believed limitations of physical existence, but were not yet adept enough to "take their place among the stars."[15] The Mystic Isles were an abode where immortals continued to refine themselves through what we would name as the alchemical work of further transmuting matter into spirit.

Mortal humans sought out the Enchanted Isles, as the islands also were known, to locate then participate in the secrets of the *xian*—secrets such as ethereal knowledge of well-being and immortality. In 221 B.C., Emperor Ch'in Shih Huang-Ti (259–210 B.C.) dispatched Hsu Fu to search for the Enchanted Isles, and "under the Emperor's orders thousands found employment in searching the seas for the Enchanted Islands."[16] As intermediaries between Heaven and

Earth, if emperors possessed well-being and immortality, then these qualities would be transmitted throughout an emperor's domain. Hsu Fu, though, never returned from his search for the Enchanted Isles.

Somewhat later Emperor Wu-Ti (140–87 B.C.) dispatched expeditions again to search the eastern seas for the Enchanted Isles. "[Voyagers], while yet far off," it was believed, "might see the islands as a cloud; as they drew closer the Three Enchanted Isles would sink beneath the waves; and when nearer still, the wind suddenly would take their barque and carry them away. In short, no one has succeeded in gaining their shores."[17] As voyagers searched the seas, emperors themselves undertook expeditions to the eastern shores to search firsthand for the islands of the *xian*. "Wu-Ti, like the First Emperor," we read, "frequented the coast interrogating seafaring folk and hoping to catch sight of the Islands in the far distance. Facing eastward, he sacrificed to the inhabitants of P'eng-lai; the Enchanted Isles, though, remained out of the experiential grasp of humans."[18] The remoteness and inaccessibility of the Enchanted Isles, the frustration of contacting *xian*, stimulated attempts to lure immortals to the realm of mortals and, in particular, to the palaces of emperors. Mirroring the form and design of the Enchanted Isles, imperial gardens subsequently were created in attempts to attract immortals to human-created doppelgänger landscapes.

Emperor Wu-Ti ordered the construction of one of the earliest garden landscapes in China, apparently meant to attract *xian*. The emperor landscaped areas surrounding venerated Lake Tai-i, west of the capital city of Chang-an, in hopes of attracting immortals. "To insure success," then, "he [Emperor Wu-Ti] resorted to sympathetic magic, constructing replicas of the Isles in his garden lake. Probably he hoped to lure some of the Immortals to a spot so similar to their own realm and so learn the secret from them."[19] "Sympathetic magic" is one name for the still-widespread cross-cultural belief that an image-likeness of something (here, the garden as iconic image of the Enchanted Isles) literally is connected to, participates in, the qualities of the actual thing of which the image is a doppelgänger-likeness.[20] Towers of stone (*Chien T'ai*, in Chinese) in the believed

FIGURE 78. In this painting the mythic island of Fang Hu is laced with garlanded groves of pine. The island is the craggy ridges of a mountain peaking from swirling seas. The apical peak of the mountain channels a waterfall flowing into a pool nested in the center of the island. A temple building rests in the foreground of the pond. Three white cranes, barely visible dots, perch on the rockery of the smaller off-shore island to the lower left. By Wang Yun (1652–1735). 1699, ink and color on silk, 141.9 x 60.3 cm.

iconic physical form of the mountain peaks of the Enchanted Isles were placed in the pond of Wu-Ti's water garden, and the composition "was so picturesque and beautiful . . . that it could have served as a palace for the Immortals."[21] Similar to Meru, the Enchanted Isles of China were believed formed from faceted jewels of stone. The jeweled Enchanted Isles were terraced, akin to Meru in India, and "upon their shores, the terraces and pleasure-towers are built of gold and jade, and the birds and flowers are all alike of unblemished white. The palaces and gates are built of yellow gold and silver."[22] The terraced slopes of the mythic island-mountains were believed inhabited by immortals of various ranks, with the rank of *xian* congruent with their level of habitation on the terraced slopes (fig. 78).

P'eng-lai, Fang Hu, and Ying Chou were differentiated with respect to size. P'eng-lai, the tallest, highest ranked island, was home to immortals "on more exalted planes. In palaces of heavenly splendor, on the peaks of P'eng-lai there live some who rank among the holiest of adepts . . . ."[23] In time, the high-ranked, physically imposing P'eng-lai alone came to stand for the Mystic Isles of the Blest. P'eng-lai often was evoked as a tall spire of stone, glinting in the midst and mists of an expansive water garden landscape.

The Enchanted Isles of China were envisioned as organic, akin to conceptions of Meru in India. Water, trees, and a variety of beings populated the slopes and summits of the Mystic Isles of the Blest. Emperors sought the Enchanted Isles in the hope of eating the gem-like flora on which *xian* nourished themselves as well as to drink juice from the fruits of the trees on the islands. The belief was that "thick groves there are [on the Enchanted Isles], laden with pearls and gems and not a flower but gives forth fragrant perfume, nor a fruit but has delicious flavor. On those who eat thereof is conferred the boon of immortality."[24] Juice from the Enchanted Isles, an elixir staving off age and death, was believed to carry immortality. The organic aspects of the Crane Island-Mountain aptly evoke the fecundity and generativity of the Enchanted Isles.

It also was believed that "the ancient crane builds its nest upon the giant limbs of its [P'eng-lai] never dying pine."[25] Cranes, and pine trees, are prominent in Chinese narratives and images of the Mystic Isles of the Blest.

The distances, again, between the eastern shores of China and the Enchanted Isles were vast; vast, as well, were the distances between the islands themselves. A related belief was that *xian* rode the backs of cranes flying between the Enchanted Isles as well as between the islands and the lands of mortal human beings. People intently searched the backs of cranes in flight for the gossamer formlessness of immortals. One would have had to persistently gaze steadily into the fabric of the sky itself, though, for *xian* "ride upon the wind, pass through water without becoming wet, and through fire without being burnt."[26] Cranes were not immortal, but were linked to immortality by virtue of their direct contagious connection to *xian*. *Xian* themselves remained unseen, but the cranes they rode with the wind were visible to mortal human beings.

FIGURE 79. *From this vantage, the Crane Island-Mountain can be experienced as evoking mythic island-mountains deep within the shadowed expanse of mythic waters.*

JAPAN AND THE EVERLASTING ETERNAL LAND

There is a remarkable correspondence of ideas about and practices toward both stones and island-mountains in India, China, and Japan. Imported legends of cosmic mountains were alive in Japan as early as the sixth century. The *Chronicles of Japan* mentions a garden constructed for Empress Suiko (554–628), within which a composition of stones named Sumeru was set.[27] Meru became Sumeru, believed to be the northern pole of Meru, and stones evoking Sumeru were referred

to as Shumisen (須弥山).²⁸ Shumisen often was evoked through compositions of stone emphasizing "a central pointed rock . . . rising from
lesser rocks around its base," of which the form and placement of the
central stone within the Island-Mountain of the Cranes remains a
fine example.²⁹ The *Chronicles of the Great Peace* recounts the dream
of a Buddhist monk who claimed to have "laid hands on the sun and
moon, taken up my abode on the summit of Mount Sumeru, and trod
on the great sea with one foot [faced death]."³⁰ P'eng-lai became Hōrai
(蓬莱; in the *Chronicles of Japan*, P'eng-lai is referred to as Hōrai).³¹
Hōrai also was known as Hōraizan (蓬莱算, Land of the Immortals),
Hōraishima (蓬莱島, Island of the Immortals), and Hōraiyama (蓬莱
山, Mountain of the Immortals).³²

As conveyed in figures 66 and 79, experience of the Crane Island-
Mountain as evocation of Hōrai is reinforced by the placement of the
composition toward the "rear part of the garden . . . deep in shadow,
which darkens the water of the lake, while the Hōrai Island, the unat-
tainable Island of the Immortals, is bathed in sunlight and seems to float
in a light haze."³³ Viewed while sitting within the Abbot's Quarters,
across the wide expanse of water, the Crane Island-Mountain indeed
evokes a palpable, felt sense of distance (figs. 3, 62). Mythic distance.

A generic Island-Mountain of the Immortals participates in archaic legends and myths from India, China, and Japan. Vast tracts
of water surround the mystic isles. Mystic isles were conceptualized
as the above-water aspect of mostly submerged mountains. Whether
conceptualized as evoking Meru, P'eng-lai, Sumeru, or Hōrai, through
awareness of its lineage ancestry the Crane Island-Mountain can be
experienced as evocation of a mythic, archetypal isle.

"We [foreigners] keep trying to make the garden . . . important."

"Well, you can make the garden important if you wish, of
course," says the priest. "But if you combine what I have been
sharing with you with your own feelings and insights that you
may have received as you looked at the garden, with your own

FIGURE 80. *The Crane Island-Mountain, glinting in the sunlight, to the right of the waterfall of stones and Bridge of Stones. In the lower-left corner, one of the Night-Mooring Stones sits in the water. From this vantage, one can discern the right-angle triangularity, the asymmetry, of the Crane-Island Mountain as a composition of stones and foliage.*

eyes, perhaps the garden by itself will become 'important.' You do not need to make the garden 'important,' forcibly. If it is 'important to you,' it will become 'important,' by itself."

Periodically sitting before the pond garden, over the years the garden itself indeed revealed to me what to notice, what to dwell upon, about what I felt deeply, what needed to be studied intensively, as well as the affecting manner, this book, in which to present the pond garden. Experiencing the presence of the Crane Island-Mountain of spaces and stones emerging from early morning mist, I often felt the memory of T. S. Eliot's animistic poem "Choruses from 'The Rock,'" where I am admonished: "Silence! and preserve respectful distance, for I perceive approaching The Rock. Who will

FIGURE 81. A sketch by a priest of the Crane Island-Mountain, emphasizing three stones of significance within the composition. The priest outlines the three stones, in the interdependent proportion of 7:5:3. These three stones also are associated with and evoke Buddha (7), Monju (5), and Fugen (3). See figure 82.

perhaps answer our doubtings. The Rock. The Watcher . . . who has seen what has happened, And who sees what is to happen. The Witness."[34] As the priest intimated, what continues to remain "important" is experience of the pond garden as epistemology. The pond garden itself is a Way of knowing.

The Wisdom of Stones

Late afternoon.

The Crane Island-Mountain is wrapped in delicate filigrees of light.

"Is there a name for this [island-mountain] group of stones?"

"We say that the stones are Buddha," says the priest. "And Bodhisattvas."

"So, Buddha is in the stones?"

"No, there is no such thing. The [stones] are the shape of Shākyamuni, as-they-are [shinnyo] . . . "

The priest is quite familiar with the tradition of conceptualizing primary stones within the Crane Island-Mountain as 7:5:3 (shichigo-san) interdependent relationship. The priest, though, further names

FIGURE 82. *Shaka Triad (Buddhist Trinity) in the Golden Hall, Hōryū-ji, Nara. Buddha, the prominent central figure, is flanked by the Bodhisattva Seishi, to the left, and Kannon, to the right (the priest replaces the two smaller flanking figures with Monju and Fugen, Bodhisattvas important to Rinzai Zen Buddhism (fig. 82). By Busshi Tori. 623 A.D., bronze. H: 175 cm.*

©Shōgakukan Publishing Company

the Crane Island-Mountain as *sanzonseki* (三尊石; three-stone composition of stones, often triangular in arrangement). The priest then diagrams the manner in which the relative masses and proportions of the *sanzon*, one to another, exhibit 7:5:3 interdependent relationship (fig. 81).

Triangular-shaped compositions of three stones in the pond gardens within many Buddhist temples also are known as the Three Buddhist Stones of the Exalted Ones (三尊仏の石, *Sanzonbutsu no Ishi*), "which literally means a composition of stones in the form of Buddha standing between two accompanying saints."[35] In Rinzai Zen Buddhism, the Three Exalted Ones are Buddha and the Bodhisattvas Monju and Fugen. The Three Exalted Ones conventionally are envisioned with the larger figure of Buddha centered between the smaller flanking figures of the other two (fig. 82).

The priest diagrams the Crane Island-Mountain, pointing to the tall central stone as evocative of Buddha and the smaller flanking stones as evocative of Monju and Fugen (fig. 83).

"When 〖Christians〗 say that God saves people," says the priest, "I take it to mean that it is the 'love' of God that saves people. In Buddhism, though, we do not use the word 'love' 〖愛〗 here. We use the word *jihi* 〖慈悲, mercy; compassion〗 to express the Buddha's gentle-heartedness. Fugen Bosatsu 〖普賢菩薩〗 is *jihi*.

FIGURE 83. *Three selected stones within the Crane Island-Mountain can be envisioned as corresponding with the interrelationship of Shākyamuni, Monju, and Fugen. Experienced as interrelated form, the three stones of significance also can be experienced as approximating a scalene triangle (fig. 58).*

Monju Bosatsu 〚文殊菩薩〛 is wisdom—as in the proverb 'the Counsel of Three can attain the wisdom of Monju.' Fugen Bosatsu and Monju Bosatsu accompany Shākyamuni, as disciples. Therefore, when I say that those stones are *sanzonseki* 〚三尊石 組, *sanzon ishigumi*〛 I mean they 〚evoke〛 Shākyamuni, Fugen Bosatsu, and Monju Bosatsu [三尊仏の石, *Sanzonbutsu no Ishi*〛."[36]

Garden specialists, on the other hand, tend to link status with the various sizes of the stones. The tall (Buddha) stone in the composition has been referred to as the Noble Central Stone, and the flanking stones (Monju and Fugen) have been referred to as Noble Side Stones. The larger side stone, evocative of Monju, has been named the First Subordinate Stone while the more horizontal side stone, evocative of Fugen, is named the Second Subordinate Stone in an arrangement of three-stones (*sanzon ishigumi*).

"Again," says the priest, "Monju Bosatsu is a Buddha who imparts wisdom to people, and Fugen Bosatsu is a Buddha who imparts the *kokoro* 〚heart/mind〛 of compassion to people."

"Is this another teaching of the garden?"

"Exactly. People vary in their characteristics and capacity, as you know. For example, there are people who possess extraordinary wisdom. Some people lack virtue, even though their wisdom is superb. On the other hand, there are people who possess excellent virtue, but lack wisdom. By teaching the importance of virtue to those who lack virtue, in spite of their wisdom, these people begin to possess virtue gradually. After a while these people possess both wisdom and virtue, and become very admirable people. In the case of people who lack wisdom, by teaching the importance of wisdom it is hoped that they will try to improve themselves . . . and eventually become excellent people."

The priest echoes a passage from the *Book of Garden* to the effect that "one who looks at my figure [the Three Exalted Ones] will be awakened to the devotional spirit."[37] For the priest, the presence in the pond of the Three Exalted Ones perhaps will stimulate in people contemplation of compassion, virtue, and wisdom.

In addition to wisdom and compassion, Monju and Fugen long have been associated with protection. The triad form and composition of stones evoking the Three Exalted Buddhas in particular "have a kind of protective function against evil spirits and illness."[38] The *Book of Garden* discusses *sanzon* and the protective function of Buddhist trinity compositions of stones set "to counter any evil, revengeful spirits entering the grounds."[39] Recalling the genesis of the Temple of the Heavenly Dragon, early in the life of the garden the three-stone composition in the pond perhaps enjoyed life in the consciousness of people, such as Takauji of the Ashikaga or Musō Kokushi, as added protection against vengeful spirits and hungry ghosts.

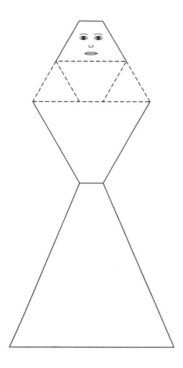

FIGURE 84. *A Jain conception of a universe, depicted as an anthropomorphic cosmic body (influencing Buddhist conceptions of Meru). The narrow center, the "waist," of the universe is the realm of the human form of being. Descending spatially from the realm of the human form of being, netherworlds proportionally increase in size; increasing spatially from the realm of the human form of being, heavenly realms within heavenly realms proportionally increase in size then terminate in a smaller privileged realm of existence* (Siddha).

The Dharma of Stones

The priest's conception of the tall stone in the Crane Island-Mountain, as evocative of Shākyamuni, touches an archaic Buddhist linkage of mountains and Buddha. In Buddhist India, Meru was the King of Mountains through belief in Buddha's direct physical contact with the mythic mountain. It was believed that Buddha traversed the universe in three steps, the Three Steps of Buddha, with the last step taken by Buddha resting on Meru.

Meru comprised four continents quartered and oriented to the four cardinal directions. The summit of Meru often was anthropomorphized as the top of a head, the face of which was the upper portions of a cosmic mountain. Figure 84 depicts Meru envisioned as a body, a *ziggurat* broad at the shoulders and gradually tapering in to the waist. The upper body of the cosmic mountain is a triangular-shaped pyramid, congruent with the above-water aspect of the Crane Island-Mountain in the pond of the garden. The lower *ziggurat* pyramid is the lower part of the body, broadening out at the base as a platform

FIGURE 85. "*The emerald feathers of ⟦birds⟧, sometimes flashing just over the lake, produce a richness of color and soften the ⟦Zen⟧ sternness of the garden.*"[185]

supporting and stabilizing the mountain-as-body, congruent with en-visioning the below-water aspect of the Crane Island-Mountain.

Ancient Indian conceptions of Meru-as-a-body are congruent with the priest's conception of the Crane-Island-Mountain-as-a-body: Buddha, and two Bodhisattvas. For the priest, in addition, "body" invariably brings to mind correspondences with *zazen*.

Buddhist interpretations of *zazen* not only reference mountains but often reference Meru specifically in that, in *zazen*, "one's self be-comes a microcosm that fuses and becomes one with the enveloping macrocosm. One's spine then becomes the Meru, an *axis mundi*, of both. Arrayed along the spine are various centers of psychic energy that one summons up, in the practice of yoga, in moving toward the supremely illuminated *samadhi* state [similar to congruencies of *chakra* in yoga and the arrangement of the Dragon-Gate Waterfall; fig. 145]. These energy centers may be viewed as the psycho physiological analogues of the heavens that the soul traverses on its path to ultimate liberation, *moksha* in Hinduism or *nirvāna* in Buddhism, whereby one is freed from the painful cycle of rebirth and made one with the infinite."[40] The priest's correspondence points to the more comprehensive principle of Buddha-Nature in which nature, people, and "enlightened" human-constructed landscapes, such as the pond garden, are believed to participate (fig. 85).

꙳

The Dharma of the stones. As embodiment of Buddha and Bodhisattva, for the priest the Crane Island-Mountain in turn evokes the *Heart Sūtra* and the story of believers in their (metaphorical) pilgrimage across the water and earth of the pond, tying boats to the Night-Mooring Stones (*Yodomari Ishi*) to be present to the Dharma of Buddha and perhaps to become aware of inherent Buddha-Nature. The Crane Island-Mountain also is linked conceptually to the priest's vision of the Dragon-Gate Waterfall (*Ryūmon no Taki*) and to the Bridge of Stones (*Hashi no Ishi*), as we will see.

6

SETTLING FLOWERS OF ICE

Early morning light.

The water shimmers, rippled slightly by polyrhythmic waves of late summer heat. The *koi* are still, massed deep within the cool recesses of the bottom of the pond.

The priest points across the pond, and over a peninsula of land and stone jutting into the water, then across and to the right of the Crane Island-Mountain (figs. 86, 87, 88). A moss-blanketed mound of earth sits within this right-side area to the rear of the pond. "*Are wa nan desu ka?* [What is that, over there?]," we ask the priest, pointing. "*Kame Shima desu* [The Turtle Island]," replies the priest, as the mound of earth conventionally is named. Concentrating, we more clearly see this pine-tree-topped earthen mound of grass and shrub as the top of an "island" strewn with stones, surrounded by the water of the pond.

The mound evocative of turtle-ness is pocked with weathered earth and small stones, strewn about by time. The rounded top of the mound, the craggy "shell" of the turtle, is sprinkled with stones glistening in the early evening light like "settling flowers of ice," as Musō wrote.[1] Prominent upended stones suggest the "head" and "tail" of the zoomorphic Turtle Island (fig. 89).[2] The "head" of the Turtle Island conventionally is associated with a large stone, almost

FIGURE 86. A view toward the northern area of the pond garden, and the coniferous tree-topped Turtle Island (a 1986 photograph; the bamboo hoops at the edge of the pond have since been removed). Slightly to the right of the island, the long slab of stone functioning as a bridge is visible. The slab of stone connects the Turtle Island to the bamboo-fenced promontory, to the right, extending into the water.

FIGURE 87. "The impression of a garden changes according not only to the time of the day, but also to the seasons. . . . You can also hear the whispering of the wind among the pine-trees, and the voices of birds on the incline."[187] The Turtle Island is just behind/above the peninsula line of stones prominently jutting into the water from the lower right.

a meter in height, the tallest stone atop the earthen mound (fig. 90). The stone associated with "tail" is placed on the opposite end of the earthen mound, set on end like the "head" stone. Stubby stones suggesting "fore legs" and "hind legs" have been set low on, and extending out from, the sides of the earthen mound, hidden among the present-day foliage.[3]

Similar to the Crane Island-Mountain, the verticality of the stones evoking the "head" and "tail" of the Turtle Island is quite affecting, aesthetically. The "head" stone and "tail" stone catch various patterns of light and shadow at different times of the day and night. The two stones are prisms reflecting and refracting light and shadow. The *chiaroscuro* effects produced by the stones, the shaded interplay of light and shadow, are captivating (fig. 91).

The island was damaged sometime in the past during one of a number of historical spasms of violence touching the pond garden. We ought not assume, then, that this present-day island is the exact composition of earth and stones set more than seven hundred years ago. Exhibiting the patina of age (寂, *sabi*) similar to other compositions of stones in the garden and the pond, the stones defining the Turtle Island are weatherworn by centuries of existence.[4] Musō experienced a composition undoubtedly more stone-studded and crisp than the weathered island presently arresting our gaze.

Mythic Turtles in India, China, and Japan

Turtles live in the origin myths of more than a few historical as well as existing cultures in the world.[5] The shell of the turtle, the amphibious behavior of the turtle, and ascribed qualities such as endurance and longevity are mythic aspects of "turtle-ness" archetypal with respect to their widespread occurrence. Our concern here is with the manner in which myths from India and China influenced and complemented references to turtles in the origin myths of Japan. A variety of archaic myths associated with turtles correspond to the physical

FIGURE 88. *The Turtle Island, in late-summer.*

FIGURE 89. *In late fall, the relative absence of foliage reveals the primary stones defining the Turtle Island. The stone plank connecting the Turtle Island to land is not contemporaneous with the initial design and construction of the pond garden, nor do priests experience this plank bridge mindful of Buddhism. Each and every stone in the pond is not experienced as evocative, or referential.*

FIGURE 90. *In the spring, the "head" stone nests within the fragrance of aza-leas and camellias in bloom.*

FIGURE 91. *Along with the plank bridge, the flat stones and signs of wear atop the Turtle Island indicate that the composition was designed to be walked upon.*

form and varied interpretations of the Turtle Island within the Temple of the Heavenly Dragon.

Similar to stones evoking qualities associated with cranes, the phenomenon of turtle islands in pond gardens was influenced by commonly understood cultural legend and myth. As with the Crane Island-Mountain, we can trace the lineage history of turtle islands, and the iconic evocation of qualities associated with turtles, from India and China then to Japan.

INDIA, AND THE WHEEL OF THE TORTOISE

In Vedic India, the earth was conceptualized as a hemisphere stabilized by and resting flat-side down upon the backs of four elephants; in turn, the elephants stood on the back of Kurma Chakra, a vast turtle. Kurma Chakra supported the earth as the cauldron of life. Fundamental attributes of these mythic turtles were strength and stability as the literal support of life itself.

Devas churned the primal Sea of Milk (echoing the generative churnings of Izanagi, in Japan, standing on the Floating Bridge of Heaven) to produce Amrita, the drink of immortality (echoing the Chinese Daoist elixir of immortality). Deva churned the Sea of Milk with Mandara, a primal mountain [Meru]. Devas wound the serpent Vasuki around the mountain, and for a thousand years Devas pulled Vasuki back and forth to turn Mandara within the Sea of Milk (Vasuki, a Nāga, precursor of the dragon, lay coiled at the base of the mountain).

The interweaving of turtle and mountain intensifies with the presence of Vishnu (Narayana). As an incarnation of Kurma Chakra, Vishnu functioned as an *axis mundi*, "the cosmic axis that steadies the world."[6] Amid the swirl of creation, Vishnu-as-axial-mountain rotated steadily. The motion was dynamic; yet, as Mandara was linked directly to Vishnu-as-tortoise, the motion was stable as well. Mount Mandara was stable and firm, yet, at the same moment, kinetic and in motion. The Wheel of the Tortoise. "Wheel" is an apt image, as

Mandara was ascribed the gyroscopic stability of a wheel in motion (images of rotating wheels later also were a sign of the Dharma of Buddha). Turtles thus came to embody the interdependence of motion and stasis, change and stability.

CHINA, AND THE ABYSS OF THE ASSEMBLY

Dynastic Chinese belief held that Heaven and Earth were created over a span of ten thousand years. Kwei was a deity important to the creation of Heaven and Earth and, after creation, Kwei took the form of an ordinary turtle and subsequently instructed humankind in the ways of truth and wisdom. Turtles thus came to be envisioned as embodiments of a deity. Turtles were believed to possess a divine nature, as turtle as well as embodiment (of truth; wisdom; compassion) of Kwei.

The aforementioned five Chinese islands of gold and jade, the Mystic Isles of the Blest, moved about in a primal sea, the Abyss of Assembly, "to which the waters from the eight points of the compass and from the uttermost parts of the earth, and from the streams of the Milky Way, all flow. And they do so without causing any appreciable change in the depth of the Abyss."[7] The five islands were swayed continually by intense underwater tides to the consternation of the *xian*, who desired stability for their abodes.

Xian dwelling on the Mystic Isles agonized that if their realm continued to exist at the whim of the waters of the Abyss of Assembly, their precious abodes eventually would drift toward the earthen shores of mortal human beings. Contagion, direct physical contact, then would transfer the immortality of the islands to the lands of humans. In large part, the five islands were "Blest" by isolation from human beings. Isolation was critical to the existence of the Mystic Isles. Correspondingly, consider the placement of the Turtle Island within the Tenryū-ji pond. The Turtle Island was set toward the rear of the pond and physically reinforces evocation of the spatial isolation of mythic isles from the lands of human beings (the stone

FIGURE 92. Mythic Mount Hōrai, supported by a turtle. The photograph is an enlargement of the upper right-hand corner of the underside of the lid of the lacquered cosmetics box in figure 93.

bridge connecting the Turtle Island to the land was placed well after the time of Musō; fig. 89).

Concerned with the drift of their islands, *xian* petitioned the Supreme Ruler of the Universe to command fifteen giant turtles inhabiting the vast floor of the Abyss of Assembly to be harnessed to support and stabilize the islands. Three turtles were ordered to support, in tripod fashion, each of the five islands.

In India, China, and Japan, odd numbers such as 3, 5, 7, and 15 in particular were associated with stability. The tripod positioning of the turtles is suggestive, as well. In effect, the turtles were positioned to form an equilateral triangle, with an island supported between each of the turtles on their slightly upturned heads.

The image of mythic Chinese turtles with slightly upturned heads is congruent iconically with the intentionally selected and placed, slightly upturned "head" stone on the Turtle Island in the pond (fig. 90). It is not necessary for pond gardens to exhibit three, or even fifteen, distinct islands evocative of turtles. Akin to the other aspects of the pond garden, the Turtle Island functions as a suggestion, a locus for evocation, not as a representation or as a symbol.

Returning to the Mystic Isles of the Blest, sometime later in mythic time a wandering Giant from Lung-po, where he lived in the undersea Kingdom of a Dragon Prince, spied the harnessed turtles within the waters of the Abyss of Assembly. The Giant snared six of the turtles in his net such that, it was speculated, he could roast the shells of the turtles until they cracked from the heat and then read the cracks as divination. Two islands (Tai Yü and Yüan Chaio) desta- bilized, and began to drift away. As we saw previously, hundreds of thousands of *xian* faded into the mist, and were lost. Three islands (Ying Chou, Fang Hu, P'eng-lai) remained tethered in place, stable amid supporting turtles (fig. 92).

Turtle islands appeared early in the pond gardens of dynastic China. Early Chinese gardens were comparatively large lakes dotted by turtle islands, the most grandiose of which was the aforemen- tioned palace of Emperor Wu-Ti. The presence of iconic turtle islands was believed to confer well-being and long life to people, by conta- gion, as well as to the human-constructed landscapes in which they were placed.

JAPAN, AND WATERY TRACES OF IMMORTALITY

The association of turtle and island was a well-known motif at the time of the birth and early life of the pond garden within the Temple of the Heavenly Dragon. Literate segments of society, in addition to Buddhist priests, would have been familiar with the legend of Hōrai (Sumeru, Shumisen), the Chinese Isles of the Blest, and with Kurma Chakra.

The Hōrai motif was widespread and prominent historically in a variety of settings, inclusive of pond gardens. Figure 93 depicts a gold-leaf-embellished lacquer cosmetics box, from the eleventh cen- tury, used by females of the *bakufu*. The hexagonal design on the surfaces of the box, formed by sprinkling powdered gold on black

FIGURE 93. *Cosmetics box (tebako).*
Thirteenth-century, lacquer, cloth,
and pewter. 2.5 x 4 x 3.5 cm.

FIGURE 94. *Full underside of the lid of*
the cosmetics box in figure 93.

lacquer, defined a distinctive tortoiseshell pattern (*kikkō tsunami mon*), subtly prefiguring a scene painted on the interior of the box (fig. 94). Similar to the design of pond gardens, where discrete areas subtly cue what is to be revealed to participants, "the tortoise shell design provides a small hint at the narrative found on the underside of the lid."[8] The scene depicted in figures 92 and 94, painted on the underside of the lid of the box, depicts Hōrai-as-mountain-island (Hōraizan, "an imaginary island shaped like a tortoise in the ocean") carried on/ supported by the back of a turtle.[9] The scene on the box lid links islands, a turtle, and cranes. The crane and the turtle, again, exist interdependently as a single archaic motif.

The base and rim of Hōraizan painted on the underside of the cosmetics box lid sprout foliage, as does the Turtle Island within the Tenryū-ji pond garden (figs. 89, 91). The turtle on the lid of the cosmetics box bears a mountain on top of its shell, coralline and convoluted, congruent with Daoist Chinese images of the jade abodes of

immortals dotting the Mystic Isles of the Blest.[10] This motif of a turtle bearing a mountain on its back also by kinship is related to Vishnu
incarnated as Kurma Chakra. In each instance, a cosmic mountain is
an island, an above-water mound of stable earth and stone supported
by a vast turtle in a boundless sea.

Influential turtle motifs continue to populate the cultural lore of
Japan. Perhaps the most pervasive, well-known lore are the legends
of Fukurokuju (Fukurokujin) and Urashima Tarō.

Fukurokuju is one of the Seven Gods of Good Fortune. He is
a composite of three deities—Fuku, the deity of happiness; Roku,
the deity of fortune; Ju, the deity of longevity. He customarily is
depicted as a white-bearded, wizened old man invariably accompanied by a turtle. Images of turtles with peacock-like tails of trailing,
seaweed-like wisps of fringe also signify Fukurokuju. Fukurokuju remains associated with good fortune and the ability to bestow long
life.

The story of Urashima, in the *Collection of Ten Thousand Leaves*
(*Man'yōshū*), dates to the eighth century, though the oral tradition
of Urashima undoubtedly is much older. As cultural lore, the story
of Urashima still is vital and conditions broad familiarity with the
mythic significance of turtles and turtle islands in gardens.

Urashima Tarō was a young fisherman, who one day freed a turtle unintentionally caught in a net.[11] Sometime later, Urashima was at
sea fishing when the turtle he had saved swam to his boat and begin
to speak to him. The turtle then "transformed itself into a young
woman of great beauty."[12] The narrative then reveals that the turtle/
person was the daughter of a Dragon King.[13] Upon her invitation,
Urashima accompanied the princess to the kingdom of the Dragon
King under the sea, where they subsequently wed.[14]

Time passed amid great happiness; yet, one day Urashima felt a
desire to return to the land above the Dragon Palace to visit his parents and to tell them that he was well. His wife presented him with
a gift, the implication of which was to ensure that he would return
to her. The gift was a lacquer-coated wooden box (akin to the gilded

box depicted in figure 93). The princess asked Urashima to promise not to open the box until he returned to her. If he opened the box while away, she said, he would never again see her. As she desired, Urashima so promised. In an instant, again, the princess transformed into a turtle and guided her husband up through the water and back to his homeland. She left Urashima on the shore and descended to the Dragon Palace under the sea. Urashima wandered about, asking of his parents, and everywhere he was told that the parents of Urashima Tarō were long dead and that their son had been lost at sea about four hundred years before.

Urashima sat on the beach pondering the blessings and the curse of long life. Perhaps an answer to his sorrow lay in the lacquered box he carried. Out of his sorrow, Urashima opened the box.

The scene on the underside of the lid of the thirteenth-century cosmetics box depicts this moment in the narrative (fig. 94). Urashima, holding the box in his hand, sits on an island (Honshū, it is believed). A turtle embodied as Hōraizan floats in the background. The scene depicted on the underside of the box lid is a frozen icon of immortality experienced, but soon to be lost. Urashima, like Pandora in another mythic time and another mythic place, opened the box only to release a maelstrom. Four hundred lost years stormed out of the box and swirled about Urashima. His hair instantly changed to gray then to white, then fell in dead wisps from his head. His body contracted, and withered. Villagers soon come upon the remnants of fabric and shreds of the bones of Urashima Tarō washing into the sand and water.

Additional imagery accompanying traditional Japanese depictions of the turtle/mountain/island motif, relevant to us, appears in both the scene of Hōraizan from the eleventh century and the scene of Urashima on the lacquer box lid from the thirteenth century. In both images cranes soar overhead, visual reminders of *xian* carried on the backs of cranes around and between the Mystic Islands of the Blest. The presence of cranes in the historical depiction of *Hōraisan* reinforces the historical linkage between the Turtle

Island and the Crane Island, the Dance of *Tsurukame*, within the pond garden.

The imagery on the underside of the lid of the thirteenth-century cosmetics box is quite intricate. Both the island of humans (Honshū) and the island of the immortals (Hōrai) are depicted. Cranes are placed carefully in linking, mediating, the space between the two islands and, metaphorically, two modes of being—mortal and immortal. The cranes in figures 92 and 94 carry sprigs of pine in their beaks, as pine is yet another ancient sign of longevity and good fortune. Precarious appearing, yet well rooted and stable. Pine trees sprout at angles on the mountain carried on the back of the turtle. Pine trees lace the craggy rock of the mountain, signaling the ability of this coniferous evergreen tree to adapt to difficult circumstances, to survive, and thus to acquire long life. Figure 94 shows Urashima shaded by trees of pine, akin to pine trees shading the Turtle Island within the pond garden (fig. 88).

The Turtle Island within the pond garden aspect of Tenryū-ji barely is seen from within the Abbot's Quarters (fig. 106). A poem from the twelfth century, in the *Chronicles of the Great Peace*, links pine trees to human salvation: "And beholding the ancient pines lowering their branches and the old trees spreading out their leaves, he likened them to bodhisattvas descending from the heavens to save living things below."[15] From a distance, the spire of the pine tree atop the earthen mound in the pond is the first aspect of the composition to be seen as we sit within the Abbot's Quarters (fig. 86).

In addition to myth and legend, still-current ideas and beliefs about turtles flowed from the observed behaviors of turtles. Turtles are comparatively long-lived; indeed, turtles are "known to be one of the longest lived creatures on earth," especially among vertebrates.[16] Reeve's turtle, the Japanese "coin" turtle, in particular is known for "the remarkable hardiness that appears inherent in the species."[17] Mythologically again, turtles live ten thousand years. Set within gardens, turtle islands often were named the Rock of 1,000 Ages.

In India, China, and Japan, the shell of the turtle was of esoteric

importance. The *Catapatha Brahmana*, one of the Vedas, conceptualized the world as composed of three parts—the Triple World.
Each world participated in the other worlds, often depicted as interconnected aspects of the shell of Kurma, a tortoise. One world
was the sky, envisioned as the inside of the upper shell of Kurma.
Another world was the earth, envisioned as the body of Kurma.
Humans perched on the world-body of Kurma and, gazing upward,
contemplated the curve of the sky, hazy in the distance, as the curve
of the upper shell of Kurma. The underworld was the lower shell
of Kurma, present but not seen by ordinary people perched on the
world-body-as-a-tortoise.

An analogy also was made between the physical characteristics
of the shell of a turtle and the existential situation of humans in the
phenomenal world, and this analogy often was imaged isomorphically
through geometric form. Turtle shells are oblong, a rough dome in
shape viewed looking down on the turtle As well, the shell of a turtle
approximates a square, when viewed from the bottom with a turtle
upended on its back. Extended by way of analogy to human cosmol-
ogy, the conception was that the roughly round top of the shell of a
turtle equals Heaven while the roughly square bottom of the shell of
a turtle equals Earth.[18] The turtle was believed to be a unique being
as the shell of the turtle combined the circle and the square, in its
form interrelating Heaven and Earth.

The shells of turtles are not seamlessly rounded like the shell
of an egg, but take their shape from the linkage of approximately
hexagonal-shaped exoskeletal plates of bone. The shells of turtles are
composite and geodesic in shape, not unlike the manner in which the
architect R. Buckminster Fuller interlinked hexagonal flat plates to
compose geodesic domes. A geodesic structure contributes to the relatively great strength and durability of the shell of a turtle. The shell
can support several times the weight of the turtle. It was a logical ex-
trapolation to envision mythic turtles supporting mountains, islands,
the earth, as well as the weight of the universe itself.

The archaic linkage of turtle, humankind, earth, and cosmos,

FIGURE 95. *A photograph from 1986 illustrates that, at the time, bamboo fencing skirted the edge of the pond in front of the Abbot's Quarters. The barrels are seats for visitors, in consideration of people sitting for long periods of time before the pond. The Crane Island-Mountain is to the left-center of the photograph, where the far edge of the water meets the trees. The Turtle Island of earth and stones is to the center-right-hand side of the photograph, beneath the boughs of the pine trees.*

was the foundation for the use of turtle shells for divination. As early as 1400 B.C., in China, oracles directed questions to the shells of turtles and sought answers from the patterning of cracks formed from placing shells into fires.[19] Divination via the shells of turtles underlay the development of the *I Ching*.[20] The Chinese custom of incising characters on the shells of turtles anticipates a similar custom practiced during the Nara period (710–94) in Japan.

The shells of turtles were decorative items in Japan and the hexagonal pattern of the turtle shell was a common motif adorning aristocratic clothing, dress, and utensils. It was the custom for aristocratic brides in Japan to wear a tortoiseshell comb in their hair as a sign of prosperity and good fortune.[21] When a vestal virgin completed her purifications and departed the aforementioned Palace-in-the-Field for the Grand Shrine at Ise, the emperor ritually would place a tortoiseshell Comb-of-Parting in her hair.

⅃

Early evening.

Late afternoon light settles both on the tall mass of vertically set stones and the pine-tree-topped, low-lying above-water mound of earth and stone. "The cold stream splashes out the Buddha's words, startling the stone tortoise from its sleep," as these words of Musō come to mind.[22]

Though by all appearances separated by the water of the pond, we now can experience the Turtle Island as interlinked with the Crane Island-Mountain (fig. 95). We become more fully aware of *Tsurukame*, the dance within the garden pond of turtle and crane as a vision, an embodiment, of interdependent relationship.

7
BRIDGE TO BUDDHA-NATURE

From within the Abbot's Quarters, the pond in the garden visually appears to us as ribbons of water woven between embracing fingers of earth, stone, and foliage. The priest points directly ahead, to a thin layer of stones in the distance spread horizontal to, and slightly above, the surface of the pond. The faint lines are a human-composed Bridge of Stones, set directly underneath the Dragon-Gate Waterfall, from this vantage appearing as the center of the embankment of earth at the rear of the pond (figs. 3, 96–102).

From this point of view, it is difficult to see a functional bridge within the myriad stones in the distance to which the priest is pointing. At this distance also, the Bridge of Stones appears to rest on smaller clumps of stones in the water—a thin line of stones resting on top of evenly spaced dots of stone.

Despite being directly across the pond, though, from our seated position on the floor of the Abbot's Quarters the faint stones appear close enough to touch.

Meditation in Movement

The composition to which the priest is pointing is held to be the oldest stone bridge within any temple garden in Japan.[1] In 1913, the

FIGURE 96. *Late afternoon. A view from the western veranda of the Guest Quarters, toward the center-rear area of the pond and the Bridge of Stones.*

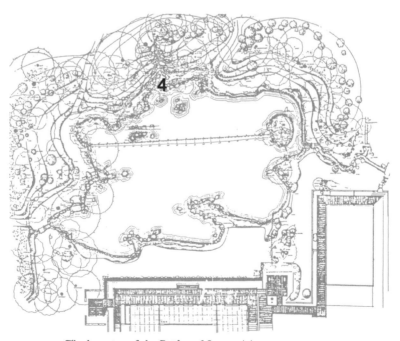

©Rikōtosho

FIGURE 97. *The location of the Bridge of Stones (4).*

FIGURE 98. *The Crane Island-Mountain rises in the water, to the right of the Bridge of Stones. From this frontal point of view, the design and composition of the bridge emphasizes the several slabs of stone, footpath stones, on top of several round support stones in the water.*

bridge was designated a National Treasure (国宝, *kokuhō*) and the temple thus does not permit people to set foot on the stones.[2]

Earlier in the history of the garden, though, priests such as Musō undoubtedly at times stood on this now-venerated Bridge of Stones.

"Can you walk on that bridge?"

"Ah, probably in the old days, but now it is no longer done because we are afraid it might be broken."

"Why do you think people [priests] walked on the bridge?"

"Probably to [experience] the waterfall."

The tall waterfall of stones, the Dragon-Gate Waterfall, would have risen above the backs of priests standing on the Bridge of Stones. The towering spire-like peak of the Crane Island-Mountain in the pond at that time perhaps would have approached the heads of priests standing on the bridge. Standing on the Bridge of Stones, priests would have been nested between the stones of the waterfall behind them and the stones of the Crane Island-Mountain before them.

The pond garden aspect of the temple landscape by design thus was not meant to be experienced exclusively from seated positions

FIGURE 99. *The horizontally composed Bridge of Stones complements the vertically composed waterfall of stones.*

FIGURE 100. *The Bridge of Stones is set lower than the earthen paths to each side of the composition. To the right, prominent rock-cut steps are visible at the northern end of the bridge, indicating that this area of the pond garden was designed to be walked upon.*

FIGURE 101. *The Bridge of Stones, to the left, has been set in intimate spatial interrelationship not only with the waterfall of stones but with the Crane Island-Mountain of stones. The curve of the Bridge of Stones is congruent with the curve of the rear embankment of the pond. The embankment of earth behind the pond rises dramatically to the left of the bridge. Several rows of stones spread across the embankment of earth, curving congruently with the curve of the bridge.*

FIGURE 102. *The footpath stones comprising the bridge were set at an oblique angle. The asymmetry of the bridge, as a composition, corresponds to the asymmetry of the Crane Island-Mountain, as a composition.*

on the verandas of the Abbot's or Guest Quarters. An earthen path on each side of, and leading up to, the Bridge of Stones is well-worn, indicating that people at times in history indeed walked around the pond garden and thus across the Bridge of Stones (fig. 100). "Walking Zen" (経行, kinhin) remains a common practice, as many priests believe that "meditation in movement has a thousand times more value than meditation in stillness."[3] The well-worn path around the garden also is a sign of the "go-around" (池泉回遊, chisenkaiyu) design of earlier pre-Buddhist landscaping in the history of the site, such as Go-Saga's pond garden.

Experienced close up, one can see that the bridge is not a single slab of stone. The footpath aspect of the bridge is composed of three slabs of stone butted end-to-end and supported at each juncture by round stones set in the water (figs. 103, 104).

The northernmost slab composing the bridge is a wide oblong stone. The bridge tapers from north to south, from a stone wide enough to support pauses while walking to narrower stones encouraging ongoing movement. The two southernmost stones are comparatively narrow and appear to have been cut from a single long slab of stone, in that "the bridge has a shape as if it was created by a master swordsman by cutting it with a sharp sword . . . in a moment."[4] Decisiveness. Will. The cut (切れ目, kireme), "cutting through"—qualities of the stones themselves embody aspects of the priest's vision of the bridge, associated with Zen and zazen, as we shall see.

The Pond Garden and the Training of Monks

The priest sketches the three flat slabs of stone composing the footpath aspect of the bridge. The topographic drawing depicts the manner in which the priest conceptualizes the Bridge of Stones in association with aspects of the training of monks (fig. 103).

Congruent with the north/south orientation of the bridge, the priest sketches one footpath stone (A) as "Place" (場所, basho), associated with the importance of place, of sangha, in the training of

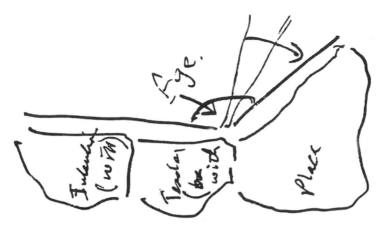

FIGURE 103. *Each of the three footpath stones of the bridge is asymmetrical in size, as well as placement. A sketch by the priest, with notations in English by the author, depicts an association between the three slabs of stone comprising the footpath and three aspects of the traditional training of monks. The bridge is irregular in shape, sharply angled. For the priest, the antiquity (寂, "age") of the bridge is associated with the obliqueness of its angularity; "newer" stone bridges, such as the plank bridge to the Turtle Island, tend to be lineal in form.*

monks; a second footpath stone (B) is associated with "Teacher" (先生, *sensei*), enlightened *rōshi*; the third footpath stone (C) is sketched as "Intention" (積もり, *tsumori*), associated with the valued character of monks in training (fig. 105).[5]

The three footpath stones of the bridge are sketched by the priest in association with three fundamental aspects of the training of monks. Two ("Place" and "Teacher") of the priest's three aspects of training are provided to monks by the temple while the third ("Intention") is a quality monks ought to bring to the temple.[6]

PLACE

Here, *basho* denotes a physical place. Young men still must apply to a temple willing to accept them for training. If accepted, the new arrival subsequently becomes part of the *sangha*.[7]

The first footstone of the bridge, associated with Place, is the largest of the three stones (fig. 104). This relatively large stone is rooted in the inlet of earth projecting into the water, providing a

FIGURE 104. The three footpath stones of the bridge, with the Crane Island-Mountain in the background.

FIGURE 105. The association of footpath stones with "Place" (A); "Teacher" (B); "Intention" (C) as well as with the 7:5:3 interrelationship.

comparative stability of footing. "Place" is large, wide, and stable, and the stone is associated with the residence of monks, the temple, as well as the community of believers as *sangha*.

Temples, bridges, concepts of "place"—each only is a helpmate "bridging between the formless and the mere forms of everyday existence."[8] Experience of Buddha-Nature, it is hoped, will reveal to monks awareness of the idea and phenomenon of place, the temple, only as a compassionate finger pointing at the moon, not the moon itself.

TEACHER

After acceptance into a temple, beginning monks subsequently establish an ongoing relationship with a senior priest:

> "This [evokes] Teacher," says the priest, pointing to the wisps of lines he has drawn of the middle stone in the bridge. "It is difficult, if not impossible, to experience Buddha-Nature without a teacher."

Rōshi periodically dialogue (独参, *dokusan*) with monks to assess each monk's experiences during *zazen*, as was the case with Bukkoku Kokushi assessing the enlightenment experience of Musō.[9] Zen is *zazen*, the priest often reminded me, and "this is why we have a teacher. With your teacher you will correct your practice [of *zazen*]."[10] Priest Taishun Satō-Rōshi adds, "to realize *satori*, it is particularly important to have the guidance of a qualified teacher."[11] The teacher-pupil relationship is fundamental to Rinzai Zen Buddhism, and flows from and keeps alive the face-to-face experiential method of training begun with Shākyamuni and Kāsyapa (Kashō-Sonja, in Japanese) on Vulture Peak in India.

Legend has it that upward of eighty thousand people would gather on Vulture Peak to be present to the Dharma of Shākyamuni. One day, after a long period of silence before those assembled,

Shākyamuni merely held up a Konbara blossom, a lotus flower. Kāsyapa alone smiled in wordless understanding. Through this well-known wordless heart-to-heart communication, Kāsyapa became Shākyamuni's disciple. The lotus then became a sign of Buddhism, a reminder of Shākyamuni (at his birth in the Gardens of Lumbini, Siddhārtha is believed to have emerged from the side of Queen Māyā and, as he began to walk, lotus flowers sprouted within his footprints).[12]

Out of all of the aspects of Buddhism on which the priest could have focused, in association with this second stone in the bridge, the association with "teacher" is telling. Rinzai Zen Buddhists often consider teaching as manifestation of the Dharma of Shākyamuni.

Teaching occurs in many guises other than through enlightened priests. Nature is a teacher, as we have seen, as nature at times was a teacher to Musō and to other priests influential in the history of the temple and pond garden. Musō's love of nature illustrates the Rinzai Zen belief that "the deeper you go in your practice the deeper you find your teacher's mind is, until you finally see that your mind and his mind are Buddha's mind."[13] Temple gardens are didactic, pedagogic; temple gardens teach, existentially expounding Dharma by virtue of their very being.

INTENTION AND WILL

"Will is most important," says the priest, referencing the third stone. "One must not give up. It is like beginners doing *zazen*. The new posture is difficult, and you want to give up. You may want to get up and go somewhere else, or do anything else except what you are doing. Your mind wanders. It is difficult to control yourself. You must discipline your will. This is important."

Two critical incidents in the life of Buddhism remain oft-cited models of intention and will: Shākyamuni's experiences under the

Bodhi tree, in India, and the experiences of Bodhidharma, in China.

As Siddhārtha sat under the Bodhi tree, the deity Māra came to him in the form of three illusions, often termed "temptations," meant to disrupt his intent and will. Siddhārtha persisted in his intent and will such that, it is believed, the earth itself shook. Siddhārtha experienced his previous lifetimes; then, out of compassion, he transformed the illusions of Māra into flowers.

Sitting on the grass mat under the tree, Siddhārtha awoke to the causes of suffering and to methods for the negation of suffering within one's lifetime. In most versions, Siddhārtha did not move from his seat for seven days, such was his intent and will. He then rose and engaged in walking meditation for another seven days, then returned to the grass mat under the pipal tree to sit for another seven days. Rather than dwelling within his subsequent awareness, though, Siddhārtha rose from his seat with an intent and will to share his experience.

A Cave, and an Image Burned

Bodhidharma (P'u-t'i-ta-mo, in Chinese; Daruma Daishi, in Japanese||) was the twenty-eighth patriarch in the line of direct succession from Shākyamuni, and he was the first patriarch of Zen (Ch'an) Buddhism in China. Bodhidharma arrived in China in 475 at the invitation of the aforementioned Emperor Wu-Ti and subsequently sought to introduce his style of Buddhism to the Shaolin (Shōrin, in Japanese) the dark Monastery in the Wu Tai Mountains of Henan Province.

One day while walking outside the monastery, Bodhidharma came upon a path leading to the entrance to a secluded cave. Over a period of nine years, in most versions, Bodhidharma every day went to sit within the cave in the physically demanding style of Buddhism he had brought from India.

The Chinese *Record of the Transmission of the Lamp* (*Ching-te Ch'uan-Teng Lu*) states that "he always sat in silence facing the wall, so people called him the 'wall-contemplating' Brahman.'"[14] *The Continued Lives of Eminent Monks* (*Hsu Kao-Seng Ch'uan*) observed, "the achievements of Bodhidharma's Mahāyāna wall contemplation are of the very highest [order]."[15] Monks from the temple often came to the cave to question him about the style of intense sitting they were observing. In a fashion we now associate with Zen priests, Bodhidharma did not respond to their questions directly but continued to sit silently with great resolve. The Buddhist scholar Seizan Yanagida concluded that "'wall contemplation' in itself was a metaphor for the inanimate, the unconscious [無心, mushin; wu-hsin, in Chinese] . . . the wall contemplates, not 'one contemplates the wall.'"[16] "Wall-contemplating" (面壁, menpeki) referred to a state of awareness associated with this legendary situation within the cave in the Wu-Tai Mountains. "Letting go" of all desire, thought, itself was "cutting through" the wall of illusion. In the cave, silently, mind contemplated mind.

Bodhidharma often refused food or warm clothing, such was his focused intent and will. Legend has it that one day a monk saw a large wolf, baring its fangs, about to pounce on the unmoving figure of Bodhidharma sitting within the cave. Bodhidharma had not flinched as the wolf approached, nor did he flinch as the monk chased away the wolf. Legend also has it that Bodhidharma cut off his eyelids to lessen the risk of falling asleep while sitting, and that he sat until his legs fell off. It is said that his intent and will was such that he sat until his image was burned into a wall of the cave.

The monk Hui-k'o (Taiso Eka, 487–593) one day visited the cave during the cold and snow of winter. Hui-k'o sought to demonstrate his intent and will to experience the intense sitting of this patriarch from India, so he cut off his left hand and presented it to Bodhidharma. Seeing his uncommon intent and will, Bodhidharma accepted Hui-k'o as his first Chinese disciple.

Bodhidharma concluded that the physical condition of the Shaolin monks was not sufficient for the type of training he wanted to initiate. He therefore introduced what came to be known as the Eighteen Lo-Han Hands system of what we term the martial arts. Bodhidharma continues to be venerated for the intent and will of his cave sitting as well as for the intent and will he sought to develop in the monks of the Shaolin Temple.

As such, during their meetings, the tradition had been for *rōshi* to "ask the monk about his purpose in coming to the monastery."[17] Why are you here? What is your intention?

After meeting several times with *rōshi*, a monk traditionally was given a *kōan* (公案) on which to meditate. Rinzai Zen Buddhism is characterized by extensive use of *kōan* in temple training programs. Ongoing relationship with a *kōan* in large part is meant to focus the intent and will of a monk.

A *kōan* is a phrase from a sūtra or from statements by venerated *rōshi* that, since the tenth century, has been used as an aid to novices in their training. A *kōan* is a paradox, a contradiction, and therefore a *kōan* cannot be "solved" or "understood" rationally. Consider these dialogues between monk and *rōshi*: "Rōshi, I am still a beginner, show me the way." "Have you had your breakfast yet?" "Yes, I have had breakfast." "Go and wash your eating bowls." And, "a monk once asked the Rōshi Jōshū, does a dog have Buddha-Nature, or not?" Rōshi Jōshū simply replied, "*Mu* [無, 'nothingness']."[18]

There isn't a "logical" connection between the questions posed by the monks and the responses offered by the *rōshi*. *Rōshi* invariably reject whatever responses novices manage to offer. Frustrated, perhaps the novices "will finally give up the attempt to find a logical solution. Only then does . . . work on the *kōan* begin. He now no longer actually thinks about the *kōan*, but he has it on his mind constantly, day and night. An intense inner dilemma then arises, in which he can neither find an answer nor any longer drop the *kōan*. If he now continues working on the *kōan* with great intensity, he will arrive at a point where . . . the entire consciousness is filled with the *kōan*. Still he perseveres and continues to practice until the *kōan* suddenly disappears from his consciousness. At this instant the consciousness has become completely emptied and not even satori, enlightenment, the aspired goal can penetrate it. Now he is very near to enlightenment."[19] Initial *kenshō* experiences, perhaps experiences of emptiness (空, $k\bar{u}$) rather than nothingness (無, mu), negate the notion of a "goal." Contradiction, logic/illogic, and internal tension and pressure disappear. For such experiences to occur, the monk must "concentrate on this 'Mu' with your 360 bones and 84,000 pores and transform your whole body into one big search. Work diligently on it day and night . . . With all of your might, work on this Mu. If you do not stop in your striving and do not waver, then you will see how darkness brightens immediately once the Dharma candle is lit."[20] *Kōan* demand intent, and will.

The *Teaching of Buddha* says that awareness of Buddha-Nature invariably is associated with "the faith to believe . . . the will to make the endeavor . . . the ability to concentrate one's mind . . . and the ability to maintain clear wisdom."[21] *Kōan* initially highlight the problematic nature of dualistic thinking, and the (often socially and culturally generated) categories privileging dualistic thinking. Akin to jazz music, a *kōan* forces monks to "go through" dualistic and categorical thinking to fashion, often on the spot in audience with a *rōshi*, spontaneous rather than formulaic responses to a standard refrain.

A Rinzai Zen tenet, exemplified by my experiences with the pond garden, is that "your true understanding must be based on your own experience."[22] There are about seventeen hundred *kōan*, organized into five ranked groups, though only about six or seven hundred presently are used in temple training.[23]

When a *rōshi* initially meets with new monks, he observes each novice and chooses a *kōan* judged most appropriate for each person. A *rōshi* must have "made his own" every *kōan* from which he then can choose for each monk. For instance, we read of a novice proclaiming to a *rōshi* that "it took me seven years to see into the meaning." "Did it really," replies the *rōshi*. "Yes, indeed." "Another seven years may have to elapse before it fully becomes yours."[24] "Fully becomes yours" defines a *kōan* as not just something apart from one to be "understood" or possessed, as the concept of understanding still embraces rationality and a separation and resultant dualism between person and understanding. A *kōan* must be integrated as an aspect of one's being, one's awareness; conversely, one must become the *kōan*. One must embody "cutting through."

Yet, will and intention eventually disappear with subsequent awareness that in fact there is nothing for which one ought to strive. *Kenshō* is entered into easily, experienced as ordinary awareness, and *satori* is experienced often.[25] "Solving" a *kōan* thus means letting go of intent and will. Like the pond garden itself, intention and will only are a means toward fashioning the "fine people" of which Musō spoke.

> "Is it wrong to compare the garden to *kōan* [[assumes separation of garden and *kōan*]]?"
>
> "It is not wrong," the priest replies, "but you do not yet fully understand *kōan*. It is true that the garden conceals [[embodies/is manifested as]] many questions that are *kōan* [[no separation of garden and *kōan*]]."

Back to the garden. Is there a significance to the differing relative sizes of the three footstones within the bridge, as a composition? Why, further, are there three slabs of stone and not, say, one or four?

> "I do not know," the priest replies, "but the differing sizes of the stones remind us of relationship. Seven, five, and three are important numbers. The three numbers [[correspond]] to the [[sizes of]] three bridge stones."

Indeed, there is a proportional increase in the relative sizes of the footpath stones as one proceeds from "Place," the largest slab of stone, to "Teacher," the middle-sized stone, then to "Intention," the smallest-sized stone. The priest conceptualizes the "Place" stone in association with the number seven, the "Teacher" stone in association with the number five, and the "Intention" stone in association with the number three (fig. 105).

We again witness the manner in which seven, five, and three

FIGURE 106. Late afternoon. The garden, from within the Abbot's Quarters.

(*shichigosan*) can be discerned with respect to the design-structure
and layout of the pond as well as primary component aspects of the
garden. *Shichigosan* continues to be associated with proportional interdependent relationship; here, seven, five, and three are associated
with the relative size-proportions of the three footpath stones.

As a composition, the bridge is not solely the three footpath
slabs of stone but also includes the four relatively large round stones
in the water upon which the slabs of stone rest (fig. 98). As a composition then, the bridge is composed of seven stones.

࿔

The Bridge of Stones in the pond is the only one of the priest's seven
features of significance in its design and function denoting the actual
presence of people in the garden. The bridge is a still-existing sign
that, historically, people directly participated in the garden.

The Bridge of Stones reminds us not to be mesmerized by the
aesthetic, affecting aspects of the temple landscape. The existential
presence of people also is considered a component aspect of the design
and layout of the pond garden (fig. 106).

8

SITTING IN THE GARDEN

The *weltanschauung*, the worldview, of Buddhism continues to condition contemplative experiences of the pond garden. The priest again
points to the far rear area of the pond, this time to a single stone in
the garden he terms *Zazen Ishi* (Zazen Stone). His name for this stone
is telling, as the priest holds that Musō, and successive priests, sat in
zazen on this stone. None of the compositions of stone highlighted
by the priest is linked so explicitly to Rinzai Zen Buddhism, with
respect to behavior, as is the stone for *zazen*.

 The stone for *zazen* was not set within the pond. The stone
sits on land near the southwestern earthen-edge of the pond, and is
not easily seen from the Abbot's Quarters or Guest Quarters (figs.
107, 108). The Zazen Stone is massive, more than a meter in length
and a meter or so in (above-ground) height. The top of the stone is
relatively flat and the base of the stone is wider than the top of the
stone. The stone widens out from top to bottom; that is, the stone
has a broad base. And thus, stability. A large stone about half the
size of the Zazen Stone was set upright and to the front of the
Zazen Stone; conical in shape, this smaller stone could not have accommodated a seated person. A space of a meter or so separates the
two stones.

 Several smaller flat stones were set in the earth in association

FIGURE 107. Early morning.

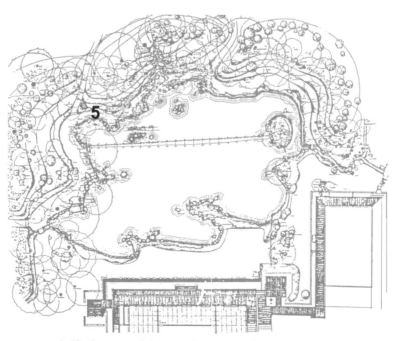

©Rikōtosho

FIGURE 108. The location of the stone (5) associated with zazen (Zazen Ishi).

with the Zazen Stone, and these stones appear to have been a footpath leading up to the Zazen Stone (figs. 109, 110). The Zazen Stone would have been approached on a slight ascent, from the path leading around the rear of the pond and across the Bridge of Stones.

The Zazen Stone is distinctive, in several respects. The stone was set noticeably to the left of other features of the pond garden highlighted by the priest, such as the spatially and visually centered (from the Abbot's Quarter's) bridge and waterfall. The Zazen Stone is a single stone, while the other features of the pond garden highlighted by the priest are compositions of stone. The name and on-land location of the stone imply that the stone was not originally placed, set, to be experienced at a distance, say, from the Abbot's Quarters or Guest Quarters. Like the Bridge of Stones, the name and spatial placement of the Zazen Stone imply that the stone was meant to be experienced directly by people.[1]

Wakeful Attention, to a Stream of Heartbeats

A stream still flows quite near the Zazen Stone. Small stones have been set in the bottom of and to the sides of the stream, indicating the intentional construction of a streambed. This stream channeled water into the garden pond from the larger stream flowing along the upper area behind the embankment of earth (fig. 48). This stream appears to have been here for some time, quite possibly during the time of Musō, as it has eroded a fairly large channel from the hillock of earth behind the pond. The Zazen Stone was placed between the middle of an upper and lower body of water, and near a stream connecting the two.

The sounds of nature here are crisp, vibrant. "Transmitting the truth [the Dharma of Shākyamuni]," we read, "relies not on teachings and written scriptures but on the sudden flashes of insight that can be triggered in a state of meditation by a single word, an action, a noise or even an arrangement of rocks."[2] Near

FIGURE 109. *The Zazen Stone was set to the right of a now slow-moving stream of water. Over time, the stream channeled the wide and deep gully to the left of the stone. The stream flows down from the larger stream of water winding around the upper area of the garden, above and behind the hillock of earth (fig. 48).*

the stone, one still can hear the sound of water in the upper stream area above the hillock of earth, the gentle sound of water slowly falling with the soothing regularity of a heartbeat along and down the streambed, as well as water fluttering about within the garden pond below.

Zazen aids being fully present, within one's body, to existence-as-it-is. In *zazen* (坐禅), *za* (坐) means "sitting" and *zen* (禅) most often is translated as "absorption."[3] "Sitting in absorption" is becoming aware of, experiencing, and dwelling within a state of "wakeful attention"; in turn, wakeful attention often is the precursor to

FIGURE 110. *The Zazen Stone, and smaller companion stone. Footpath stones to the left of the stones lead up to the Zazen Stone. Thick moss presently blankets the stones.*

experiences of *kenshō* and *satori*. Zen-is-zazen and *zazen*-is-Zen, for "although *zazen* is certainly not all there is to Zen, a Zen which lacks *zazen* may be said to be no Zen at all."[4] *Zazen* is the experience of Zen.

Stones within gardens, by legend associated with *zazen*, still are conceptualized by priests as platforms, "seats," for sitting. "In *zazen*, one sits cross-legged in silence. The right foot is placed on the left thigh. The back and the neck must be kept straight. Hands are folded on top of the legs, with the right hand placed on the left leg, palms facing upward and cupped into each other with the thumbs just touching to form a circle in front of the lower abdomen. . . . When we cross our legs like this, even though we have a right leg and a left leg, they have become one. The position expresses [takes the form of] the oneness of duality."[5] The Great Buddha (Daibutsu) of Kamakura is a bronze figure of Amida Buddha, in *zazen*. Well-known and well-visited public iconic imagery such as the Great Buddha condition in people a familiarity with the posture of *zazen* (fig. 111).

FIGURE 111. *The Great Buddha (Daibutsu). This venerated statue within Kōtoku-in, Kamakura, was bronze cast in 1252 then covered by a protective building to replace an earlier statue of wood destroyed by storms in 1248. A tidal wave destroyed the protective building in 1495, and since then the statue has remained in the open.*

There are no "objects" contemplated or meditated upon while sitting in *zazen*:

"Why, then, do priests not just go into nature to meditate?"

"Some do," the priest responds. "Many priests go into the woods, if that is the place best suited to them. Musō Kokushi spent many years alone in a hut in the woods surrounding Kamakura. Other priests become overwhelmed by the distractions, the noises, in nature."

Aspects of nature such as stones and mountains invariably are present in narratives about *zazen*. "After Tōin-Rōshi effortlessly crossed his legs in the full-lotus position," for instance, "he gradually began to move the upper part of his body. Little by little the Rōshi's body seemed to rise up. At the moment he lowered the physical focal point of his body to a point located in the center of his clasped hands, his body movement stopped abruptly, and he seemed to be as massive as great Mount Tai of China."[6] Features of nature are not "symbolized" in such accounts of *zazen*. The narrative search appears to be for words expressing the collapse of illusory distinctions between qualities of nature and corresponding qualities of people in *zazen*. "But this comparison is still far too weak. Actually, one should say: *zazen* is a feeling, so solid that . . . the whole world was filling the abdomen. The green mountains stand immovable. The white clouds come and go and in this seated position the body becomes like a rock, and the mind gains the strength of immovability beneath the everchanging flow of thoughts."[7] Descriptive accounts of *zazen* invariably fashion an interdependent, participatory correspondence, not a symbolic comparison, between people and nature as when Musō would "sit in the stillness [of nature], and [he] still."[8] Both nature and people, in *zazen*, are "natural," and both are associated with Original Face/Buddha-Nature.

"Facing through the Garden"

The priest holds that past and present priests within the temple sat in *zazen* on the stone in the garden, while other priests also hold that "a flat stone under a moonlit tree was considered to be as fitting a place for meditation . . . as the meditation platform of the monk's hall."[9] And, for Musō, we know of "those places, or rather types of places, where, sitting in meditation, he felt instinctively connected to the world around him. These were the places where he chose a rock to be his *zazen seki* [meditation rock]."[10] Flat stones. *Zazen* out of doors amid dusk; and then, moonlight.

Venerated stones in and around the pond garden, such as the Zazen Stone, are not ends unto themselves as "objects" of meditative contemplation. "In all circumstances," Musō wrote, "whether under a tree, upon a rock, in the darkness of a cave or deep in a glen, the Law has been set forth and transmitted."[11] For the priest, the stone for *zazen* is but another instance of the temple landscape as manifestation of the Dharma experienced by Musō.

"In the old days, when Musō Kokushi was alive, he must have 〚sat in〛 *zazen* on the Zazen Stone."

"When they make gardens, they don't experience it from one place only.

"Therefore, I suppose that Musō Kokushi recognized the garden in many perspectives, looking at it from various spots. So it is not that he made the garden standing here 〚pointing to the pond〛 with his stick in his hand."

"But after that, was the stone used in the same way? Did other priests sit on the stone?"

"Yes. Several priests must have 'sat' there. It is improbable that the garden had been left alone. It was not only Musō Kokushi who sat in *zazen* on the stone, so . . . up until now thousands of priests have appeared 〚to live in the temple〛. Many of them must have done *zazen* in the garden, I presume."

The priest is speaking of Rōshi. As concerns *unsui*, he says:

"There is a building called *Zendō*. Inside the building there is a place to sit 〚in *zazen*〛. They 〚monks〛 sit there for the period we set aside for it. At nine P.M. we put out the lights, so after that they can leave the *Zendō* and continue *zazen* on the porch 〚veranda〛, on a stone 〚the Zazen Stone〛, wherever they wish. These are the things they do."

"So it does not have to be in front of the garden . . . The garden is just one more place to meditate?"

"Right."

In the *Zendō*, monks still sit on cushions on a raised platform spanning the length of one wall. In contrast, the priest speaks of monks being permitted to sit individually out of doors around the pond garden, after required sessions of sitting within the *Zendō*:

> "There is a *zazen-ishi* a little bit over there . . . [the Zazen Stone is not easily seen from the Abbot's Quarters] those who wish to sit in *zazen*, do it."

The pond garden is experienced by the priest as a gift from Musō, out of enlightened compassion, to successive generations of priests. The pond garden is conceptualized as an aid to the experience of Buddha-Nature.

> "We look at . . . nothing. When we do *zazen*, we face through the garden to Musō Kokushi who made the garden. By 'seeing' [facing through] the garden we get to know Musō Kokushi. Thus, we sit this way. And it will trigger us to enter into the world of *satori*. Therefore, some may sit before the stones in the garden. . . . However, although the tracks may vary, the terminal station is the same . . . to meet Musō Kokushi. Our temple garden is [the essence of] nature as the heart [*kokoro*] of Muso Kokushi. . . . "

And, through Musō, the priest glimpses the enlightened mind of Shākyamuni:

> "We call Muso Kokushi Buddha. Shākyamuni saw through *kyōchi kyōgai* [境地境界, a state of mind reminding us of our limitations]. We have to go through *kyōchi kyōgai*, as did Shākyamuni. In the sense about which I have been talking, Musō Kokushi and Shākyamuni are the same."

Temple as Flowing Spring

Several other temple landscapes associated with Musō also exhibit features specifically linked to *zazen*, none more prominently so than

Zuisen-ji (瑞泉寺, Flowing Spring Temple) in the mountains of north Kamakura.[12] The design of the Flowing Spring Temple dramatically illustrates Musō's preference for *zazen* within nature as well as the stones for *zazen* associated with Musō.

The Flowing Spring Temple was constructed from 1327 to 1332. We remember that prior to his becoming first abbot of this temple, Musō for some time previously had been living within forests and on mountains. The design of the Flowing Spring Temple tightly integrates buildings and aspects of nature into a landscape physically permitting Musō, and successive generations of priests, to sit in *zazen* out-of-doors.

A shallow cave carved into the side of the mountain facing the rear of the Abbot's Quarters is a prominent feature of the Flowing Spring Temple. The cave-in-the-mountain design of Zuisen-ji illustrates Musō's allegiance to the style of Zen (*zazen*) lived by venerated ancestors in Buddhist India and China.[13] Shākyamuni (India) and Bodhidharma (China) both were known to prefer *zazen* within nature, often within caves, as we have seen.

CAVES, MOUNTAINS, AND GARDENS

Buddhist cave temples in India invariably were mountain monasteries, corresponding in several physical respects to the Flowing Spring Temple. The cave temples at Bihar, for instance, were constructed for monks by the Mauryan Emperor Ashoka who, we recall, converted to and aided the growth of Buddhism in India. Rock-cut monasteries (*vihara*, in Sanskrit), the construction of which often were sponsored by Emperor Ashoka, contained residence quarters for monks along with chambers for meditation such that "the earliest form of *vihara* or monastery cave seems to have been that of one or more cells with a verandah or porch in front."[14] Cave temples in India also often contained a pond, what we would term a pond garden, as an aspect of the landscape.[15]

Influential Buddhist cave temples in China were constructed

FIGURE 112. *The rear of the Abbot's Quarters of the Flowing Spring Temple (Zuisen-ji).*

along the Silk Road, the most prominent of which were the Mogao Grottoes at Dunhuang, Gansu Province. Also known as the Caves of the Thousand Buddhas, the complex at Dunhuang was carved throughout the fifth to fourteenth centuries. The later cave temples at Dunhuang were carved contemporaneous with the carving of the cave aspect of the Flowing Spring Temple. Similar to the siting and layout of the Flowing Spring Temple, the Mogao Grottoes were carved into the face of a sixteen-hundred-meter-long north-to-south

FIGURE 113. *During construction of Zuisen-ji, a cave was carved from the lower face of the mountain.*

running cliff. The cave chambers at Dunhuang include numerous single-room cells serving as living quarters for monks as well as cavernous assembly halls.

The Abbot's Quarters within the Flowing Spring Temple was placed quite close to the base of a plateau leveled from the south-facing side of the Kamakura mountain range (fig. 112). A small three-chamber cave was carved from the southern face of the mountain to the rear of the Abbot's Quarters, and a pond placed between the Abbot's Quarters and the cave. The cave is shallow in depth, about three meters deep, with a ceiling height of about two meters. The central cave area is flanked on each side by a smaller chamber. The inside walls of the cave are curvilinear, with bibulous pockets expanding the experiential size of the chamber (fig. 113).

THE DHARMA SEAT

Priests at Zuisen-ji refer to the cave as *zazen kutsu* (座禅窟, "zazen cave"). The temple legend is that Musō and successive generations of priests sat in *zazen* within the cave as a *dokusan tei* (独参庭, garden in which one sits alone).[16] A flat stone, a *Zazen Ishi* (Zazen Stone), sometime in history was placed on the floor of the cave chamber and priests say that this stone evokes Musō's "Dharma Seat" (fig. 115).

The phrase "Dharma Seat" reveals a number of relevant Buddhist correspondences. In Buddhist India, "the seat is the third stage in the *Yoga Sūtra*. The seat is also the prerequisite of Buddhist meditation."[17] We recall the Dharma Seat, the throne-like dais, ascended by *roshi* when delivering lectures within the Tenryū-ji Dharma Hall (fig. 114). We remember Shākyamuni sitting on a flat stone, the Dharma Seat in the *Heart Sūtra*, atop Vulture Peak.

The Zazen Stone within the cave in the Flowing Spring Temple mirrors the Zazen Stone within the garden in the Temple of the Heavenly Dragon. In both instances, priests at Tenryū-ji and Zuisen-ji name stones in association with Musō's preference for *zazen* within nature.

§

The priest daily sits through long sessions of *zazen*:

> "We do *zazen* about five hours a day, usually from five to ten
> [in the later afternoon, and evening] straight."

FIGURE 114. A Cloud Dragon (雲龍図, Unryūzu), painted by Matsutoshi
Suzuki in 1899, covers the ceiling of the Lecture Hall. Beneath the painting
is the elaborate chair and platform (shumidan, meaning that the platform is
linked to Mount Sumeru, the center of the Buddhist cosmos), a seat, to which
senior priests ascend when delivering lectures. In 1997, this painting was
replaced by a new Unryūzu painted by Matazo Kayama.

FIGURE 115. The Zazen Stone at Zuisen-ji.

Zazen is an epistemology, a Way of knowing, of experiencing. *Zazen* is the posture, a physical Way of being, still preferred by many priests for experience of the pond garden.

> "You will 'learn' more by practicing *zazen* facing the garden," says the priest. "That is the way to 'know' the garden."
>
> "And just . . . sit, before the garden?"
>
> "Yes . . . in the evening, around five o'clock, when the sun sets in that [pointing to the west, across the pond] direction, you should look at the garden—face to face. Then, you probably will receive feelings from the garden . . . You are the one who has to [feel/understand] the garden. You have to sense what the garden is talking to you . . . about yourself. This is what we call 'talking with the stone,' 'to talk with the earth,' 'to talk with the water,' and so forth. If you look at the garden next morning from the porch [veranda of the Abbot's

FIGURE 116. Mid-afternoon.

Quarters] silently and calmly with your own eyes . . . the question comes out by itself."

By extension, the stone for *zazen* by temple legend designates the Way, and place, by which past generations of priests also perhaps came to "know," to experience, the pond garden (fig. 116).

9

ANCHORS ALONG THE JOURNEY

Contemplating this area to the rear of the pond, it is easy to overlook, literally look over, a row of low-lying stones set in the water to the left of the imposing Crane Island-Mountain of stones. Concentrating, though, we discern a line of five comparatively small stones from this vantage appearing to rest quietly on the water (figs. 3, 117–21).

The row of five stones in the water long has been named Night-Mooring Stones. "What does it mean," it has been asked, "this mysterious straight line of stones across the ponds of old gardens? No one knows."[1] Prevailing interpretations of this line of stones conclude that the composition at one time functioned as an aspect of now-desiccated building architecture, or that the line of stones evokes cultural myth and legend, or that the line of stones references aspects of Shintō and Buddhism.

The Rhythm of Number and Interrelationship

One view envisions the row of five stones at one time functioning as piers for posts supporting pavilions extending into an area of the pond, this most likely during the time of the boating activities we surveyed within the villa of Emperor Go-Saga.[2] "It has been suggested," the position holds, "that here these stones might be nothing more

FIGURE 117. *The Night-Mooring Stones are the crescent-shaped row of five stones in the water, to the center-left, with the rear of the Guest Quarters in the background.*

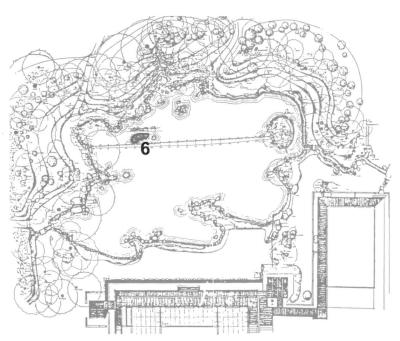

FIGURE 118. *The location of the Night-Mooring Stones (6).*

FIGURE 119. The Night-Mooring Stones.

FIGURE 120. The Night-Mooring Stones are the curved row of stones that from this vantage appear placed close in front of the Crane Island-Mountain of stones, towering in the background.

FIGURE 121. *As a composition, the Night-Mooring Stones comprise four comparatively large stones and a small center stone (a turtle is sunning on the stone second from the right). During rainy seasons in the spring and fall, the water level of the pond rises to nearly submerge the small center stone.*

than one-time foundations for some building which overhung this small pond [though the previous pond was not 'small']. Since the stones are sometimes pointed and are all irregularly spaced, this seems very unlikely."[3] There are more convincing examples in other pond gardens of rows of stones arguably functioning as post-supporting stones for a pavilion built out over the water.

The Temple of the Golden Pavilion (Kinkaku-ji), for instance, is located to the north of the Temple of the Heavenly Dragon and dates to 1394 when the complex was named Deer Park Temple (Rokuon-ji). Constructed at the behest of Ashikaga Yoshimitsu (1358–1408), the complex sat amid an extensive garden with a three-story pavilion still extended out into the water of the pond (fig. 122).

The row of five stones bordering the present-day Golden Pavilion has been interpreted as functional post-supporting stones, and these "old *yodomari* [夜留まり], the night mooring stones . . . were placed in a straight line parallel to the building (fig. 123)."⁴ These five stones are fairly flat on top and indeed could have supported the posts of a pavilion extending over the water. Not so, though, with respect to the convex form and asymmetrical placement of the five stones in the pond garden within the Temple of the Heavenly Dragon.

The Night-Mooring Stones within the Tenryū-ji garden pond, in addition, were set in a curving line, and this distinctive curving is not easily seen when the five stones customarily are experienced at a distance from the area around the Abbot's Quarters or Guest Quarters.⁵ The curving arrangement of the five stones (asymmetrical in number as well as asymmetrical in arrangement) points to non-architectural functions of the Tenryū-ji Night-Mooring Stones.

Viewed frontally and up close, further, each one of the Night-Mooring Stones exhibits a unique size and shape; none of these five stones are the same height or width (figs. 121, 126). The five stones exhibit a prominent asymmetrical rhythmic balance. Visually beginning at either end of the composition, one proceeds inward to notice that the next stone is either higher or lower, larger or smaller, than each end stone. Starting at the left-end stone and proceeding inward, the next stone, second from the left, is a larger and higher-set stone; starting at the right-end stone and proceeding inward, the next stone, second from the right, is a smaller and lower-set stone. Low-to-high from the left and high-to-low from the right. The middle stone, barely visible frontally, is the smallest (above water) stone in the composition. The easily overlooked middle stone mediates the complementary opposition and alternating rhythm of the stones to each side of it. The undulating up-and-down rhythm of the Night-Mooring Stones-as-they-are (*shinnyo*) is graceful, when contemplated via sustained attention to the composition as a whole.

The Treasures of Paradise

Another prevalent view of the row of five stones, by students of the

FIGURE 122. *The Temple of the Golden Pavilion (Kinkaku-ji). A row of Night-Mooring Stones sits in the water (under the white panels on the lower-level of the pavilion) next to the veranda on the right side of the building.*

FIGURE 123. *The straight-line design of the row of stones in the pond within the Temple of the Golden Pavilion in their form and placement could have supported the posts of pavilions extended out into the water, unlike the curving-placement of the Night-Mooring Stones within the Tenryū-ji pond.*

garden, is that the Night-Mooring Stones at one time functioned as pilings for the mooring of boats, "a mooring place for pleasure boats."[6] The pond in the villa garden of Emperor Go-Saga, prior to the present-day temple, as we have seen, was extensive enough for boating. Boats still sit within the waters and under the boathouse of the pond within the garden of the Temple of the Golden Pavilion. In

FIGURE 124. *Te-hua porcelain carving of Seven Immortals in a celestial boat. Early seventeenth century. H: 29 cm.*

lieu of wooden pilings, it is argued that the row of stones in the ponds of both gardens actually could have moored boats.

Conceptualizations of the Night-Mooring Stones in association with boats link the row of stones with cultural myth and legend, to emphasize "stones placed . . . in the pond . . . symbolizing ships at anchor, ready to set out to seek the treasures of paradise."[7] Ships. Paradise. Treasures.

The Night-Mooring Stones have been linked by students of the garden to the archaic though still vital sociocultural belief in the Seven Deities of Good Fortune and their fabled Treasure Ship (fig. 124).[8] An ongoing sociocultural belief is that during the first three days of the New Year the Seven Deities of Good Fortune come together, board a Treasure Ship, and sail from the realm of the deities to the realm of humans. The ship carries "treasure valuables" associated with each of the seven deities. An ongoing practice, for children especially, is to place a picture of the deities and the Treasure Ship under pillows at the New Year. If the seven deities and their ship appear in a dream, the dream is taken as a sign that the dreamer throughout the coming year will participate in the qualities associated with each deity. As with Go-Daigo, Musō Kokushi, and Tadayoshi of the Ashikaga, dreams still are experienced as harbingers of future events and personal states of being.

The view here is that the Night-Mooring Stones evoke a ship having sailed from the realm of deities to lie "moored" at the realm of humans. "These rocks," we are told, "which are characteristic of the Heian style of garden, were . . . known as 'night mooring stones' . . . they represented ships anchored at night, in a harbor on their way to quest our treasure."⁹ The ship arrives then departs; arrives, then again departs . . . with expectation of future returns. The Night-Mooring Stones thus are situated within a still current mythic event.

There are, finally, explicitly religious conceptualizations of the Night-Mooring Stones. The cultural legend of the Seven Deities of Good Fortune and their Treasure Ship has a corresponding mythic life within Shintō and Buddhism.

The *Record of Ancient Matters* describes the *kami* Amanosa-kume loading a Heavenly Ship (Amenoishifune, the Heavenly-Rock Boat) with gold, silver, and precious jewels and sailing from the High Plain of Heaven to the earth below.¹⁰ The Heavenly-Rock-Boat of Amanosakume is well known socioculturally, as is the Ship of the Seven Deities, and often is commemorated in contemporary performances of Noh.

A variation of this view is the cultural association of the Night-Mooring Stones with the Island-Mountain of the Immortals (Hōraizan); here, the "yodomari-ishi [Night-Mooring Stones] were rocks symbolizing Hōrai bound ships lying at anchor."¹¹ A passage from the *Diary of Konoe Michitsugu (Gukanki)*, written in 1348, records "a vision of the Three Isles [Islands of the Blest] and a ship [Treasure Ship] sailing to them could not be fairer than this."¹² Here, the stones in the pond evoke "rocks representing ships anchored in the water . . . as if on their way to or from Hōrai on a treasure-seeking expedition."¹³ This view fuses a correspondence between the line of stones in the pond, deities, longevity and good fortune, and an archaic myth of eternal return.¹⁴ Other compositions of stone in the pond and around the garden, such as the Crane Island-Mountain and the Turtle Island, also are linked socioculturally to deities, longevity and good fortune as well as to cycles of myth, legend, and nature. Akin to the Crane Island-Mountain and Turtle Island in particular, the Night-Mooring Stones live in broad social and cultural corre-spondences widely accessible to people. The pond garden, again, for the most part is not esoteric and can be experienced freely by visitors who possess varying degrees of familiarity with myth, legend, and social and cultural history.

Treasure Ships and Heavenly Boats appear in each of the afore-mentioned conceptualizations of the Night-Mooring Stones. Stones in the iconic shape of boats and ships themselves do not appear in the pond garden, only stones evocative of treasure ships and heavenly boats. As with other compositions of stone in the pond and around the garden, the Night-Mooring Stones *evoke* rather than "symbolize" or "represent."[15]

Conceptions of the Night-Mooring Stones all share a vision of the pond garden as participating in socio-cultural myths and leg-ends involving boats, travel, and the sea. The name "Night-Mooring Stones" also refers us back, interestingly, to the priests' story and Buddhist legend of believers traveling and assembling to be present to the Dharma of Shākyamuni.

Sitting Within the Shores of Night

Early evening.

Fading light presses between grains of sand carpeting the front of the Abbot's Quarters, as well as between the distant leaves of maple trees above the far earthen edges of the pond. Fading light dissolves and flows like liquid along the sinuous branches of trees. A breeze moves across the rear of the pond and waning light is tossed about, in a frantic sparkle, within the leafy tangles of tree limbs.

Quite suddenly, evening dusk quiets the breeze into a stillness all at once blanketing the pond garden. In profound stillness, darkness begins to rise from within fading light.

FIGURE 125. *The Night-Mooring Stones, bathed in moonlight.*

During the day, amid steady showers of light, the backs of myriad leaves and the interstices of myriad grains of sand are nests for stray flecks of darkness. In darkness, deep into the night, the edges of tree trunks and the corners of stones remain nesting places for stray flecks of struggling light.

Darkness appears to swell animistically from within grains of sand and from within the twinkling light-strewn spaces between the leaves of trees, as when Musō experienced the manner in which "the moon-trees keep growing and growing."[16] Slivers of fading light cling to the cracks of stones in the pond, and ripples of light linger on rippling curls of water. Darkness emerges as a quality of things themselves, swelling into being in its own ever-recurring time.

Gradually. Until one is startled to notice that . . . it is dark.

The shining darkness reveals a quite different garden pond from the one existing during the light of day. In the deep of night, the pond exists indirectly. In the deep of night, the pond is defined by refracted and reflected light in contradistinction to the clear and crisp definition of the pond by the direct light of day. On evenings not favored by the presence of the moon, the pond appears pockmarked with random sprinklings of light—light refracted from the subtle movement of eddies in the pond, reflected light clinging to the edges of stones, light filtered from faint clouds high above seemingly overlooked by darkness, and flecks of light lingering within the boughs of trees. On nights such as this, even at a distance, one feels the vibrant animistic presence of "the churning genesis of glowing and growing stones that live on . . . in the cold."[17] On nights such as this, favored by the presence of the moon, the pond in the garden is alive and shining within a dark brilliance reminiscent of priest Minakami's memorable phrase that "the eternal is moonlight on the pond."[18] In the deep of night, one must concentrate to see what one sees easily during the day. Darkness demands attention (fig. 125).

Night-Mooring Stones. In addition to associations with myth and legend, the telling name for the subtle row of stones in the rear area of the pond also has been associated with being "moored for the night in some safe haven."[19] Night.

The name for these stones speaks to a primal participation, interdependence, of the pond garden with night itself. A privileged experience of the pond garden continues to be at dusk, and deep into the night.

The priest prefers to sit in *zazen* before the pond garden at dusk, within the stillness between fading light and emerging darkness (fig. 126). Musō wrote that he would "sit in the stillness, and am still. . . ."[20]

"When you sit, is there a time of day or season better suited for meditation within the garden?"

"Usually sitting is better during the time of *hakubō* [薄暮]," says the priest.

FIGURE 126. *The Night-Mooring Stones in late afternoon light, touching the reflection on the water of the roof of the Abbot's Quarters.*

"Hakubō?"

"Sunset, from dusk to night and at night."

"At night, too?"

"Yes, at night."

"Why?"

"Like your studies, don't you think? It is better to study when the body is good. You will have a good experience. So, it is not such a good experience for me to sit for long periods in the middle of the day or in midsummer. I prefer autumn and the spring, like now. The [human] body moves with the sun, when the sun comes up the body is more awake, so the body is more distracted when the sun is up or coming up and I go to sit. It is just my preference.

"It is a better experience to sit when the body is slowing

down, not moving so much, when it is getting dark. Also, it is quiet here then [no visitors, or novices moving about], less distractions.

"The body [and heart- mind] better adapts to sitting when it is quiet."

Musō also frequently sat before the pond at night, and he once wrote, "in the dead of night, the moonlight strikes the middle of the pond."[21] Experience of the pond often occurred at night. The experiences of Musō and the priest further introduce consideration of the Night-Mooring Stones from the point of view of Buddhist ideology as practice. Within the context of early Buddhism, Night-Mooring Stones exist in association with Arhats and thus can be linked to the diffusion of Buddhism out of India after the death of Shākyamuni. An Arhat was a person who had experienced sufficient insight into existence to pass into *nirvāna* upon death, and thus not be subject to future rounds of incarnation (*samsāra*). The interpretation here is that the Night-Mooring "stones are intended for the Arhat, the five hundred disciples of the Buddha, to cross on."[22] Shākyamuni directed that some disciples remain in this world to travel to and dwell in different lands, and thus disseminate Dharma. The interpretation here is that the Night-Mooring Stones, and images of travel and boats and the sea, evoke the diffusion of Buddhism out of India, into China, and then into Japan.

The Theravāda (Teaching of the Elders) tradition of Buddhism developed during the first century after the death of the historical Buddha. Recall that Hinayāna (小乗仏教, *Shōjō Bukkyō*, "Small Vehicle") was the disparaging name given by later Mahāyāna (大乗仏教, *Daijō Bukkyō*, "Great Vehicle") Buddhists to the early Theravāda tradition.

In the Mahāyāna tradition, within which Rinzai Zen was born, the Heart/Mind of Shākyamuni is believed to be the Great Vehicle and Dharma to be disseminated to distant shores. Bodhisattvas (菩薩; *bosatsu*, Enlightened Being) were prominent in the

Mahāyāna tradition of Buddhism. A Bodhisattva had seen through suffering, yet renounced *nirvāna* until all beings similarly are liberated. Bodhisattvas embody the Mahāyāna ideal of insight and wisdom, merged with compassion. A connotation of Mahāyāna as Great Vehicle is that the "great" vehicle is more encompassing, can embrace more beings, and thus can help more beings to salvation from suffering than the "small" vehicle of the Theravāda tradition. Jen Chen (Humanity Vehicle) Buddhism, for instance, likens "The Greater Vehicle" to a ship carrying all forms of being (animals, deities, ghosts, people) across seas of suffering to shores of awareness. Yet, the early Theravāda tradition also spoke of liberation from suffering and the rounds of *samsāra* as "reaching/experiencing the other shore" (Bhandra, for example, was known as "The Arhat Who Crossed the River").

Shākyamuni, Dharma, and Bodhisattvas thus often exist in association with boats, travel by water, and with places for mooring. "The Buddha," for instance, "likened his teaching to a raft, to be used for crossing over to the other shore, and suggested that having arrived, a man would then lay down the raft rather than continue on his way with it."[23] During the ceremony opening the Temple of the Heavenly Dragon, Musō took the Dharma Seat and, mirroring Shākyamuni on Vulture Peak, reminded the assembled that "the appearance in this world of all Buddhas, past, present, and future, is solely for the purpose of preaching the Law and helping all creatures to cross over to the shore of Liberation."[24] As a *sangha*, the Temple of the Heavenly Dragon itself became "moored," so to speak, so as to help people "cross the shore" to liberation.

The Theravāda and Mahāyāna traditions of Buddhism both speak of enlightenment-awareness using words and images of travel, the sea, and boats. Both traditions have been viewed as "a necessary vehicle for crossing the stream to enlightenment."[25] Whether "great" or "small," Buddhism speaks of itself in terms of "vehicles" for the literal transmission of Dharma. It is in this manner that the

FIGURE 127. *Early evening, with the Night-Mooring Stones in the center of the water, below the trees.*

Night-Mooring Stones, evoking "mooring places," participate in core beliefs and practices of Buddhism (fig. 127).

※

The priest looks out over the veranda of the Abbot's Quarters and is reminded of an encompassing image and narrative of believers and believers-to-be, traveling to be present to the Dharma experienced by Shākyamuni. Here, the priest refers to the Dharma of Shākyamuni as *sekkyō*.[26]

Sekkyō (説教) here means to attend, experience, and participate in a sermon and/or to be taught a religious lesson. In the priest's re-telling of the old temple and Buddhist story, *riku* (陸) was used as an active verb meaning pilgrimage travel toward a distant shore.

Words central to the priest's story combine the active and the passive, traveling and listening, within the context of religious voyaging we would term a pilgrimage. We remember that the pond earlier in the history of the garden was referred to as *Sōgenchi*, a physical place corresponding to a state of awareness, again, "where ordinary people [*sō*], like myriad drops of water, begin a journey revealing a river . . . of which people are yet unaware."[27] The Night-Mooring Stones are yet another composition of stones in the pond "moored" to an aspect of the old Buddhist story with which the priest began our contemplative survey of the garden.

IO

THE DRAGON GATE

The deep roof eaves of the Abbot's Quarters catch early evening light, as shadows begin to seep across the *tatami* on which we sit. Above and to the rear of the pond, myriad tree leaves quiver amid the emerging dusk.

The priest is pointing to his final selected composition of stones, set here on the embankment of earth on the far side of the pond across from the rear of the Abbot's Quarters (figs. 128, 129). The composition is a waterfall of stones presently devoid of flowing water. Large slabs of stone centuries ago were set upright on the lower front of the embankment of earth behind the pond. The stones presently are about two-and-a-half meters in height, and nearly a meter and a half in width. Other than soil erosion of the embankment occurring over the centuries, contributing to a slight inward tilt of slabs intended to stand upright, the waterless waterfall of stones remains as it was set at least some seven hundred years or so ago.[1] The distinctive waterfall of stones commands a spatially, and visually, central position with respect to experience of the pond in the garden from the Abbot's Quarters (fig. 3).

During the Tokugawa period (1615–1868), the composition of stones functioned as an actual waterfall. Water apparently was channeled (from Turtle Mountain) to the waterfall then into the pond through a sinuous arrangement of stones, and perhaps tubes of

FIGURE 128. *From the veranda of the Abbot's Quarters, the Bridge of Stones, the Crane Island-Mountain of stones, and the waterfall of stones are the visual center of the pond garden.*

bamboo, on top of and to the rear of the embankment of earth.[2] The winding design of the channel of stones, twisting about in cascading descent, itself mimics a torrent of moving water (figs. 130–34). In the process of directing water into the pond, though, the tops of the upright slabs of stone at some point in time were nicked and the original stonework slightly damaged. At the time, it was concluded that the temple priests responsible for damaging the upright slabs of stone were not enlightened, "unable [unlike Musō] to imagine the visual stream," unable to accommodate the earlier waterless waterfall of stones as-it-is.[3] Efforts to divert water into the serpentine channel of stones then into the pond subsequently were abandoned. The waterfall again became a "dry" composition of stones.[4]

Though presently not frequented by water, the design of the waterless waterfall of stones continues to be experienced as embodying qualities of water such as movement and associations with music.

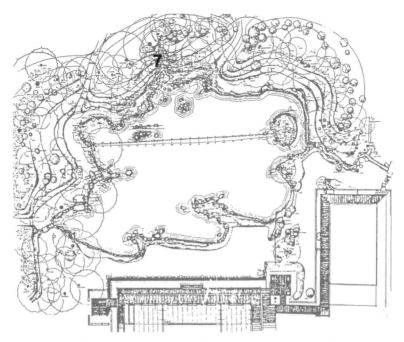

FIGURE 129. *The location of the waterfall of stones (7).*

"Originally, this fall had no water whatsoever," we read. "Wind in the Pines, and the far murmur of a river [Ōigawa] were the only sounds. The garden represented a vast seascape, and echoes the faint music of a mighty cascade."[5] In "Dry Mountain," Musō wrote, "a waterfall plunges, without a drop of water."[6] Interestingly, aptly, in "The Waste Land" T. S. Eliot envisioned "stony places . . . no water but only rock . . . mountains of rock without water."[7] Parenthetically, in *Stones of the Sky*, Pablo Neruda envisioned a place where "every-thing had been turned into stone, into sheer rock: teardrop or rain-drop, water kept on running into stone."[8] Many cultures of course recognize the affecting effects of combinations of water and stone.

Cascading Water, and the Third Moon

The priest refers to this final feature of significance as a *Ryūmon no Taki* (龍門の滝, Dragon-Gate Waterfall, evoking an ascent up a water-fall [*taki*], to pass through the gate [*mon*] of a dragon [*ryū*]). *Ryūmon*

FIGURE 130. *The Dragon-Gate Waterfall, as a composition, reaches from the top of the Bridge of Stones to the top of the earthen mound behind the pond.*

principally means passage through a difficult portal, to experience a dragon. *Taki* is a "dry" waterfall, evocative of a cascade of falling water again in association with a dragon. Dragon-Gate Waterfall.

The name "Dragon-Gate Waterfall," applied to the waterfall of stones, is traced to an archaic Chinese legend. The well-known legend concerns the waterfalls lacing upper streams of the Yellow River (黄河, Huang He, in Chinese) as the river flows through Shanxi and Shaanxi provinces, channeling water from myriad streams threaded like capillaries throughout mountainous north China. The Yellow

FIGURE 131. The Dragon-Gate Waterfall, in visual interrelationship with
the Bridge of Stones.

FIGURE 132. As a composition, the
Dragon-Gate Waterfall was set to
spread out along the front of the
embankment of earth to the rear of
the pond. At one time, water flowed
along the channel of stones winding
above the prominent upright slabs of
stone. The dragon/satori-stone is the
large triangular-shaped stone atop the
embankment (figs. 137, 147).

FIGURE 133. Stones border the desic-cated, winding channel through which water once flowed down through the waterfall and into the pond.

FIGURE 134. The serpentine channel of stones, strewn across the embank-ment of earth, along which water once flowed into the pond. The form of the waterfall is asymmetrical.

River itself was envisioned as a great dragon, its body nearly five thousand kilometers in length. The head of the dragon was held to be the mouth of the river, originating in the northern Bayan Har Mountains. The terminus of the river, in the Gulf of Bohai to the south, was envisioned as the tail of the dragon.[9]

The well-known legend centers on the cataracts along the Yellow River in north Shanxi and Shaanxi provinces and on the fish, primarily sturgeon and carp, seasonally attempting to swim against the current of the river and up the falls. After a nearly two-thousand-kilometer swim during spawning season, surviving fish mass at the bottom of the cataracts of the river. Fish then make dramatic leaps up the falls of cascading water, in efforts to reach the calm waters of spawning grounds above the cataracts. Flogged by cascading water, most fish are pushed back into what become pools of death at the bottom of the falls. Some fish, though, persist in swimming against the thunderous current of the upper reaches of the river, leap up the falls, and into waters within which they subsequently will bring forth life. The final cataract of the Yellow River traditionally has been named the Dragon Gate (龍門, *Lung Men*, in Chinese). Fish deemed of exceptional will, persisting to and over this final cataract, were said to have passed through the Gate (the final cataract) of the Dragon (the Yellow River).[10] Chinese and Japanese art often depicts spawning fish leaping up and twisting about in the froth and torrent of cascading water (fig. 135).

There is a compelling metaphysical aspect of this legend. Fish, carp in particular, and dragons are held to embody aspects of each other as it is envisioned that "carp shape might conceal dragon soul."[11] Both carp and dragon are believed to share the vital attribute of transformation.

A metaphysical aspect of the archaic Chinese legend has it that a fish reaching the top of the falls transforms itself into a dragon and then, in most versions of the legend, flies off into the sky (generally, to the west). "*Sankyūgan* 〖三級巌; the Yellow River cataracts, as a three-tiered waterfall〗 was so steep that many fish could not leap up the falls. Subsequently, those fish remained within the waters beneath

FIGURE 135. *Fish and dragon were envisioned as aspects of each other. A Daoist sculpture captures a fish (the upper portion of the figure) at the moment of transformation into a dragon (the lower portion of the figure). Temple roof ornament from China. Ch'ing dynasty (1644–1911), glazed pottery. H: 24 cm.*

the falls. If there was any carp which could swim up this waterfall, though, it would at once transform into a dragon."[12] Dragon-fish often were envisioned with wings and, like cranes, often were depicted being ridden by *xian*. The Daoist adept Tsze Ying Sien-Jen, for instance, by legend tended a young carp until it had matured. In return, the fins of the fish changed to wings, the fish invited Tsze Ying Sien-Jen to mount its back, and both then flew up into the sky.

Persistence. Strength of will. Will and persistence are required for the legendary transformation of fish into dragon. These attributes are "admired because it [the fish] struggles against the current, and it therefore has become an emblem of perseverance. The fish of the Yellow River are said to make an ascent of the stream in the third moon of each year, when those which succeed in passing above the rapids of Lung Men are transformed into dragons."[13] As each is an aspect of the other, the transformation of fish into a dragon then merely is a drawing out, through will and persistence, of that which already is present.

The priest, as we will see, conceptualizes the Dragon-Gate Waterfall within the pond garden with respect to fish metaphorically swimming up the waterfall at the legendary moment of transformation into a dragon. Again, we experience dragons in association with the Temple of the Heavenly Dragon. Both the Dragon-Gate Waterfall in the pond garden as well as the cataracts of the Yellow River are associated with transformation as a vital aspect of dragons. But, let us consider further aspects of Chinese Dragon-Gate waterfalls.

Dragon Ponds and Dangerous Places

The perennial Chinese legend emphasizes three specific cataracts along the upper Yellow River in north Shanxi Province. Mimetic of the Yellow River cataracts, Dragon-Gate waterfalls within garden landscapes in Japan often were constructed as three-tiered ("three-drop") waterfalls (*sankyūgan*).

Water at one time flowed over three horizontally placed primary ledges of stone within the waterfall, then into the pond within the garden aspect of Tenryū-ji (fig. 136). The ledges within the waterfall of stones are said to correspond to the ledges of mythic significance within the Chinese Dragon-Gate cataracts. "They built a waterfall in the garden," Mirei Shigemori notes, "to imitate the great waterfall located in the upper streams of the Yellow River in China. The waterfall is called *Sankyū-gan* [waterfall-on-three-levels] as the falls are terraced on three levels. The waterfall of stones within Tenryū-ji garden was also named *Sankyū-gan* after it."[14] At the time of the ceremonies "opening the mountain" of the Temple of the Heavenly Dragon, the waterfall was known as *Ryūmon Sankyū* (龍門三級, Three-Step Dragon-Gate Waterfall). "Last year," priest Tsutomo Minakami wrote, "I visited the area of the *Ryūmon* [Dragon-Gate] in China, on the upper stream

FIGURE 136. An interpretive drawing of the Dragon-Gate Waterfall, depicting channeled water flowing down into the pond. To the right foreground, the Crane Island-Mountain of stones peaks above water.

of the [Yellow River]. The landscape touched me, very much. As I walked the cliffs, I remembered the garden of the Tenryū temple, as I experienced it when I was young. Of course, the Dragon-Gate in the Tenryū-ji garden is an arrangement of stones fashioned as a waterfall. The [composition of stones] is beautiful, and skillfully done."[15] In "Three-Step Waterfall," Musō wrote, "at dangerous places, awesome ledges, three barriers, so many fish have fallen back."[16] Musō wrote of his awareness of correspondences between the Chinese Gate of the Dragon and the Dragon-Gate Waterfall at Tenryū-ji. Interestingly, Musō's awareness of the training of monks is, as we will see, similar to points made by the priest within the temple about the relationship between the training of priests and the Dragon-Gate Waterfall.

DEEP VALLEYS AND AWESOME LEDGES

The somewhat atrophied three tiers of stones comprising the pond-garden waterfall at present still form a broad isosceles triangle. The still-discernable isosceles triangle form of the waterfall is envisioned as composed of: (1) a broad lower tier, with its center between the upright slabs of stone (compare figs. 144 and 148); (2) a comparatively narrow middle section, emphasizing a "carp stone" (compare figs. 144

and 146); (3) a comparatively narrow top section of the composition emphasizing a "dragon stone" atop the embankment of earth, reaching up as if to pierce the sky (compare figs. 144, 145, 147).[17]

The (triangular-shaped) Dragon-Gate Waterfall itself was set amid clusters of smaller stones dotting the peak, front slope, and piedmont of the (triangular-shaped) earthen embankment behind the pond. The myriad stones surrounding the upright slabs of the water-fall within the Tenryū-ji garden pond were set on several still-distinct levels across the front slope of the embankment of earth. These dis-tinct horizontal bands of smaller stones reiterate the tiered arrange-ment and overall form of the waterfall itself (figs. 146, 148).[18] The vertical axis of the broad triangle of the embankment of earth broad-ens and visually stabilizes the waterfall of stones as a composition. The tiered arrangement of the stones dotting the front of the em-bankment of earth is apparent when the waterfall is experienced from the veranda of the Abbot's Quarters, especially apparent during fall and winter seasons when the embankment of earth is relatively shorn of flora (figs. 137–39).

The stony landscape immediately surrounding the Dragon-Gate Waterfall, in addition, evokes the landscape surrounding the upper reaches of the Yellow River in China. The cataracts of the Chinese Dragon Gate are situated within a legendary landscape of mountains, ravines, and rivers. The area near Luoyang, the old capital of the Sung Dynasty near the cataracts, is known as the Walls of the Dragon Gate. The cliffs surrounding the river near Luoyang are punctuated with cave temples filled with carved images of Buddhas. The area near Luoyang remains the venerated Buddhist landscape within which the Gate of the Dragon is situated, as the mountains and cliffs and ravines themselves are envisioned as the Walls of the Dragon Gate.

In writing about his visits to the Walls of the Dragon Gate along the upper reaches of the Yellow River in China, Priest Minakami felt that "the landscape of the [Dragon Gate] waterfalls appeared as if countless dragons were living there and the scene affected me very much. To me, both the Tenryū-ji waterfall and the natural stones . . .

FIGURE 137. *The broadly triangular shape of the Dragon-Gate Waterfall repeats the broadly triangular shape of the piled-up embankment of earth, distinctive against light filtering between the trees.*

are a group of huge dragons. . . . [In the Tenryū-ji garden] marvelously skillful layers of old mossy stones are all rough and natural, and they are exactly like a crowd of dragons."[19]

Priest Minakami envisioned the hillock behind the pond within the Tenryū-ji garden as the back of a dragon, as the land itself "helps the imagination to discover the outlines of the dragon."[20] From this perspective, consider again the embankment of earth and stones on which the Tenryū-ji Dragon-Gate Waterfall was set. During the birth

FIGURE 138. *The central stones of the Dragon-Gate Waterfall are surrounded by stones that appear to have been set on (three) tiered bands across the face of the embankment of earth. A long line of stones extends from each side of the horizontal Bridge of Stones, at the base of the two upright slabs of stone. There is a second row of fewer stones midway up and to either side of the central waterfall stones, beginning with the relatively big stones at the top of the upright slab of waterfall stones. Still fewer tertiary-level stones are on either side of the satori-stone at the top of, and slightly to the left of, the central channel through which water once flowed (fig. 137). All of these horizontal bands of smaller stones reiterate the tiered arrangement of the waterfall itself (figs 139, 146, 148)*

and early life of the pond garden, fewer trees than at present permitted a panoramic view of Turtle Mountain and the Mountain of Storms above and beyond the embankment of earth behind the pond. The Dragon-Gate Waterfall then would have appeared as a visually distinctive group of tall faceted stones clustered in the valley-like rear-center of the pond, with Turtle Mountain and the Mountain of Storms as background (figs. 3, 63, 96). We remember that the pond itself earlier on was considered the lair of a dragon; indeed, "the valley is so deep [that] the dragon comes out [of the pond garden] late," as Musō wrote. [21]

Dragon-as-landscape and landscape-as-dragon reveal the kinship

FIGURE 139. *The Dragon-Gate Waterfall can be experienced as the visual center of the pond garden, in relationship to the rear verandas of the Abbot's Quarters (the lower center roof). From the point of view of this interpretive drawing, the pond appears embraced by surrounding mountains. The Dragon-Gate Waterfall can be experienced as evoking a narrow valley between and to the foreground of surrounding mountains.*

between the Dragon-Gate waterfall of stones within the Tenryū-ji pond garden and the venerated landscape of north China. Priest Minakami concludes that the rear of the pond garden "looks like the view along the upper stream of the Yellow River."[22] Along with the pond, in each instance the form of aspects of the earth itself were envisioned as a dragon.[23]

A FISH . . . CHANGED

Imagine a waterfall. Undoubtedly, the mind's eye follows the downward flow of cascading water—as water once cascaded through the winding channel of stones atop the embankment of earth, then down through the now-waterless waterfall of stones. Here, though, we must envision movement *up* the Dragon-Gate Waterfall. Seated within the Abbot's Quarters, as the eye moves out and over the pond to the Dragon-Gate Waterfall, there is a shift in eye movement up the waterfall and embankment of earth, then up and into Turtle Mountain, the trees, then up again and into the Mountain of Storms across the Ōi River (fig. 46). Looking across the pond then up and over the Dragon-Gate Waterfall into the distant mountains is a visual ascent upward and over features both naturally occurring and human-made—pond; embankment of earth; waterfall; mountains; sky.

The physical form of the tiered cataracts along the upper Yellow River in China, similarly, conditioned an emphasis on ascent in widespread legends of fish transforming into dragons. Transformation was envisioned as a vertical phenomenon, as ascent—leaping carp; ascents up waterfalls; mythic flights into the sky. Correspondingly, there is a pronounced emphasis on the vertical—on ascent in the physical form, metaphysical meaning, as well as the visual experience of the Tenryū-ji Dragon-Gate Waterfall.

There is an additional historical significance to the Dragon-Gate Waterfall, in that the waterfall influenced the naming of the Temple of the Heavenly Dragon. "And in the Tenryū-ji garden . . . a risen carp changing into a dragon was carved. The name 'Tenryū-ji [Temple of the Heavenly Dragon],'" we read, "expresses that a dragon rises to the sky."[24] Musō was well aware of the link between legends from China and the Dragon-Gate Waterfall of stones, especially as concern of the onccept of transformation. The *Recorded Annals of the Temple of the Heavenly Dragon* (*Tenryū-ji Jukkyō*) notes that during commemoration ceremonies in the temple, Musō proclaimed that "a fish changed at Sankyū-gen [three-tiered waterfall]."[25] The "fish" mentioned by Musō most likely referred to the civil war, ignorance manifested as war, to which the temple was an offering of redemption. The birth of the temple indeed was a transformation of vengefulness, dishonor, and death ("fish" consciousness, so to speak) into a dragon, the Temple of the Heavenly Dragon. For Musō, the birth of the temple appears associated with the transformation of fish into dragon, and he associated both the temple and transformation with the Dragon-Gate Waterfall. Indeed, the Dragon-Gate Waterfall was considered synonymous with the temple itself. During the time of Musō, the temple also was known as *Sankyūgen* 〚three-tiered waterfall〛 then somewhat later as *Ryūmon sankyū* (the three-tiered waterfall of the dragon gate).

It is important to reiterate that dragons were not demonic, or associated with death and dissolution.[26] In China and Japan, dragons were an embodiment of life.

A Cascade of Consciousness

Night seeps through the *shōji* of the Guest Quarters. Moonlight and shadow seep across the interior *fusuma* walls of the room. As *shōji* are pulled back, the room opens to the night and is enveloped in stillness. The moon cannot be seen; yet, moonlight blankets the night sky and flows as liquid strands of pearl along the wood grain of the expansive floor of the veranda (fig. 140).

Earlier in the evening, after esoteric conversation, the priest patiently again brought me back to the importance of my own experiences with the garden:

> "You are too concerned with my understanding 〚of the temple and pond garden〛. My understanding is only my understanding," he admonished. "I think you must stay here at the temple, to let the garden speak to you so that you will have your own understanding . . . In the early evening, say, at this time of the year, around five o'clock, when the sun sets 〚pointing to the west, across the pond〛 in that direction, you should look at the garden . . . face to face."

So, quite often I sat on either the veranda of the Abbot's Quarters or on *tatami* within the Guest Quarters until deep into the night as well as early in the morning. The tone and language of the writing composing this book, the inclusion of sensate experiences of the temple and pond garden, archaeological and historical and cross-cultural perspectives, as well as incorporation of varied points

FIGURE 140. *Moonlight highlights the Crane Island-Mountain, in front of the Dragon-Gate Waterfall.*

of view, all convey that which came to life over decades of periodic face-to-face experiences with the pond within the garden.

Deep at night the pond is blue, tempered by the cold. Moonlight appears as filigree, ethereal lace on stones strewn upon still water.

Original Face and Transformation

As with other aspects of the garden pond and temple landscape, the priest's conception of the Dragon-Gate Waterfall largely is conditioned by Rinzai Zen Buddhism. The priest in large part conceptualizes the waterfall as evocative of the existential "suchness" (*shinnyo*) of Rinzai Zen Buddhism.

The priest reiterates that the Dragon-Gate Waterfall exists in the pond garden through the compassion of enlightened Rinzai Zen Buddhist priests, whether Chinese (Rankei Doryū) or Japanese (Musō Kokushi).

Images of Dragon-Gate waterfalls in China and Japan invariably emphasize the moment of fish-to-dragon transformation (fig. 135). In considering the Dragon-Gate Waterfall and Rinzai Zen Buddhism, the priest speaks of the often sudden transformation (変化, henka) of ordinary awareness and initial (kenshō) awareness/experience of Bud-dha-Nature. Experience of the waterfall for the priest is associated with experience of states of awareness, states of being (figs. 142, 145).

For the priest, initial awareness of Buddha-Nature is akin to the transformation relationship between carp (koi) and dragon (ryū) associated with the Chinese Gate of the Dragon. For the priest, carp swimming in the pond evoke the ordinary awareness of monks in training as well as the ordinary consciousness of laypeople not yet aware of their Original Face, their Buddha-Nature. People swim in illusion, dash here and there, moved by desire in particular, the priest says, much as carp in the pond reflexively swim to tossed crumbs of bread (figs. 25, 141). The rigors of Zen training and temple life are analogous to fish attempting to swim up the Yellow River waterfalls. Sustained training is a necessary though not exclusive experience for the spontaneous breaking-through of ordinary awareness to initial awareness of Buddha-Nature. Metaphorically, the priest fashions an analogy of ordinary awareness as a carp (koi) and awareness of Buddha-Nature as a dragon (ryū). Initial awareness of Buddha-Nature is conceptualized as an often-sudden rupture of ordinary awareness, then sudden awareness of Buddha-Nature (awareness of oneness with Buddha-Nature).

SWIMMING WITH THE WIND

We have seen that Buddhist temples, historically, for the most part were inhabited by males and that temple priests, for the most part, were and are male. Carp (鯉, koi; Cyprinus carpio haematopterus)

FIGURE 141. *The pond is stocked with a brocade of* koi (nishikigoi). *Koi bring vibrant colors to the water of the pond.* Kōhaku (color combinations of red and white), ōgon (color combinations of golds, yellows, and oranges), *and* shōwa sanke (color combinations of blacks, whites, and reds) *remain popular colors bred into koi. The colors of the koi in the pond change with the temperature of the water and fade somewhat during the winter while deepening in spring and summer. Transient beauty* (mono no aware).

FIGURE 142. Paintings of dragons wind their way along the inner (fusuma) walls of the Abbot's Quarter's. This serpentine dragon appears to guard the Dragon-Gate Waterfall in the garden, reflected on the wall. Dragons are sentinels. When the priest sits in zazen before the garden, he is surrounded by dragons—the dragon/satori-stone and Dragon-Gate Waterfall are before him; the dragon on the walls of the Abbot's Quarters is behind him.

remain prominent in Japanese culture and society, and *koi*, for the most part, remain associated with males.

Young males culturally are encouraged to display qualities attributed to *koi*—endurance, persistence, and strength of will. *Koi* are known as "samurai fish" because a carp is said to not flinch and flop about when flayed. Fish often are flayed alive. It is considered a delicacy by many people, a freshness, to eat flayed fish and feel still-living flesh on one's palate. For most people, it remains desirable for male children to behave as *koi* behave; that is, not flinching amid adversity.[27]

On Children's Day, May 5, the tradition is to fly colorful kite tubes (*koinobori*) in the shape of *koi* from the roof of family houses. Banners, some approaching seven meters in length, are flown on poles by families celebrating the sons, especially, in their homes (fig. 143). Kite-like, the banners twist and turn in catching the wind. The

*FIGURE 143. "Kite tubes (koinobori).'
Black carp tubes (magoi), usually the
longest, traditionally are associated
with male children within the house
while shorter red carp tubes (higoi) are
associated with female children within
the house.*

twisting and turning, the swimming with the wind, is a vibrant correspondence to fish swimming up the Chinese Yellow River cascades.
The banners signal that the sons, especially, in the house are as strong
as legendary Dragon-Gate fish and that they will grow to be tena-
cious, to not give up, to persist and flourish.

Koi in the waters of the pond; legends of fish changing into dragons; a waterfall embodying a fish and a dragon. Salient features of the
pond garden thus would not be inscrutable, esoteric, or inaccessible
to most people experiencing the pond garden aspect of the Temple of
the Heavenly Dragon.

CHOOSING THE WAY

The priest continues. He renders a drawing illustrating that, by
way of analogy, if one attempts to go *up* the waterfall (choosing the
Dharma of Shākyamuni) and persists, there often is a sudden transfor-
mation of ordinary awareness (*koi*, carp) as one initially experiences
Buddha-Nature (*ryū*, a dragon; fig. 135).[28] By way of analogy with the
Dragon-Gate Waterfall, the priest's drawings say that experience of

FIGURE 144. *The Dragon-Gate Water-fall, with the carp-stone prominent to the center-left.*

Buddha-Nature (initial *kenshō*, especially), though spontaneous, is envisioned as an ascent. In turn, the Dragon-Gate Waterfall is not a static composition of stones but is conceptualized by the priest as movement, dynamic motion (fig. 145).

The priest defines two interrelated sets of movement: the experience of Buddha-Nature envisioned as movement and, secondly, this same movement superimposed upon an image of the Dragon-Gate Waterfall. The priest's graphic analogy has carp swim from the waters of the pond, to and under the Bridge of Stones, then *up* the Dragon-Gate Waterfall. As we have seen, the Bridge of Stones, with its present-day evocation of intention and will, place and teacher, was sited in the pond in intimate association with the Dragon-Gate Waterfall. The Bridge of Stones and the Dragon-Gate Waterfall both participate in the priest's conception of compositions of stones in the pond garden evoking salient aspects of Rinzai Zen Buddhism and the training of acolytes (figs. 145, 146, 148).

The priest's graphic analogy flows from his long-term detailed observations of the Dragon-Gate Waterfall. The priest therefore readily points to two specific stones within the intricate composition as critical to his analogy and to transformational "movement" associated with the Dragon-Gate Waterfall: one, a stone (鯉魚石, *rigyoseki*, carp stone) in the middle of the composition, which the priest by way of analogy

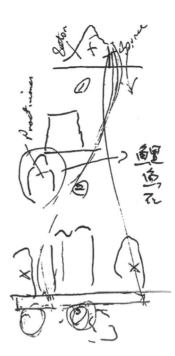

FIGURE 145. A sketch by the priest, emphasizing the (metaphorical) winding ascent up the Dragon-Gate Waterfall.

associates with a carp leaping up the waterfall at the moment of transformation into a dragon; two, a stone (龍石, ryūseki, dragon stone) on the very top of the embankment of earth, which the priest by way of analogy associates with a carp transformed into a dragon (figs. 137, 147). The carp stone is curved in shape, and was set into the earth at an upright angle. It is offset spatially and set lower in height to the left of the dragon stone on top of the piedmont of earth. The carp stone appears set, composed, to "face" the dragon stone perched on top of the embankment of earth. The dragon stone distinctly is triangular in shape, and appears especially as such when experienced visually from in front of the waterfall (fig. 79).

WHEELS OF LIGHT, MOUNTAINS OF INFINITE STILLNESS

The priest draws a spiraling line across his sketch of the Dragon-Gate Waterfall (fig. 145). The designed spatial interdependent relationship of the carp stone and the dragon stone is asymmetrical. The asymmetrical spatial placement of these two prominent stones defines a zigzag

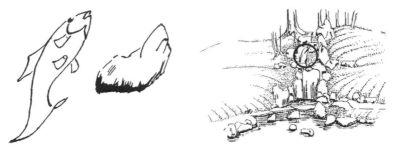

FIGURE 146. *The shape of the carp-stone is envisioned as reinforcing the shape of a carp leaping up the waterfall (the circle denotes the "mid-stream" placement of the carp stone, within the waterfall of stones).*

pattern, as one visually perceives "carp" to move upward, diagonally, toward "dragon" (fig. 146). The priest's spiral pen-line moves from the Bridge of Stones, to the carp stone, then diagonally across and up to the dragon stone (fig. 145).[29] The spiral line graphs the ascending movement of carp-to-dragon transformation, analogous to the rupture of ordinary awareness in people and the often-sudden experience of Buddha-Nature for the priest, invariably associated with a person sitting in *zazen*. The analogies, metaphors, and graphic imagery employed by the priest in communicating his vision of the Dragon-Gate Waterfall reveal the kinship of *zazen* to aspects of the parent Indian tradition of yoga.

The posture of *zazen* is an offspring of the yoga posture within the Indian tradition of Yogācāra. Texts such as the Upanishads say that there are seven nodes, *chakra* (Wheels of Light), what we might term spiritual energy, congruent with seven major glands and organs within the body. Nodes of *chakra* are interrelated vertically in the body, from the genitals to the brain.

Each Wheel of Light is believed to be its own consciousness, and thus the body is "simply an area or realm of existing or potential consciousness."[30] Each node of spiritual energy is considered a distinct, autonomous presence. *Chakra* are ranked with respect to each other, as "lower" or "higher," and the practice of yoga is believed to stimulate awakening of yogacara consciousness as awakening moves from its "lower" aspects to its "higher" aspects. *Chakra* are composed of complementary-opposed aspects: Ida (female) and Pengali (male), and the

FIGURE 147. *The dragon/satori stone atop the mound of earth is distinctive against light flowing between the trees. The dragon has long been the guardian of Buddhists and Buddhism, and from this vantage the dragon/satori stone appears to guard the buildings and pond below.*

movement of Ida and Pengali is the Fire of the Serpent—Kundalini.[31] Kundalini often is depicted as a coiled serpent, or dragon, at the tip of the coccyx. When stimulated by meditation, the Fire of the Serpent is envisioned as a dragon ascending up the *chakra* of the body. The Fire of the Serpent is movement from "lower" *chakra* to "higher" *chakra*. As it rises, the Kundalini·dragon is said to "awaken" each of the seven nodes of successively "higher" consciousness/spiritual energy. By force of meditative will, the dragon as the Fire of the Serpent spirals up the spine to and through the head of one's body.

In yoga, the node of consciousness/spiritual energy associated with the head of a body traditionally was termed the Brahma Gate (analogous to the dragon stone at the "head," the top of the pied-mont of earth, of the Dragon-Gate Waterfall). Gates and the theme of ascent also appear in Chinese Daoist practices of seated meditation, influencing Zen Buddhism, where "the spinal column, in particular, turns into a magnificent road of ascent to a range of magical moun-tains which rise beyond the head. These represent the ultimate home

FIGURE 148. *The priest's conception of triangularity and 7:5:3 proportions as design aspects of the Dragon-Gate Waterfall. The priest identifies seven triangular-shaped stones of significance within the waterfall; these stones then are combined, forming progressively larger triangles. The large triangle of the Dragon-Gate Waterfall is subdivided horizontally into three bands, with respect to compositional space, interrelated in the proportion of 7:5:3. The small figure to the lower left is the priest's sketch of a person in zazen. Correspondence of triangular form interrelates the small figure of a person in zazen and the form of the Dragon-Gate Waterfall.*

of the immortal 'mountain man.' The road up passes through three gates. The lowest is at the base of the spine; the second in the back; the third, the jade gate, is where the spine joins the skull."[32] Ida and Pengali often were depicted as two entwined serpents/dragons.[33] The spine of the body was Merudanda [the rod of Meru], in reference to Meru, the aforementioned primal mountain of Buddhist myth.

The dragon lives in both yoga and Zen images of transformation of awareness. Yogi sought to move the dragon, the Fire of the Serpent, from "lower" to "higher" regions of the body. The curved ascent of the Kundalini dragon is the spiraling Fire of the Serpent. Its movement is isomorphic with the manner in which the priest envisions carp-to-dragon transformation as movement from "lower" to "higher" stones, or nodes, along the Dragon-Gate Waterfall. The generative intertwining of Ida and Pengali corresponds to the priest's drawings of a carp's curved ascent up the Dragon-Gate Waterfall.

The dragon as Fire of the Serpent, traversing the seven nodes of consciousness/spiritual energy, is believed to preexist within the body; yet, without meditation, one is not aware of what already is present. Similarly, Rinzai Zen Buddhists hold that Buddha-Nature is preexistent—one simply is not aware of inherent Buddha-Nature.

TISSUES OF THE SOUL

Nature is a prominent aspect of conceptions of transformations of awareness in yoga and *zazen*. Musō's initial experience of Buddha-Nature, it will be remembered, occurred amid mountains and forests and not within a temple building. In the yoga tradition of India and the Buddhism of China and Japan, embodied in Musō's Zen, we recall that nature was a preexistent animistic condition and situation (Buddha-Nature) in which people participated. Similarly, the priest experiences the Dragon-Gate Waterfall as a physical reminder that the polar-opposed distinctions people make, say, between people and nature, are illusion.[34]

The priest's conceptualization of transformation of awareness associated with *zazen* is analogous to metamorphosis in nature. Biological metamorphosis is not growth. Biological metamorphosis is a literal transformation of the physical form, function, and behavior of organisms.[35] A caterpillar transforming into a butterfly is metamorphosis, a familiar metaphor of the nature of life itself. Life is change, literally: the possibility of new forms and ways of being, already present ("fish: dragon") as an existential aspect of being.

Human beings, to date, exhibit a lack of biological metamorphosis as a characteristic of the species. Yet, metamorphosis is a pervasive theme in the cultural imagination, the religious imagination in particular, of many societies.[36] The human body invariably is the cauldron for metamorphosis in cross-cultural accounts of transformations of awareness. Influenced by the tradition of Hermes Trismegistus, alchemists of medieval Anglo-Europe, for instance, conceived of the body as the arena for transformation of awareness. Athanor was the alchemist furnace where lead, what the priest would term "carp-awareness," was transformed into gold, what the priest would term "awareness of Buddha-Nature." Athanor was embodied; that is, Athanor was envisioned as "a tissue of powers of the soul which have the body as their support" and Athanor therefore was accessible via one's own body.[37] For alchemists, the work of transforming lead into gold was the life's work of transforming consciousness—within one's body, also as envisioned by the priest at Tenryū-ji.

THE FORM OF POSSIBILITY

The priest sketches his perceived congruence between the form of a body in *zazen* and the form of the Dragon-Gate Waterfall (fig. 148).[38] The broad shape of the embankment of earth on which the waterfall is raised as well as the shape of the waterfall itself, again, roughly is triangular in form. The priest envisions a correspondence between the triangular form of the waterfall, the embankment of earth, and the triangular form of a person in *zazen*. Rather than the popular image of the circle in association with *zazen*, the triangle and the spiral are the graphic forms recurring within the priest's visual conceptualization and interpretations of the waterfall as well as with respect to other core aspects of the temple and pond garden.

Viewed frontally, the broad form of the waterfall approximates an isosceles triangle; thus, a conceptual line drawn from the apex downward divides the triangle of the waterfall into two approximately bilaterally symmetrical halves. Rinzai Zen Buddhism, though, eschews the bilateral symmetry and polar-opposed dualism of an isosceles triangle. Bilateral symmetry does not embody the creative tension, or possibility, manifested as asymmetry (非対称, *hitaishō*).

The priest thus deconstructs the broad triangular form of the waterfall to reveal the asymmetry inherent within bilateral symmetry. The priest first highlights seven stones of significance from all of the stones composing the waterfall. All of the seven stones are envisioned as smaller triangles interlocking to compose the broad triangle of the waterfall. The priest then draws three *horizontal* lines subdividing the large triangle of the Dragon-Gate Waterfall into three horizontal segments (fig. 148). The priest conceptualizes these three horizontal planes, segmented spatial areas of the waterfall, as interrelated, interdependent, in the proportion of 7:5:3.[39]

The creation of asymmetry, here, is the negation of axial symmetry as the final resting place of awareness. The priest creates awareness of asymmetry by visually apprehending the asymmetrical proportions of 7:5:3 within an apparently bilaterally symmetrical triangle. Asymmetry is revealed as an inherent aspect of symmetry. The waterfall indeed is "balance," the dynamic balance of asymmetry rather than the static balance of symmetry.

We continue to see 7:5:3 envisioned as a pervasive proportion defining salient physical aspects, and spatial interdependent relationships, of the pond garden. We can note here at least three characteristics of this proportion often appearing subtly within Rinzai Zen Buddhism.

7:5:3 is an arithmetic proportion exhibiting an equality of difference, yet an inequality of ratio; that is, $7-5 = 2$ and $5-3 = 2$. The arithmetic difference between 7, 5, and 3 does not affect the resultant sum, in each instance, of 2. Differences between 7, 5, and 3 result in an equality. On the other hand, $7/5 = 1.4$ and $5/3 = 1.6$—the ratio difference between 7, 5, and 3 results in an inequality.

The proportion 7:5:3 at once is similarity and difference, equality and inequality. For Pythagoras of Samos (582–500 B.C.), proportion was a Divine Harmony embodying the manner in which contrasting elements form a whole while maintaining difference. "The triangle," as proportional interdependent relationship, "symbolizes a method of organization through the joining or mediating of differences."[40] If difference (not inequality) in this respect does not exist, then relationship (not equality) in this respect is not possible.

Asymmetrical triangles, embodiments of dynamic equilibrium, are "capable of endless continuation even beyond rigid boundaries, and [open] up possibilities of cosmological interpretations accorded closely with both Japanese aesthetic feelings and Zen ideas."[41] 7:5:3 triangular interdependent relationships, for instance, occur as the form and spatial structure of flower arrangements (ikebana) and venerated stones displayed in trays (suiseki and bonseki), and in the subtle proportions of rooms for tea ceremony (chaseki).[42] That which people find beautiful, compelling, and affecting often is proportional in form.

The Music of Stones

Across the centuries, people visiting the pond garden aspect of the Temple of the Heavenly Dragon often expressed deeply affecting experiences of the landscape through the language of music. Music in place during the construction of the temple had been introduced from China in the seventh century. The Seven-Notes-in-All-Positions (七世書く具, nanasei kakugu) became the basis of Buddhist music. More specifically, music (声明, shōmyō) accompanying Buddhist chants was composed around a yo and an in scale. The yo scale was pentatonic (C, D, F, G, and A in ascending intervals). Incorporating two, three, two, two, and three semitones/half-steps would bring in the in scale. A rhythmic prelude (序, jo) followed by a transitional development of meter (破, ha) gradually leading to a culmination (急, kyū) was the larger structure of the movement of compositions.

Indeed, "everything has *jo*, *ha*, and *kyū*."[44] Zeami Motokiyo (1363–1443) compared this movement pattern of musical composition to the movements of a river that began slowly, gained speed and intensity in flowing and widening, then merged powerfully with a tranquil, encompassing sea.

Falling water earlier on caressed the stones composing the Dragon-Gate Waterfall, and it was felt that the water would "splash out the Buddha's sermon."[45] The flow of water across the top of the piedmont of earth and down the waterfall at one time by design actually produced sounds experienced as musical effects. In its serpentine descent through a network of bamboo and a channel of stone, water was led into a concave ring of stones to the rear of the embankment of earth behind the pond. "At Saga, near Kyōto, is the garden of Tenryū-ji," it was noted, "a garden designed for sound . . . tranquillity is magnified by the placing of a deeply hollowed stone [presumably still present under earth to the rear of the waterfall] beneath the upper drop of the waterfall."[46] The hollowed-out stone, now covered with moss, was deemed a "sounding stone."[47]

Later, the Dragon-Gate Waterfall often was experienced as an "orchestrated composition" of stones. Samuel Newsom and Mirei Shigemori experienced the Dragon-Gate Waterfall as "the faint music of a mighty cascade."[48] In his poem "Three-Step Waterfall," Musō wrote of this complex of stones as evoking "the loud water rushes; the spray of the falls hovers."[49] Indeed, "the academic voices debating the historical origins of this dry rock waterfall are drowned beneath the overwhelming beauty of its presence."[50] The profound silence of the Dragon-Gate Waterfall still flows, musically, directly, into one's heart.

The present-day Dragon-Gate Waterfall can be experienced musically as a rhythmic composition of "initial prologue stones" (myriad lower base stones, experienced as *jo*), transitional mid-placed stones (at the level around the carp stone, experienced as *ha*), and the culminating dragon stone (experienced as *kyū*).[51] That is, the myriad low-lying horizontal stones sprinkled across the lower aspect of the

FIGURE 149. *Early morning.*

embankment of earth (fig. 128) can be experienced as the initial rhythmic (*jo*) prelude of the composition. As the eye gradually moves inward and up the waterfall, as the triangle of the waterfall narrows,
gains intensity, stones set roughly on three levels across the mid-as-
pect of the embankment (fig. 138) establish a transitional, "midrange"
(*ha*) rhythm. The dragon stone apex of the waterfall (fig. 147) then
can be experienced as the dramatic (*kyū*) culmination of the rhythmic
experience of the composition.

Experienced musically as a composition in stone, the waterfall
exhibits a distinct tempo. The myriad stones raised on the embankment of earth increase in size, then cluster and gather intensity in
moving from the outer edges of the waterfall inward toward the
centrally placed upright slabs of stone. The tempo of the waterfall
increases, visually, toward an apical conclusion, as one's awareness

moves from broadly placed, lower initial stones upward and inward to the (*kyū*) dragon stone.

Experienced musically as a composition in stone, the prevalent *shichigosan* proportion of 7:5:3 (or 7 and 5, with respect to the numbers of musical notes) becomes a progression of harmonic tones and rhythmic interdependent relationship.[52] The waterfall thus can be experienced as *wa* (harmony), manifested as stones in proportional interdependent relationship. It is in this manner that the Dragon-Gate Waterfall can be experienced as "frozen music."[53]

The realization here is that, however compelling, stones experienced solely as "things" tend to stop, hold, and limit our awareness. Proportion, music-as-proportion, reminds us that our attention ought to swim in the music of interrelationship, not in things themselves.

¿

Early morning, eyes fall away into emptiness.

Seated within the Abbot's Quarters, our eyes are cast slightly downward, contemplatively, such that "when your eyelids have fallen across the whole of the empty world," as Musō promised, "the gate [Buddha-Nature] will open at the snap of a finger."[54] Our awareness rests lightly, quietly, on the Dragon-Gate Waterfall deeply nested within the mist-shadow and stillness that is the pond in the garden (figs. 3, 149).

III Garden as Life and Spirit

The ancient Japanese believed,

in fact,

that rocks grew.

This idea is repeated

in the poem which is sung today

as the Japanese national anthem:—

"May the nation live and thrive

thousands of years

till pebbles

have grown to be boulders

covered with moss."

T. KAORI KITAO[1]

We have experienced, vicariously, an influential Rinzai Zen Buddhist temple and its celebrated pond garden—the circumstances of their genesis and salient ongoing life experiences. The presence of people as a vital aspect of the life of the pond garden, not merely as spectators, has been emphasized. Emotions such as fear and guilt, compassion and love in particular participated in the birth and ongoing experiences of the landscape aspect of the temple. To speak of "garden," then, is to speak of the lived lives of people . . . their ancestors and their deities. The pond garden aspect of the Temple of the Heavenly Dragon embodies properties of as well as remains a compelling entrée into Japanese culture, history, and society. To speak of "garden," then, is to name a fundamental aspect of Japan.

In this final section, from within the Temple of the Heavenly Dragon we briefly will move deep into prehistory to illustrate the significance of gardens of stone, such as the pond garden within Tenryū-ji, to humanity and world history as well as to Japan. To demonstrate the significance of stones rather than foliage to the archetypal idea of garden itself, we will peruse stone circles from prehistoric Japan and Sumerian narratives on a sacred garden of stones. We reiterate the importance of conceptualizing garden, and of experiencing gardens, inclusive of the vital concepts of animism and spirit.

Teiji Itoh reminds us that "gardens were first and foremost of the spiritual world."[2] Aesthetic, historical, and sociocultural conceptions of and approaches to the study of gardens, while compelling, ought not overshadow the spiritual 〖霊的な面, *reiteki na men*〗. Our contemplative study of the ongoing life of the Temple of the Heavenly Dragon revealed the specific manners in which the pond garden is conceptualized as a physical manifestation of beliefs and behaviors conditioned by several religious traditions through which spirit largely is experienced. Consider the concept of *mononoke* 〖物の怪〗, meaning "spirit of things." Often envisioned as malevolent forces nowadays, especially in contemporary *anime*, earlier animistic conceptions of *mononoke* emphasized the vitalism of life as an aspect

old. Surface as well as excavated sites along the Kada Gona River in Ethiopia reveal numerous intentionally flaked fragments of mostly quartzite stone as well as stones themselves appearing to have been used as tools.[12] Fossilized remains of a hominin named *Australopithecus garhi* were found in association with these early stones used as tools from Ethiopia. Stones used as tools found in association with the earliest fossilized species of our *Homo* genus, *Homo habilis*, date to around 2.5 million years ago. These stones used as tools, the Oldowan tool tradition, continue to be unearthed in the Olduvai Gorge area in present-day Tanzania, East Africa, as well as around Lake Turkana in Kenya. A prevalent Oldowan tool was rounded "core" stones most likely used for killing then breaking the bones of animals. The fist-sized stones were used to strike sharp-edged flakes from quartzite, which then most likely were used to dismember animals and to break open the marrow of bones.

Around 1.7 million years ago, the Achulean stone-tool tradition began to appear at Olduvai Gorge in association with the fossilized remains of *Homo erectus* hominids. Selected quartzite stones used as tools were chipped on both sides to produce a symmetrical (bifacial) cutting edge. Tear-drop in shape, better fitting the human hand, these sharpened stones were used as tools to kill then butcher fairly large animals. The Achulean stone-tool tradition remained fairly constant for some 800,000 years and, along with the Oldowan tradition of stone tools, enabled migration out of Africa and subsequent human survival in varied geographical regions of the world.

Around 300,000 years ago, the Mousterian tool tradition began to appear in what we know as northern Africa, the Near East, and in Europe. Relatively small, very sharp flakes primarily were struck from quartzite. These (Levalloisian) flakes then were used as spear points, as scrapers for tanning animal hides, and, most likely, for making holes for sewing shoes, clothing, bedding, and carrying-sacks. Traditions of stones used as tools continued to be of survival importance for humanity until the advent of primary dependence on

horticulture and agriculture—anticipating the next relevant historic
and prehistoric event in our conclusion.

A Walk to the Garden

Teiji Itoh's conclusion that gardens, the gardens of Japan, first and
foremost were "of the spiritual world" is telling, and is important in
a more comprehensive respect. *Extended to humanity as a whole*, the
primordial idea as well as the phenomenon of "garden," in particular gardens of stone, can be seen as participating in spirit—in life.

The pond garden aspect of the Temple of the Heavenly Dragon
preserves in stone ancient ideas of materiality as embodiment of spirit.
The pond garden privileges stones, and compositions of stone. And,
as we have seen, human culture has a deep temporal familiarity with
stones. In this often taken-for-granted respect, privileging stones as
it does, the pond garden is a compelling physical manifestation and
reminder of a primordial idea of garden—the archaic idea of garden as
composed principally with stones rather than foliage.

Our earliest recorded idea of garden envisions stones as participating animistically in spirit/life. The nature and character of the
pond garden aspect of the Temple of the Heavenly Dragon leads us
deeper into prehistory to a human-wide primordial idea of garden-as-
spirit/life, embodied as stones.

The priest reminded us to not stop our experiences of the landscape aspect of the temple with things themselves, to not stop contemplation while lingering amid the pond in the garden. Echoing our
introductory walk through the temple to the pond garden, to conclude our study let us briefly walk *through* our experiences of the
beautiful pond garden aspect of the Temple of the Heavenly Dragon
to a deeper, primal idea of garden itself.

Conventionally, "garden" is conceptualized as a horticultural
phenomenon. One's conventional mental image of garden reflexively
brings to mind the horticultural—flower gardens, plant gardens, vegetable and herb gardens, and the like . . . as garden. This pervasive

idea of garden-as-horticulture can be attached to human dependence on cultivated/domesticated plants dating to 11,000–9,000 B.C. in various geographical regions of the world. For our purposes, let us consider several formative conceptualizations of garden within the context of the "Fertile Crescent" arena encompassing present-day southern Turkey, western Iran, and northern Iraq.

About six thousand years ago, Sumerians began to occupy the southern portion of present-day Iraq. The intensive cultivation/domestication of plants supported the advent of sedentary urban life within walled cities such as Unu (Uruk in Akkadian, present-day Tel al Warka).

Two Sumerian narratives and primal conceptualizations of garden are relevant here. The *Epic of Gilgamesh*, composed in cuneiform characters incised on tablets of clay, dates to ca. 2000 B.C. though scholars conclude that this written narrative recorded older orally transmitted narratives. The cuneiform characters for *The Huluppu Tree*, secondly, a narrative pertaining to Inanna, date to ca. 1750 BC. Inanna was related to Gilgamesh in that both were descended from, shared divinity with, a mating of the sky-deity An and the earth-goddess Ki. (Ninsun, a deity, was Gilgamesh's mother while Lugalbanda, the third king of Uruk, was Gilgamesh's father. Ningal, a deity, was the mother of Inanna while Nanna, a deity, was the father of Inanna.) Inanna was the sister-in-law of Gilgamesh through her mating with Dumuzi Tammuz, the brother of Gilgamesh. Uruk was the patron city of both Inanna and Gilgamesh.

The Huluppu Tree and *The Epic of Gilgamesh* to date contain our earliest written descriptions, conceptions, of garden. Let us consider the idea of garden within *The Huluppu Tree*, then the description of a somewhat earlier garden in "The Search for Everlasting Life" within *The Epic of Gilgamesh*.

Inanna, and the Idea of Garden

Inanna was Queen of Heaven and Earth and her palace, the House of Heaven [E'Anna], remains one of the oldest preserved temples in present-day Tel al Warka. Inanna was an embodiment of the Morning and Evening Star (Venus), and she "was responsible for the growth of plants and animals and fertility in humankind."¹³ Cuneiform characters tell us that "gardens flourished luxuriantly" within and around Inanna's House of Heaven.¹⁴ We read of a petition to deities that "in the gardens, may the lettuce and cress grow high" amid "the lush gardens and orchards, the green reeds and trees."¹⁵ The idea of garden here, in association with the innovation of intensive agricultural traditions in early Mesopotamia, most likely is the earliest archetype of our conventional idea of garden as flora, cultivated plants, and source of domesticated food.

The Huluppu Tree begins with Inanna engaged in an act of cultivation/domestication of plants, in association with this early conception of garden as a horticultured phenomenon. "In the first days, in the very first days," we read, "at that time, a tree, a single tree, a huluppu-tree [most likely a date palm, or willow tree] was planted by the banks of the Euphrates. The tree was nurtured by the waters of the Euphrates. The Whirling South Wind arose, pulling at its roots and ripping at its branches, until the waters of the Euphrates carried it away. A woman who walked in fear of the word of the Sky God, An, who walked in fear of the word of the Air God, Enilil, plucked the tree from the River and spoke: 'I shall bring this tree to Uruk. I shall plant this tree in my holy garden [my italics].' Inanna cared for the tree with her hand. She settled the earth around the tree with her foot."¹⁶ Inanna rescues a tree, resurrecting then physically bringing primal nature within the realm of her cultivated garden.¹⁷ We are not told the origin and character of Inanna's garden, though deities are mentioned by way of association with her horticultured landscape. Her garden is referred to as holy (participating in divinity), and Inanna herself by birth also participates in divinity.

The Huluppu Tree emphasizes people as an aspect of garden, as Inanna invests the energy of her own (divine) body in the cultivation of the tree. The primal idea of garden here is the generative interplay

of nature, people (a female presence), and divinity within a horticultured setting.

Gilgamesh, and the Idea of Garden

The historical Gilgamesh was the fifth king of Uruk. With the death
of his companion Enkidu, Gilgamesh began to venture far outside the
walls of Uruk in search of the secret of immortality.[18] The trials of Gilgamesh eventually led him to the Mountains of Mashu, where he was
confronted by guardian beings "half man and half dragon [dragons-as-
guardians, see pp. 80–82]."[19] After seeing his great intent and will, the
dragon guardians "opened the gate of the mountain" and permitted
Gilgamesh to pass (mountains associated with deities; dragon guardians; a 'gate' through which one must pass; intent, and will—there
are startling correspondences between *The Epic of Gilgamesh* and the
priest's conception of aspects of Zen training in association with aspects of the pond garden—see especially pp. 279–85).[20] After passing
through the gate-of-the-mountain, a toilsome path led Gilgamesh to
the Garden of the Sun. "This was the garden of the gods," we read,
"all round him stood bushes bearing gems. Seeing it he went down at
once, for there was fruit of carnelian with the vine hanging from it,
beautiful to look at; lapis lazuli leaves hung thick with fruit, sweet to
see. For thorns and thistles there were hematite and rare stones, agate,
and pearls from the sea."[21] Inanna's garden was horticultured. The
more distant (spatially; temporally earlier) *extant* garden experienced
by her brother-in-law was an *in situ* garden . . . of stones.

The presence of stones in association with an idea of garden thus
appears slightly older than the presence of flora in association with an
idea of garden. The Garden of the Gods in *The Epic of Gilgamesh* was
the garden of a deity—Shamash, the Sun. The Garden of the Sun lay
at a physical (and thus spatiotemporal; experiential) distance from the
realm of urbanizing humans, from Uruk, and from the horticultured
garden of Inanna.

The Garden of the Gods flourished at the edge of a vast sea, the

Waters of Death. The Abyss (see p. 201). The Garden of the Gods bordered, participated in, an even more distant sacred place. Utnapishtim the Faraway lived on the far side of the waters of The Abyss, in Dilmun (held to be present-day Bahrain). Gilgamesh meant to venture into Dilmun to seek out Utnapishtim, who had been granted immortality by the gods after the flood. The Garden of the Gods bordered the human-side of sacred Dilmun—Dilmun, across the Waters of Death, where the Sun (life) forever was born anew.

The idea of garden in *The Epic of Gilgamesh* is of a mid-space, separated by water, between the realm of humans and the realm of deities. The Garden of the Sun, a primal garden of stones, participated in the divinity of Shamash . . . as did the stones themselves. The garden of Inanna, a garden of flora, participated in the divinity of the Queen of Heaven and Earth. Akin to the pond within the Temple of the Heavenly Dragon, here "garden," the Garden of the Sun, is a hierophany—a meeting place of people, nature, and deities (or, in the case of Japanese Rinzai Zen Buddhism, venerated ancestors).

The Garden of the Sun was composed of stones. On Tablet IX of *The Epic of Gilgamesh*, several of the stones comprised in the Garden of the Sun are mentioned by name: agate; carnelian; hematite (in his hymn to stones, *Stones of the Sky*, Pablo Neruda interestingly envisions a place where "agate and carnelian and sparkle replaced sap and wood").[22] These comparatively hard and faceted stones tell us the colors and textures of the Garden of the Sun, the very name of which evokes ever-present movements of variegated light. Iron oxides are prevalent aspects of carnelian and hematite and would have given the Garden of the Sun a golden, reddish quality varying in hue with the movements of sunlight. Agate and carnelian are microcrystalline stones and would have glistened and glinted in sunlight. Carnelian is translucent and agate, within the chalcedony family of stones, is vibrantly striped and banded. These stones, in addition to pearls, would have given a rich shimmering quality of depth to experiences of the Garden of the Sun. The colors and textures of the Garden of the Sun would have been quite effervescent, in contrast with the subtle earth-tone colors and muted textures of Inanna's garden of foliage.

Sumerians associated lapis lazuli with Venus, and therefore with Inanna. In *The Huluppu Tree*, we read of Inanna being "outfitted . . . with lapis lazuli diadem" and of her tying "small lapis lazuli beads around her neck."[23] Lapis lazuli (stone-of-azure) is a rich deep blue in color, and opaque. The mineral lazurite compacts under the pressures of the earth, and aggregates of lapis lazuli often are formed with intricate spiderweb veins of lighter-colored trace minerals of calcite and pyrite. *The Epic of Gilgamesh* frequently mentions "rare stones" such as lapis lazuli, as in Sumer there was "very little stone and timber" apart from imported stone and timber.[24] The presence of rare stones such as lapis lazuli within the Garden of the Gods is another sign of divinity as an aspect of this early idea of garden.

We recall that Mirei Shigemori, writing of his experiences within the garden aspect of the Temple of the Heavenly Dragon, felt that "the water of the pond is lapis [lapis lazuli] and the exceedingly beautiful stones in the pond are beyond compare."[25] The pond garden within the Temple of the Heavenly Dragon as well as the Garden of the Sun both were experienced as beautiful, "sweet to see," in association with lapis lazuli.

The Garden of the Sun presumably was described further on Tablet IX of *The Epic of Gilgamesh*. Tablet IX, though, is damaged at this point of description of specific stones composing the Garden of the Sun.

The advent of human dependence on cultivated/domesticated plants, the material basis for our conventional idea of garden-as-horticulture, is comparatively recent. Rather than flora, the defining presence of stones is the *leitmotif* of the more archaic idea of garden in *The Epic of Gilgamesh*—as well as of the pond garden aspect of the Temple of the Heavenly Dragon.

"JUST AS BEFORE"

Myriad stones appear to float on water
    softened by a shimmering late afternoon haze,
    caressing the pond.
The garden
    is a mosaic of water and stones, foliage and sky,
experienced as . . .
tranquillity.

The initial lines of this book foreshadow the significance of the long experience of human familiarity with, dependence upon, and un-doubted veneration of stones. The gardens of Japan traditionally have been composed around stones, embellished by landscapes of foli-age. Without animistic awareness of garden as embodiment of spirit, though, one is left with an idolatrous experience of stones—one "sees" only form and shadow . . . akin to the captives of illusion in Plato's cave; in Buddhist terms, one will mistake the finger pointing at the moon for the moon.[1]

The significance of the gardens of Japan does not stop *at* the gardens of Japan. With Tenryū-ji.

The intricate pond garden aspect of Tenryū-ji, an eminent gar-den composed around revered stones embellished by landscapes of foliage and water and sky, preserves and remains a still-compelling reminder of our earliest conception of a garden.[2] Contemplative study of the Temple of the Heavenly Dragon has revealed that, indeed, gar-dens first and foremost are of the spiritual world. In and of itself, a garden is a sacred space and place.

We began our experiences together, here, seated before the pond garden aspect of Tenryū-ji, the Temple of the Heavenly Dragon. Throughout our study, perhaps the garden began to disassemble into archetypal ideas, beautifully pregnant shapes and architectured forms, interpretive meanings, myth and legend, and sociocultural belief and practice. Through our experiences here, perhaps the garden became something other than itself.

In his poem "Bamboo Garden," Musō gently returns us to "this garden continuing in its green shade . . . just as before."[3] As we rise, the pond garden continues as *shinnyo*, as "suchness." . . .

> . . . just as before.
> The garden,
> again,
>   is a garden.

ENDNOTES

Notes for photograph captions correspond to their respective figure numbers and appear at the end of the Endnotes.

THE POND IN THE GARDEN

1. The current address of the temple is 68 Saga, Suskinobaba-chō, Ukyōku, Kyōto-shi.
2. Itoh (1983:28). Influential studies of the gardens of Japan for the most part remain overview presentations of the history of gardening in Japan. Specific gardens routinely are presented as apt examples illustrating general principles and characteristics of garden design or to exemplify phases in the history of gardening in Japan. We know little about the life-history of individual gardens, with notable exceptions (Berthier and Parkes 2000, on Ryōan-ji; Covell and Yamada 1974, on Daitoku-ji; Davidson 2007, on Saihō-ji). Case studies of individual gardens, after the fashion of case studies in law and medicine, remain rare. It is hoped that this book will stimulate intensive studies of individual gardens, especially gardens of influence.
3. Günter Nitschke (1987) elaborates upon affecting spaces such as these as architectured "places of stillness." See also the elegant book by Carver (1955) as well as Inoue's (1985) excellent study, *Space in Japanese Architecture*.
4. On *karesansui* see especially Casalis (1983), Kawase (1968),

and Yoshikawa (1971).
5. Minakami (1976:69).
6. Harvey (2006:xi).
7. Minakami, 74. Hunt (1975), Matsubayashi (1992), and Vatsyayan (1991) give cross-cultural examples and nuanced interpretations of the concept of *genius loci* (spirit of place).
8. Minakami, 68.
9. There is increasing reconceptualization of the concept of animism, an otherwise pejorative and immutable hierarchy-maintaining negative concept in particular associated with the unilineal evolutionalism of Edward Burnett Tylor and Robert Ranulph Marrett (cf. especially *Animism: Respecting the Living World*, Graham Harvey's critique and intricate reconception of animism). Animism in the main was coined negatively to disassociate the "rationality" of "civilized" societies from colonized societies deemed "primitive" "who could not or did not distinguish correctly between objects and subjects, or between things and persons. The new animism names worldviews and lifeways in which people seek to know how they might respectfully and properly engage with other persons . . . human and other-than-human" (Harvey 2006:xiv). As such, approached from ideas embedded within the term itself rather than the sordid intellectual history of the use, the misuse, of the term (cf.

William McDoughall's *Body and Mind: A History and Defense of Animism* for a thorough history of the idea of animism), I find the concept of animism quite useful to the interpretation of gardens. *Anima*, the (feminine) Latin root of animism, meant life/being with a connotation of spirit associated with breath/breathing-as-life. *Anima* is a verb, rather than a noun. Far from early pejorative misuses of *anima*, contemporary embrace of the primal meaning of *anima*/animism by theorists such as Mikhail Bakhtin (1981), Linda Hogan (1995a, 1995b), and David Young and Jean-Guy Goulet (1994) is an important resurrection of an important concept. For our purposes here, animism is useful as a conceptualization of life as an aspect of the idea of garden. Life is much more comprehensive a phenomenon than that which is confined to and/or limited by dualisms such as the present polar distinction between, say, organic/inorganic (cf. Lynn Margulis and Dorian Sagan's *What is Life?* for a critique of this distinction) where life is deemed the exclusive property of the category "organic." As well, reconceptualization of animism importantly places emphasis on the reality of spirit as an aspect of life. The concept of animism therefore encourages us not to blithely dismiss as "confused thinking" ongoing cross-cultural realities such as "stones that grow" (see p. 293).

10 Armstrong (1971:43).

11 Contemplative experience of gardens is an epistemology, what I coin as *Niwadō* (庭道, Way of Garden). Prolonged involvement with gardens is as meditative and consciousness-raising as is taking up of the Way of Tea (*Chadō*), the Way of Softness (*Jūdō*), or the Way of the Sword (*Kendō*). The suffix -*dō* (道) is attached to these various Ways of knowing and doing. Each is a path, a method, and a state of becoming aware of existential stillness amid the apparent swirl of the world. To take up the Way of the Sword, though, one is not expected to design then forge and temper metal blades. Both the Sumerian Garden of the Sun and the pond garden within the Temple of the Heavenly Dragon were not constructed by those experiencing the gardens. Gilgamesh did not fashion the Garden of the Sun and the priest did not fashion the pond garden within the temple; yet, both incorporated a garden as an aspect, a Way, of their lives. To take up the Way of Garden, one is not expected to construct a garden—except, possibly, one's own life as garden. In the conclusion of *Candide*, François Marie Arouet (Voltaire) has Pangloss declare that "all events are linked together in the best of possible worlds . . . " "That is very well put," Candide replies, weary of words, but " . . . we must cultivate our garden" (Adams 1966:77). Consider an interpretation of this well-known passage: one can "cultivate" one's being-as-garden

(Musō's "excellent people"). The pond in the temple declares that gardens, and people, do not exist autonomously; as such, cultivating one's garden also involves cultivating (as do Bodhisattvas) the garden that is each and every person. In his masterful work *Gardens: An Essay on the Human Condition*, Robert Pogue Harrison (2008:x) agrees:"When Voltaire ends *Candide* with the famous dictum '*Il faut cultiver notre jardin . . .*' the emphasis on cultivation is essential. We must seek out healing or redemptive forces and allow them to grow in us. That is what it means to tend our garden . . . *Notre jardin* is never a garden of merely private concerns . . . " An aspect of the Way of Garden, then, is compassionate interdependent relationship (see also Johnson 2010).

12 Neruda (1970:17).

13 Moir and Merritt (1977:142). See also Nakane's (1970a) reflection on the "Character of Japanese Gardens."

14 On page five (personal communication) of a translation by Christian Tschumi of Mirei Shigemori's review of the *Book of Garden* (*Sakuteiki*; see Tschumi and Saito 2005 and Takei and Keane 2001).

15 *Turning the Wheel: Essays on Buddhism and writing*, by Charles Johnson (2003), is a fine meditation on the manner in which creative processes mirror aspects of Buddhism such as mindfulness, dependent co-arising, and *sangha*.

16 Armstrong (1971:83).

17 Autret et al. (1987).

18 *The Art of Setting Stones*, by Marc Peter Keane (2002), is a model for researching, writing about, and presenting gardens of Japan. In humanistic fashion the book combines first-person narratives of on-site research and physical work within gardens, lyrical descriptions of the author's emotions as affected by gardens, historical and cross-cultural perspectives, as well as the author's exceptionally fine drawings illustrating aspects of gardens (see Johnson 2010).

PART I: LAND, LANDSCAPE, AND THE SPIRIT OF PLACE

1 Ōta (1991:62).

2 On this conception of "temple" see Fox (1988:105–29), Johnson (1989), and Turner (1979). Davidson (2007:69–79) provides an in-depth overview discussion of this vital concept of *ma*, while Pilgrim (1986) discusses *ma* within religion and aesthetics. See Fujimori (1990), Hayakawa (1984:144–73), and Morse (1972:234–46) on the importance of the veranda to the subtle generation of an "interval" (*ma*) space resulting from the architectured interrelationship of interior and exterior.

3 Research for and the writing of Part I in particular was informed by Ōta et al. (1967), Horiguchi (1977, 1963), Mori (1960:87–103), Naramoto (1978, 1976), Seki (1976), Minakami and Seki (1976), Shigemori (1936–39:2,2), and Tatsui (1939). Works in

English informing the research for and writing of Part I in particular include Collcutt (1982, 1981), Hall (1983), Hall and Takeshi (1977), Hayakawa (1984), Itoh (1985), Kuck (1968:113–24, 1940:85–100), Kuitert (1988:28–99), Mass (1997, 1982, 1979), Schaarschmidt-Richter and Mori (1979), and Slawson (1985).

CHAPTER 1: MOUNTAINS, WATER, AND FRAGRANT TREES

1 George Sansom (1958:99) underscores the point that "certainly superstitious dread had a great part in the decision to change to a new site; and after diviners and geomancers had been consulted . . . work was begun on the new capital."

2 The interpretation here of landscape *feng shui* in particular was informed by Feuchtwang (1974), Hay (1983), and Potter (1970). In Dynastic China at the time there was a Form School and a Compass School (*Kanyu*, Chariot of Heaven and Earth, was an earlier name for the Compass School) of Wind/Water, both of which influenced the siting and spatial layout of Buddhist temples in Japan.

3 Sansom (1958:212). George Sansom (212) adds "scarcely any action could be taken by a Fujiwara nobleman in his public or private life without consulting the oracles—the verdicts of astrologers or geomancers or necromancers or other practitioners of the science of divination and

prophecy."

4 Skinner (1982:9).

5 Higuchi (1988:146–47). Also, see Critchlow (1980:221–22) and Zuritsky (1986). The Mountain of Storms is a prominent feature of Kyōto's white tiger range of mountains "balanced" locally by the emphasis on dragons at Tenryū-ji.

6 On the architectonics of Kyōto, see Ponsonby-Fane (1956:129), Sadler (1962:60–63), and Hayashiya and Nelson (1977:15–36).

7 Morris (1964:28).

8 Morris, 18–19.

9 According to Chamberlain (1981:26), *Yamato* (人和) for instance early meant "place-between-mountains" / "mountain gate." The early word for Japan participated in a specific feature of what later, and generically, would be termed "nature" (自然, *shizen*). On the genesis of concepts of nature in Japan, see Tellenbach and Kimura (1989). See Berque (1986), Bruun and Kalland (1992), and Shaner (1989) for studies of concepts of nature in Japan.

10 Critchlow (1980:220).

11 Higuchi (1988:153).

12 See Arthur Waley (1960, 1925) for authoritative translations of the *Tale of Genji*. The Grand Shrine at Ise is organized around two principal arenas: an Inner Shrine (*Naiku*) area devoted to the sun-deity Amaterasu-ō-mi-Kami (from whom emperors are believed descended), and an Outer Shrine (*Geku*) area devoted to Toyuke-no-ō-Kami,

a deity historically associated with bounteous harvests of rice (cf. also Kuroda 1981, Tange and Kawazoe 1965, and Watanabe 1974:11–84).

13 In addition see Blacker (1975:127–39), Hori (1975), Schafer (1973:11–15), and Tonomura (1997) on female shamans.

14 See Aston (1972,1:48–50), Ono (1962:51–52), and Picken (1980:49–56) on varieties of traditional Shintō purification by water (潔斎, kessai; 禊, misogi;御祓い, oharai).

15 Waley (1960:192).

16 Waley, 194.

17 Tanizaki (1993:80–81).

18 The present-day Forest Temple continues to be associated with fecundity. The still-pervasive legend is that Lady Tachibana was barren until she prayed for children within her Buddhist complex. Subsequently, she gave birth to the future Emperor Ninmyō (reigned 833 to 850). See Paul (1985) for an interesting study of females within Buddhism.

19 Anesaki (1963:67).

20 Lyons and Peters (1985:6). On the Rinzai Zen Buddhist concept of Original Face refer to Cleary (1978), Hisamatsu (1982), and Schloegl (1976, 1975).

21 Lyons and Peters (1985:6).

22 Eliade and Couliano (1991:28). See also The Teaching of Buddha, published by the Society for the Promotion of Buddhism (Bukkyo Dendo Kyokai; 1966). For comprehensive overviews of Mahāyāna Buddhism see Corless (1989), Hirakawa (1990), and Wil-

liams (1989).

23 Chan (1963:126). Pivotal moments in the life of Shākyamuni occurred within nature: the garden within which he was born; the fig tree in Bodhi Gaya under which he was "awakened"; Deer Park, where he delivered his first sermon; the hills near Vaisali where, it is held, he passed away.

24 Fischer-Schreiber et al. (1991:263). Cleary (1978), Hisamatsu (1982), and Schloegl (1976, 1975) especially influenced this interpretation of the Rinzai vision of Zen Buddhism.

25 Yoshioka (1984:113).

26 Conze (1982:114).

27 The Pali "Three Baskets" (Tripitaka) are the Higher Knowledge or Special Teachings Basket (philosophical writings, with emphasis on the life of Buddha), the Discourse Basket (focusing on Dharma, the teachings of Buddha, and Sangha), and the Discipline Basket (with emphasis on the monastic community).

28 Anesaki (1963:68).

29 A major reconstruction of Danrin-ji occurred in 1964.

30 Shigemori (1936–39:2,2:44–45).

31 Shigemori, 44. The "grass house" most likely was an early form of detached palace. Ivan T. Morris (1964:26) tells us "there were several detached palaces outside the Greater Imperial Palace. It was here that Imperial consorts were lodged during confinements, which, according to Shintō beliefs, would have made the imperial residence ritually unclean. Sometimes the Emperors themselves were obliged

to move to these outside palaces, since their own buildings had the unfortunate habit of burning down at frequent intervals."

32 Shigemori (1936–39:2,2:45).

33 Teiji Itoh (1983:25) adds that perhaps Turtle Mountain also was experienced as "*shinsentō* 〖神仙島〗, an unearthly mountain island in a mythical sea." This conclusion in turn evokes the Chinese Daoist idea of Hōrai, the mountain paradise surrounded by impenetrable seas, home to the Immortals. Kameyama (1249–1305), a son of Go-Saga, was so affected by Turtle Mountain (*Kameyama*) that he took his name with respect to the mountain.

34 Itoh (1983:25).

35 See Chamberlain (1981:lxii).

36 For comprehensive overviews of *kami* see Holtom (1940), Hori (1969), Kitagawa (1980), Muraoka (1988), and Ono (1962). On historical conceptions of spaces/ places especially deemed participating in *kami* see also Anesaki (1963:41–43), Kato and Hanayama (1988), and Picken (1994, 1980).

37 Shigemori (1936–39:2,2:45).

38 Itoh (1983:25).

39 Frederic (1972:27–28). Ivan Morris (1964:34) elaborates upon "the murkiness of their houses. Women in particular lived in a state of almost perpetual twilight."

40 Shigemori (1936–39:2,2:48).

41 McCullough (1990:6–7).

42 See Shigemori (1936–39:2,2:47).

43 Frederic (1972:106–7).

44 Ōta (1967:110).

45 Itoh (1983:26).

46 Shigemori (1936–39:2,2:48). This type of Heian-period (794–1185) pond often is classified as *chisen shūyu shiki* (池泉周遊式), a garden pond for boating.

47 Shigemori, 47.

48 McCullough (1990:32).

49 Mosher (1964:29).

50 Takeda (1993:27). See also Blacker (1975:208–34).

51 Yoshifumi (1993:48).

52 Shigemori (1936–39:2,2:46).

CHAPTER 2: DEATH, DREAM, AND THE GENESIS OF A TEMPLE

1 Sansom (1961:16).

2 Sansom, 43.

3 Sansom, 61.

4 The Three Treasures are a mirror (*Yata no Kagami*), a sword (*Kusanagi no Tsurugi*), and jewels (*Yasakani no Magatama*). The Three Treasures are emblems of the Divine Right of an emperor to rule by virtue of believed descent from Heavenly Kami. Heavenly Kami presented the Three Treasures to Ninigi, grandson of Amaterasu-ō-mi-Kami. The mirror carried by Ninigi, in particular, is said to rest on a sheltered post at the center of the Inner Shrine at Ise (see Aston 1972,1:177–78). On the Three Treasures and the Regalia, see Sansom (1961:9).

5 Primary writings on Musō Kokushi are Cleary (1996), Collcutt (1981, 1977), Davidson (2007), Hayakawa (1984:62–69), Kino (1978), Kraft (1981), Merwin and Shigematsu (1989, 1987), Tamamura (1958), and Tatsui (1942).

6 Priests often conducted esoteric practices behind screens, literally out of sight of the uninitiated.

7 Sadler (1962:115–16).

8 Seki (1976:82).

9 Davidson (2007:25).

10 Davidson, 26.

11 Ikeda (1976:12).

12 Lyons and Peters (1985:6).

13 Davidson (2007:36).

14 Periodic "wandering about to test and settle his insight" was expected of monks such as Musō (Schloegl, 1976:8). See also Keir Davidson's (2007:15–51) fine account of this period of Musō's life.

15 Kraft (1981:90).

16 Sekida (1975:102–3).

17 Davidson (2007:37).

18 Sekida (1975:99).

19 Sekida, 150.

20 Sekida, 158–59.

21 Musō's *satori* poem ("*Tōki no Ge*"), in Merwin and Shigematsu (1989:120). See Merwin and Shigematsu (1987:25) and Davidson (2007:38) for slightly varying translations of this important poem.

22 Sekida (1975:29).

23 Sekida, 12.

24 Sekida, 95.

25 Kraft (1981:90).

26 Merwin and Shigematsu (1989:64).

27 Association with Musō was attractive to the emperor owing to Musō's noble birth. Musō was descended from Genji and also by birth was related to the Ashikaga (as a maternal great-grandson of the daughter of Yoriuji Ashikaga, 1189–1254).

28 In the dream of Tadayoshi, the linkage of dragons and emperors to carriages in the sky corresponds to dynastic Chinese legend and lore. The birth of Emperor Wu (156–87 BC) of the Han Dynasty (207 BC–AD 220) "was heralded by a dream in which his father saw a red fog descend from the clouds into the palace and enter the Exalted Fragrance Corridor . . . a cinnabar-colored vapour arose and curled itself dragon-wise in the rafters" (Huxley 1979:30).

29 Sansom (1958:215). On "hungry ghosts," see also Masaharu Anesaki (1933:75–80).

30 Sansom (1961:99).

31 Sansom, 100.

32 Collcutt (1981:104).

33 Yi-fu Tuan (1979:6) perceptively observed that "landscape is a construct of the mind as well as a physical and measurable entity. 'Landscapes of fear' refers both to psychological states and to tangible environments."

34 Kraft (1981:81).

35 Tsunoda et al. (1958:254).

36 de Visser (1913:166).

37 de Visser, 167.

38 Chamberlain (1981:2–3).

39 See Cleary (1996), Foster et al. (1996), and Kraft (1981) on Musō's "dream conversations."

40 Minakami (1976:69). Helen Craig McCullough (1990:342) adds that "many times in China and Japan, when there was need of a virtuous sovereign, a wise counselor, or a man skilled in making war, a monk was returned to the world or a retired monarch was set upon the throne. So Chia Tao the Hermit of the Waves

[a T'ang dynasty poet] left the cloister to be a servant of the court, and Temmu and Koken of our country gave up their holy retirement to sit upon the throne. Which is best for the sake of the state; that as an abbot I should dwell in a retired valley on Mount Hiei, or that as the chief of His Majesty's military government I should keep peace in all the realm?"

41 de Visser (1913:154). Ryūjin was a *kami* dragon associated with female ascetics, shamans, and mystics (see Blacker 1975). In early Japan, Shinto shrines often were dedicated to dragon *kami*.

42 In the *Chronicles of Japan*, Izanami-no-mikoto gives birth to the deity Kagutsuchi (*kami* of fire), then dies. Out of grief over the death of his sister, Izanagi-no-mikoto cuts the newborn deity into three pieces. Blood dripping from the sword of Izanagi changed into three *kami*, one of which was a goddess in the form of a snake-dragon (*okami*). Though embodiments of fecundity, dragons in Japan were born amid violence and blood.

43 Aston (1972, 2:248–49).

44 Huxley (1979:28).

45 Huxley, 30.

46 Allen and Griffiths (1979:42–43). De Visser (1913:10) adds that "in the fifth week after reaching perfect Enlightenment, the Buddha went to Lake Mucilinda, and the *Naga* of the same name, who resided there, came out of the water and with his coils and hoods shielded [Shākyamuni] from the rain for seven days."

Dragons also have long accompanied, protected, and been associated with Buddhist priests. For instance, "a blue dragon appeared to the Tendai priest Eisai, when in 1168 he ascended the Chinese T'ai [T'ai shan, in China]" (de Visser 1913:193). See Munsterberg (1971) for an overview of images of dragons in Dynastic China.

47 Huxley (1979:30).

48 McCullough (1990:378).

49 de Visser (1913:225).

50 de Visser, 180.

51 Seki (1976:86).

52 *Kami* often came to people through dreams, and dreams thus came to be considered messengers of *kami* (see Blacker 1975:37). Ivan T. Morris (1964:14) elaborates upon "the great network of superstitious fears—the belief in avenging ghosts, in possession by living spirits." See Dorson (1962), McAlpine and McAlpine (1958), and Piggott (1983) on historical conceptions of ghosts and spirits.

CHAPTER 3: CLOUDS OF
FLOWERS PRESERVE THE WAY

1 On correspondences in the design of Chinese and Japanese Buddhist temples, see especially Collcutt (1981:172–82), Paine and Soper (1955:377–405), and Wheatley (1971:411–76). Lessa (1968:17) underscores the very important conclusion that "correspondence has great significance . . . for the Chinese it replaces the idea of causality." Here, dynastic Chinese theory

negated dualism, in that iconic (image) correspondence was sympathetic influence—congruence with respect to form was considered a physical manifestation of what we would term a metaphysical connection and influence.

2 The architecture here was the Zen Style (唐様, *Karayō*), from China.

3 The site of the original mountain gate (*Sanmon*) is to the west of present-day entrance gates (*Honmon*; *Chokushimon*; fig. 6). People not members of the *sangha* originally were required to approach the complex indirectly, as "the medieval Zen monastery was not open to casual entrance" (Collcutt 1981:190). These present-day public outer gates were not among the original seven central structures of the complex.

4 In a note to me, Marc P. Keane concludes that this bridge and small pond most likely materialized a division of the profane ("outer" world) and the sacred ("inner" world of the temple).

5 Collcutt (1981:206).

6 Morris (1964:202).

7 See Collcutt (1981:171–220). Robert Lawlor (1980:33) adds "architecture means in Greek 'the way or method of structuring what is archetypal.'" See also Johnson (1988), Jung (1980:3–41; 275–89) and Marc (1977) on architecture approached via the concept of archetype.

8 See Mountain (1982), Preston (1988), and van de Wetering (1974) for interesting studies

of Zen Buddhist temples as environments.

9 Nishimura, Satō, and Smith (1973:9).

10 Pilgrim (1981:34).

11 Pilgrim, 33.

12 Correspondence theory, derived from Aristotle, assumes participation; that is, correspondence of shape and/or form was not considered symbolic in our conventional sense of the term "symbol." Correspondence of shape and/or form is one manner in which subtle connection is revealed via what is termed the principle of sympathy, where things of similar form are held by believers to be (invisibly) connected (cf. Barfield 1988, Eco 1986:52–64, and Hay 1983). Correspondences, especially with respect to physical form, direct awareness to synthesis and to other familiar concepts such as ecology and holism.

13 Eliade (1959:162–213), Lawlor (1982), and Snodgrass (1988:353–377) elaborate upon the temple = body: body = temple correspondence. The temple = body: body = temple correspondence appears in a variety of cultures around the world, and appears in many periods throughout human history (see Beck 1976, de Lubicz 1977, Johnson 1988, Paul 1976, and Wheatley 1971:423–36).

14 Pilgrim (1981:33).

15 Sato (1984:171).

16 Grube (1992:187).

17 The words are by Kūkai, in Pilgrim (1981:30).

18 Shaner (1985:58).

19 Merwin and Shigematsu (1989),

especially pp.109–40.

20 Seki (1976:95). Also, see a trans-
    lation by Tatsui (1942:123).

21 Higuchi (1988:26).

22 See Seki (1976:94).

23 Higuchi (1988:26).

24 Higuchi, 26. Higuchi (26) adds
    that "the wall-like mountainside
    was the central feature, from the
    gardener's vantage," emphasiz-
    ing the manner in which the
    Mountain of Storms dominated
    the visual landscape.

25 Higuchi, 60.

26 Itoh (1983:24). Teiji Itoh con-
    cludes that "borrowed scenery"
    did not exist at this site until the
    redesign of the Turtle Mountain
    villa of Go-Saga into a Zen Bud-
    dhist temple complex. "It is even
    possible to think," he says (27),
    "that Arashi-yama could not
    have been seen at all from the
    garden of the Kame-yama Palace
    if the trees in the garden had
    formed a tall enough screen to
    block it from view." The inter-
    relationship of the Mountain of
    Storms and Turtle Mountain is
    subtle, geographically as well as
    historically. Itoh (27) concludes:
    "It was only after the building of
    the Tenryū-ji that Arashiyama
    became an attraction. Kameyama,
    which had once served as an aus-
    picious symbol of an unearthly
    realm, at last faded from promi-
    nence, and Arashiyama, rising
    behind it, dominated the view
    [from the verandas of the Ab-
    bot's Quarters]."

27 Itoh, 15.

28 Davidson (2007:185).

29 Seki (1976:95).

30 Davidson (2007:34) adds that

"over the winter of 1301–2
Soseki apparently spent more
and more time meditating at the
mouth of the small cave . . . looking out over the pool [at Ungan-
ji]." See also Johnson (1999a;
1999b; 1993a; 1993b; 1991b).

31 Tellenbach and Kimura
    (1989:155).

32 Dumoulin (1963:182). Heinrich
    Dumoulin (182) goes on to say
    "inspired by a deep Buddhist
    faith, and in keeping with the
    syncretistic tendencies of his
    time to regard the Japanese kami
    as manifestations of the primal
    Hotoke or Buddha, he [Musō] co-
    ordinated his native Shinto cult
    with Buddhism."

33 Dumoulin, 182.

34 Harada (1985:34). Also, see
    the translation by Shigemori
    (1936–39:2,2:51).

35 Snodgrass (1988:354).

36 Sansom (1961:101).

37 Collcutt (1981:107). See Victoria
    (1997) for, perhaps unexpected,
    accounts of Zen Buddhist par-
    ticipation in warfare.

38 Shigemori (1936–39:2,2:56).

39 Hachimangū, a shrine dedicated
    to Emperor Ōjin (approximately
    201–310).

40 The present-day bridge is not the
    original bridge, though, as rem-
    nants of the original bridge have
    been unearthed about 200 me-
    ters upstream of the present-day
    bridge. Teiji Itoh (1983:27) for
    instance notes that "a map drawn
    in 1426 shows that the Tenryū-ji
    compound extended quite close
    to the river . . . also, at that time,
    the Togetsu Bridge was located
    farther upstream and could be

seen from the compound."

41 Shigemori (1936–39:2,2:52). The bridge still is the destination of pilgrimages in the spring to view cherry trees in bloom on the Mountain of Storms.

42 Itoh (1983:27).

43 Tanizaki (1993:80).

44 Shigemori (1936–39:2,2:46).

45 de Visser (1913:167–68).

46 Merwin and Shigematsu (1989:27).

47 The area for the new pond apparently was layered with chestnut shells. A layer of clay then was laid to render the bottom of the pond area relatively leakproof. The layer of clay filtered sediment and helped to keep the pond water clear. Finally, a layer of sand and gravel appears to then have been laid over the clay.

48 Shigemori (1936–39:2,2:58). *Tsukiyama* (築山) named the mound of earth to the rear of a *chitei* (池庭), or hill-and-water type of garden. See also Davidson (1982:13–30) and Schaarschmidt-Richter and Mori (1979:20–28, 100–110).

49 Shigemori, 58.

50 On the experience of motion as a design aspect of gardens, see Conan (2003) and Johnson (2003).

51 Tatsui (1942:138).

52 Horiguchi (1977:123). See also Naramoto (1976:31).

53 Horiguchi, 123. See also Shigemori (1936–39:2,2:52–54). *Sōgen* perhaps also referenced the Rinzai Zen priest Sōgen (Bukkō Zenji, 1226–86), from China, the founding priest of Engaku-ji in Kamakura.

54 Horiguchi (1977:123).

55 Cf. Kuitert (1988:89).

56 Dumoulin (1990:32). On Rankei Doryū at Saga-in, see Itoh (1985:101–10).

57 Collcutt (1981:66).

58 Ōta (1967:114).

59 Tatsui (1942:138).

60 Seki (1976:80).

61 Itoh (1983:26).

62 Shigemori (1936–39:2,2:49). Yet, Martin Collcutt (1981:183) concludes that "the natural environment was further shaped and refined in the gardens designed by monks like Musō." But Samuel Newsom (Newsom and Shigemori 1988:229) argues that "Musō altered the existing design of and oversaw the reconstruction of the [Tenryū-ji] site." See also Kinsaku Nakane's (1970b) comment on "Zen and Japanese Gardens."

63 Merwin and Shigematsu (1989:162).

64 Merwin and Shigematsu, 162–63.

65 Horiguchi (1977:123).

66 See Johnson (2001).

67 Minakami (1976:68). See Kino (1978:67) for a slightly varying translation of this passage.

68 Yoshioka (1984:45).

69 Dunn (1972:144).

70 Frederic (1972:16). On River-Bank Gardeners and stone-setting priests refer also to Itoh (1985:79–83), Kuitert (1988:132–37), and Schaarschmidt-Richter and Mori (1979:248–58). Sōetsu Yanagi's (1972) beautiful acknowledgment of the unnamed makers of now-celebrated Korean *chanoyu* pottery parallels my effort here to acknowledge the

contribution of the unnamed makers of gardens.

71 Morris (1964:85).

72 McCullough (1990:xx).

73 Consider Keir Davidson's (2007:181) nuanced *homage* to those to whom I refer as The Despised: "These were the experts who knew how to fill in or clean out Kyōto's swampy landscape, survey new garden sites, lay out, dig, and line new ponds and streambeds; who could find, transport, and set up rocks needed for the 'pile-up' arrangements . . . and who provided the plants, labor, management, and tools to create the gardens, whether they did the designing themselves or worked with others . . . their presence on a garden site removed it from the everyday, secular world and gave it to the other-worldly dimension that, even today in some places, is part of the special experience of Japanese gardens."

74 Itoh (1985:80).

75 The name of the person known as Zen'ami is unknown. "Ami" was the generic "pass-name" given to lower-caste persons permitted to labor for higher-caste persons. Despite his skill as a designer of gardens, Zen'ami "was still a social outcast and was required to live in the areas relegated to such people" (Itoh 1985:82). Despite relentless oppression, Zen'ami went on to design still-venerated garden landscapes such as Daijō-in in Nara and the Imperial Palace in Kyōto.

76 Davidson (2007:180).

77 *Ishitate so* (priests who set stones).

78 *Notes on the Making of Gardens (Sakuteiki)* was the most influential of the *zōen hiden sho* (see Keane and Takei 2001 and 1996:37–39). *Notes on the Making of Gardens* would have been of little use for instructions on the actual "making" of a garden—working earth; digging; hauling stones. See Slawson (1985, 1987) for a definitive discussion of the esoteric manuals of gardening.

79 Horiguchi (1963:24).

80 Itoh (1985:103).

81 Tatsui (1939:350).

82 Minakami (1976:68).

83 Itoh (1985:82).

84 Itoh, 104.

85 Itoh, 83.

86 Tsunoda et al. (1958:252).

87 Itoh (1985:184).

88 Merwin and Shigematsu (1989:xx).

89 Collcutt (1981:106).

90 Tsunoda et al. (1958:254).

91 Shigemori (1936–39:2,2:51). Tadahiko Higuchi (1988:56) adds that "in the past a similar situation must have existed at the Tenryū-ji where Mount Arashi, as viewed across Sōgen pond from the garden of the priest's residence, was said to resemble an 'elaborate brocade,' a textured backdrop of sorts. This effect is lost today because the trees in the garden block off from view everything but the top of the mountain."

92 Itoh (1983:27). Also, see the translation by Bokuō Seki (1976:95).

93 Tsunoda et al. (1958:252).

94 See Martin Collcutt (1981:92–119) on the effect of Tenryū-ji on the Five Mountains, and Akamatsu and Yamplonsky (1977) on Zen Buddhism and the Gozan system.

95 Shigemori (1936–39:2,2:51).

96 Hamaguri Gomon no Sen, the Hamaguri Gomon Incident within the Kinmon War (Kinmon no Hen). This section was paraphrased from Bokuō Seki's (1976:97–100) dramatic, moving account of the Incident.

97 Seki (1976:97).

98 Seki, 97.

99 Naramoto (1978:114).

100 The present-day *Kuri* and *Dai Hōjō* date from rebuildings in 1899, while the latest rebuilding of the *Ko Hōjō* occurred in 1924.

101 Mirei Shigemori (1936–39:2,2:53) brings us to our consideration of the present-day pond garden in reminding us that "in the *Tsuki-yama Teizo Den* [*Story of Making Artificial Hills*], this garden was mentioned as a noted garden. . . . All of these aspects of the temple landscape are the same as the present landscape. The Tenryū-ji garden has been preserved, in spite of the devastations of the temple."

102 Several other researchers also have been invited to live periodically within Tenryū-ji, enabling a firsthand study of the pond garden (cf. Merwin and Shigematsu 1989; Sawyers 1985).

PART II: A GARDEN IN GREEN SHADE

1 Yoshioka (1984:13).

2 The words of "the priest," as I will refer to him, were transcribed into English from taped conversations then edited for readability. To protect the priest's privacy, his name is not revealed. I do not know the views on or interpretations, if at all, of the pond garden held by other priests at Tenryū-ji. People invariably directed me to the senior priest with whom I was permitted to study, with respect to a consensus concerning his singular knowledge of the garden. In no uncertain words, though, the priest told me not to attempt to speak with monks (*unsui*) in training.

The hermeneutics of this book emphasize inclusion of first-person narratives in writing about landscapes, a methodology in particular influenced by Wilhelm Dilthey (Rickman 1976) with respect to his concept of *Erlebnis* ("living through"); see also Armstrong (1971), Sawyers (1985), and Tuan (1977). The periodic inclusion of my lived experiences within the temple, as well as the priest's points of view on the pond garden, might increase the reader's sense of a felt-experience, however vicarious, of the Temple of the Heavenly Dragon. Dilthey emphasized that writing to include an author's "living through" experiences was "sharing lived experiences," echoing what the anthropologists Victor Turner and Edward Bruner (1986) termed "putting experience into circulation." Dilthey emphasized experience-as-epistemology, interestingly, a stance congruent with Rinzai Zen Buddhist emphasis on heart-to-heart communication of experience. The idea of hermeneutics here suggests that fine-tuned description is a mode of interpretation (see also Bachelard 1958; Basso 1996; Shaner 1985).

3 It is not to be assumed that most people in Japan, especially younger people, are familiar with traditional meanings and contemporary interpretations of the landscapes of premodern shrines and temples. Much like monks living at Tenryū-ji, for many people in Japan temple gardens in particular are just . . . there, an aspect of culture. Even Kinsaku Nakane-san, the celebrated designer and connoisseur of gardens admitted that "as a Japanese, I am embarrassed to say it, but at that point [in my life] I really had no idea that such splendid culture existed in Japan. I think it is a necessity first to understand these superb traditional works [gardens]. To begin with that is most essential" (Moir and Merritt 1977:140). For both Japanese and non-Japanese students of gardens, I would add.

4 Marc Peter Keane (2002:154) also comes to this conclusion, in writing that "the garden is an ocean that surrenders its mysteries only to the abiding, casts them up for only the watchful to find. If you

come to a garden, it will not disappoint, but you must come as to an ocean . . . dreamy yet alert."

5 Chambers (1896:21).
6 Walker (1989:97).
7 Black (1929:68).
8 The terms "symbol" and "representation" are not used in this book, especially with respect to the study and presentation of the garden aspect of Buddhist temples. The concepts of symbol and representation in and of themselves assume a dualism and manifest opposition between what we would term subject and object, things and ideas. Both terms denote that there is something "there," say, a garden, that is to be represented or symbolized by . . . something, say, the "meanings" of gardens. Spatial distance, conceptual distance, between phenomena and meaning, is embedded in conventional conceptions of representation and symbol. Symbol and representation inherently are referential, and referential meaning forces a separation of person and, say, garden. See Cirlot (1984:xi–lv), Evans-Pritchard (1956:123–43) on "The Problem of Symbols," and Raine (1967:105–22) for nondual conceptions of symbol.

CHAPTER 4: A POND OF SHADOW AND SHIMMERING STONES

1 Shigemori (1957:5).
2 Soper (1942:376). See also Ienaga (1973) and Shimizu (1981).
3 Shigemori (1936–39:2,2:50). Dragon ponds were recorded as

early as 796. Takeiwa Tatsu no Mikoto (Dragon Deity of the Strong Rock) was believed to dwell in a sacred pond in present-day Kyūshū, Chikuzen Province. Emperor Kanmu ordered people to pray to the dragon-deity in the pond that it might rise and thereby bring rain and cessation of a prolonged drought (see also Itoh 1985:83). Dragons were linked to emperors, as we continue to see, and dragons in ponds also were believed to protect emperors visiting particular sites. The relevant historical example here is the Garden of Divine Waters (Shinsen_En) of the Imperial Palace, in Kyōto. The Garden of Divine Waters was laid out under the direction of Emperor Kanmu. The venerable Shingon priest Kōbō Daishi directed that "a pond be dug before the [Emperor's] Palace and filled with pure water, whereupon Kōbō invited the Dragon-king to come and live there. And behold, a gold-coloured dragon, eight *sun* long, appeared, seated on the head of a snake, more than nine *shaku* [尺; approximately 8.95 feet] in length, and entered the pond" (de Visser 1913:164). Another translation of the incident has it that "the Emperor, who at once caused a lake to be dug in front of the palace enclosure, filled it with cool water, and prayed the dragon king to come there. The dragon king Zenno indeed came to the lake in the guise of a golden dragon ten inches long, riding on a nine-foot snake" (Mc-

Cullough 1990:377). Subsequently, the pond in the garden of the Imperial Palace was referred to as Dragon Pond. Shigeno no Sadanushi (785–852), a visitor to the Imperial Palace in the ninth century, wrote that "the path . . . is a clean sweep and shadows of willows laying across catch a pure spring bubbling up, to run off in a narrow stream-let. If we climb the low hill, we may often catch sight of birds, startle the wood doves. . . . In the dragon pond glimmers the sun, moon and stars" (Morris 1964:26). The presence of water in the pond, and the corresponding presence of a dragon, assured peace and prosperity in the land. The Garden of Divine Waters, though, became desiccated and "the waters of the lake were shallow, as though the dragon king had gone away to another place" (McCullough 1990:378). With the departure of the dragon, with the desiccation of the pond, conflicts and war ensued. "Assuredly is this displeasing to the dragon king! We must bring peace to the land by restoring the garden with all speed" (Mc-Cullough, 379). Restoration of the pond, the presence of water, invited a dragon to return to the area. Behavior toward the pond within the Imperial Palace complex mirrors beliefs about the pond within the old Imperial villa at Turtle Mountain, and both of these examples prefigure later ideas about and behaviors toward the pond within the Tenryū-ji compound.

4 See Shigemori (1936–39:2,2:57) for an additional critique of the often-assumed *kokoro* character-shape of the pond.

5 The words are by Kūkai, in Pilgrim (1981:30).

6 Myokyo-ni (1987:25).

7 Myokyo-ni, 61.

8 Myokyo-ni, 70.

9 Pilgrim (1981:33).

10 Sato (1984:171). Plato (428–348 B.C.) also understood the idolatry danger of "stopping" at forms themselves. In Book VII of *The Republic*, Plato fashioned the well-known allegory of people living deep within a cave, mesmerized by compelling forms and images cast as shadows of "reality" on the walls of the cave such that "the prisoners [ordinary people] would in every way believe that the truth is nothing other than the shadows" (Grube 1992:187).

11 Louis Frederic (1972:107) adds that the pond is "not designed to distract attention, but on the contrary to . . . turn it toward the heart of things [心, *kokoro*]."

12 Rinzai Zen Buddhists often consider *zazen* a "natural" posture of the body. Correspondingly, triangles often are the natural forms and patterns of growth in nature. Many plants blossom radially, from a center point on the stem, in a geometrically proportional manner stimulating Pythagoras of Samos to conclude that proportion was a Divine Harmony (cf. Guthrie 1987). The growth pattern of the plants unfolds *ad infinitum* in forms and patterns of interdependent relationship we experience as triangular, and the proportions of a triangle are "incommensurable ratios unique in their ability to consistently replicate through endless divisions in space" (Fletcher 1988:46). As plants continue to grow, these forms and patterns of interrelationship continue to exhibit the same geometric proportions (cf. Doczi 1981:1–13). Aristotle thus concluded that nature, experienced as triangles, is gnomonic, meaning that "certain things suffer no alteration, save that of magnitude, when they grow" (Thompson 1961:181). See Ball (1999) for a thorough analysis of nature experienced as geometry.

13 Sekida (1975:39).

14 Fletcher (1988:48).

15 After his conversion to Buddhism, it is said that King Ashoka began to venerate the Bodhi tree to such an extent that his (jealous?) wife had him cut down the tree. The stump did not die, though, and the tree at various times in history sprang to life only to be cut down another three times. The present-day Bodhi tree is venerated as the fourth direct descendent of the original tree under which Siddhārtha became aware of Buddha-Nature.

16 The third turning of the Wheel of the Dharma, on Mount Malaya in south India, occurred near the end of his life. The Third Turning of the Wheel reinforced the doctrine of emptiness (*kū*), around which the *Heart Sūtra* is based, as the nature of existence.

17 Conze (2001:82).

18 Conze, 119. This theme also is
    evident in comparatively recent
    writings such as "A Raft to
    Cross the Ocean of Indian Bud-
    dhist Thought" by the 2nd Dalai
    Lama (1476–1542).

19 The priest reiterates that "there
    are no ancient documents that
    tell us the 〖意味 imi, "meaning"〗
    of each and every stone."

20 Tatsui (1942:138).

21 Itoh (1985:35).

22 Minakami (1976:68). No one to
    my knowledge has claimed that
    Musō was not competent to
    raise stones. Bokuō Seki (1976:87)
    noted that "Musō Kokushi made
    the garden for his disciples at
    Rinsen-ji," the temple where he
    passed away in 1351.

23 Eyama (1942:88) observed that
    "in the Tenryū-ji garden, there
    is an island shaped like a turtle.
    . . . A turtle may be lonely with-
    out a crane, and it was not so
    long ago that a turtle and crane
    were thought of together. Ac-
    cording to an Indian legend, a
    turtle supports an elephant on
    its back. This idea is just like the
    idea that a dragon surrounds the
    world and the idea that a turtle
    and a dragon both were togeth-
    er. . . . So all together I conclude
    that the islands in the Tenryū-
    ji garden are an expression of
    Ryūchi 〖Dragon Pond〗, based
    on the sūtras." Mirei Shigemori
    (1936–39:2,2:26) elaborated upon
    the spatial interrelationship of
    the Crane Island-Mountain and
    the Turtle Island in adding that
    "the Tsuru Islet 〖Crane Island-
    Mountain〗 is composed of sev-

eral big stones. The Kame Islet
〖Turtle Island〗 which is placed
at the north is 〖aligned〗 with the
Tsuru Islet 〖when viewed from
the veranda of the Guest Quarters, as in fig. 63〗."

24 See Gisei Takakuwa and Kiichi
    Asano (1973:129) on the manner
    in which gender often is ascribed
    to garden compositions of earth
    and stones. In addition to gen-
    der, these two compositions of
    earth and stones also have been
    interpreted with respect to age.
    David Slawson (1987:128–29),
    writing about turtle islands, for
    instance notes that "the effect
    〖of the Turtle Island〗 is that of
    very old mountains worn down
    by erosion. Its companion 〖the
    Crane Island-Mountain〗 on
    the other hand, resembles the
    Never Aging Rock 〖or the rock
    of the Spirit Kings〗 in its use of
    sharp-edged rocks in the vertical
    position—these may be likened
    to the wings of the crane—to
    convey the impression of steep,
    jagged new mountains. . . . It is
    this contrast, between newly
    formed peaks and well-eroded
    old mountains, that so effectively
    triggers the aesthetic experience
    of ageless vitality."

25 November fifteenth celebrates
    the health and long life of boys
    (and girls) ages three, five, and
    seven. At Shintō shrines, visit-
    ing children are presented with
    a stick of candy, said to be thou-
    sand-year candy (chitoseame),
    which traditionally was stuffed
    into bags adorned with pictures
    of cranes and turtles. Broad so-
    ciocultural ideas and behaviors

such as these, again, condition in people the potential to recognize obvious associations, presented here, stimulated by the Turtle Island and the Crane Island in the pond garden.

26 The attributed characteristic of exceptionally long life may not be misplaced. Cranes in zoos have lived to eighty years, in addition to their age at captivity. In their natural habitats, cranes routinely live to fifty years of age.

CHAPTER 5: FOOTPRINTS IN THE SKY

1 Shigemori (1936–39:2,2:46).
2 Kuck (1968:121).
3 Merwin and Shigematsu (1989:37).
4 Britton and Hayashida (1986:11). Historically, it had been the custom for people of privilege to gain merit through bird-freeing ceremonies. In the tenth century, for instance, Yoshiie Minamoto of the Kawachi Genji conducted legendary bird-freeing ceremonies at the Hachiman Shrine in Kamakura. Captured cranes, with gold and silver strips of sacred cloth (gohei) tied to their legs, ceremoniously were released then prompted to fly up and away. The strips of cloth attached to their legs carried offerings to kami, petitions for the repose of the souls of those killed by Yoshiie in battles with rival clansmen. Yoshiie's crane-freeing ceremonies, concerned with the repose of potentially restless souls freed during battle,

were akin to the carp-freeing ceremonies held during the establishment of Tenryū-ji, similarly concerned with the repose of potentially restless souls freed during battle.

5 Schaarschmidt-Richter and Mori (1979:37).
6 Neruda (1970:3).
7 Shibumi (渋み) is an aesthetic concept prominent around the sixteenth century. See Covello and Yoshimura (1984:26–32), Itoh et al. (1993), and Koren (1994).
8 Other students of the landscape aspect of the temple also have noticed, from specific points of view, the visual alignments of particular compositions of stones in the pond and around the garden. Mirei Shigemori (1936–39:2,2:57), for instance, found that "islets [the Crane Island and the Turtle Island] are on a line [oblique, to the Guest Quarters]."
9 Shigemori (1936–39:2,2:62).
10 Huxley (1979:28).
11 Meru is believed to be either the Pamir Mountains of central Eurasia or Mount Kailasa (Kailas) in Tibet. Conceptualized topographically, the legendary form of Meru often was imaged as four isosceles triangles interlocked to define a square; from this topographic point of view, we would experience Meru as a mandala. In Sanskrit, mandala names designs formed from various combinations of the circle, square, and triangle. Mandala designs are believed to focus and quiet one's mind and heart (see

Argüelles 1972; Mabbett 1981).
On *mandala* in Japan, with an
emphasis on geography and landscape, see ten Grotenhuis (1999).

12 Schaarschmidt-Richter and Mori
(1979:25).

13 Schwartzberg (1992:369). See
also Haldar (1977:1–2).

14 Buddhism virtually disappeared
from India during the Delhi Sul-
tanate, beginning around 1206.

15 Schaarschmidt-Richter and
Mori (1979:32). Yetts (1919) is
the primary reference for this
section on the Islands of the Immortals. See also Grapard (1981),
Wales (1953), and Wheatley
(1971:138–40).

16 Yetts (1919:58).

17 Yetts, 42.

18 Yetts, 58–59.

19 Kuck (1940:9). See also Kuck
(1968:38–45) and Yetts
(1919:58–59).

20 Byzantines (approximately 476 to
1453), for instance, believed that
iconic images of Mary or of Jesus
literally were physical manifestations of the Spirit of the Virgin
Mary and of Christ (Ladner
1953). The sand paintings of the
Diné (Navajo) likewise are believed to be sacred images, iconic
manifestations, of the Holy Family; the images function, it is believed, to restore people to states
of psychophysical and spiritual
balance (*Hózhó*) (see Newcomb
and Reichard 1975).

21 Kuck (1968:43).

22 Yetts (1919:40, 42).

23 Yetts, 43. See also
Schaarschmidt-Richter and Mori
(1979:36).

24 Yetts, 40.

25 Aston (1972,1:368).

26 Yetts (1919:38).

27 Yetts, 38. Penelope Mason
(1993:18) discusses the archaeological site of Towadamachi, in
Akita Prefecture; standing-stones
there, perhaps, also referenced
Sumeru. The earliest surviving
example of garden stones pre-
sumed to evoke the Island of the
Immortals is in Lake Ozawaike,
dated to the eighth century,
Kyōto.

28 The crane and the dragon are
linked through archaic legends of
a mythic mountain within a vast
cosmic sea. Jnanranjan Haldar
(1977:3) notes that "according to
the Shumisen theory, a dragon
lived in the sea right under the
Shumisen [Crane Island], and
there is a story in the sūtras that
dragons surround the root of
the Shumisen. If the pond is expressed as a dragon pond according to the sūtras, it is possible to
evoke the presence of a dragon
in the pond by reference to the
Shumisen." Experienced as evocation of Shumisen, the Crane Island by kinship thus is linked to
the previously discussed dragons
at one time believed to inhabit
the pond area.

29 Kuck (1940:11).

30 McCullough (1990:369).

31 Aston (1972,1:368). Archaic
legends also speak of Shinsentō
(神仙島), a mystical mountain-
island in an expansive cosmic
sea. Other legends mention an
Everlasting, Eternal Land (Tokoyo no Kuni,常世の国) stable
in the swirl of endless seas quite
distant from the realm of human

beings. The Everlasting Eternal Land was believed to be lush with the fruits of immortality and thus became the object of extensive searches by emperors.

32 Itoh (1985:70, 1983:25).

33 Schaarschmidt-Richter and Mori (1979:32). Claire E. Sawyers (1985:67) worked with a *niwashi* (庭師, gardener; caretaker of gardens) at Tenryū-ji who also told her that "the middle rock is the peak of Mt. Hōrai" and, evoking a non-Buddhist interpretation of the pond, the peak of Mount Hōrai is "barely rising above the cloud layer of lake water."

34 Eliot (1972:73).

35 Takakuwa and Asano (1973.123). The priest's selection of three stones here is consistent with the *Book of the Garden*, which notes that "when you place a vertical stone, you must also place other accompanying stones such as the side stones on both sides of it as well as the sideways stone in front." (Tachibana 1976:32).

36 The priest also considers the stones of the Three Exalted Buddhas as evocative of Hōrai, as he further says that "Hōraizan is 〚呼び起こされる, *yobiokosareru*, 'evoked'〛 by placing the *sanzon seki* there. It is not the case that Hōraizan is there already, and various 〚things〛 are made up with respect to it. On the contrary, Hōrai is 〚evoked〛 by placing the *sanzon seki* there." Jiro Harada (1956:11) reminds us that "it does not seem that priests in general regarded these rocks as images of deities; rather they tried to express aesthetic principles by means of Buddhist doctrines with which the people were more or less familiar."

37 Tachibana (1976:16). According to the *Chronicles of the Great Peace (Taiheiki)*, during the time of Musō rites of esoteric Buddhism routinely invoked Monju and Fugen. Go-Daigo at one time ordered Buddhist monks to offer prayers and "mystic (Tendai) rites for the healthy birth of a pregnant Princess. The monks recited the eight-word Monju formula and Fugen longevity prayers. . . . Smoke from their sacred fires filled the Inner Princesses garden" (McCullough 1990:12).

38 Schaarschmidt-Richter and Mori (1979:38).

39 Tachibana (1976:26).

40 Schwartzberg (1992:381).

CHAPTER 6: SETTLING FLOWERS OF ICE

1 Merwin and Shigematsu (1989:28). Turtle islands are prominent within several other present-day temple landscapes associated with Musō Kokushi. A distinctive Turtle Island of stones rests in the moss of the upper-garden area of the Temple of the Western Fragrance (Saihō-ji, 1339) in Kyōto, within which Musō served as the initial abbot. There also are a number of turtle islands, explicitly named as such, within the lower pond of the Temple of the Golden Pavilion (Kinkaku-ji). Kinkaku-ji is a Muromachi-period (1392–1573) compound, the design of which

was influenced by the Temple of
the Heavenly Dragon.

2 The "head" stone of the Turtle
Island faces north, to the right-
hand side of the pond. The Turtle Island is the most northerly
placed composition of primary
stones within the pond and thus
can be experienced as "guard-
ing" the north. In Sung Dynasty
China, the Black Tortoise (Kwei,
in Chinese) of the North was one
of Four Divine Creatures (Sze
Ling, in Chinese: Red Phoenix
= South; Azure Dragon = East;
White Tiger = West). Chinese
feng shui and Japanese hōgaku
both deem north a direction from
which one ought to be protected.

3 Josiah Conder (1964:51) discusses
the principal stones traditionally
composing a kame shima.

4 Cf. Covello and Yoshimura
(1984:30–32).

5 See especially Dupre et al. (2006).

6 Eliade (1978:213).

7 Perceval W. Yetts (1919:40),
quoting from the Book of Lieh
(Lao) Tzu, sixth century B.C. (see
Chan 1963).

8 Yetts, 19.

9 Harada (1956:9).

10 Loraine Kuck (1968:97) adds that
"with the presence of a tortoise
island we are back to the ancient
Chinese tale of the Mystic Isles
which were stabilized by giant
tortoises." See also Hay (1985),
Little (1988), and Rawson and
Legeza (1979).

11 Compassion. Among Buddhists,
the act of freeing animals still is
considered an act of merit. Perhaps Buddhists would recognize
Urashima's setting the turtle

free as an act of compassion.
Buddhists in Myanmar (Burma)
still decorate the shells of turtles
with gold leaf then ceremonially
release the turtles into rivers, as
a meritorious act of compassion.

12 Piggott (1983:123–34).

13 Ponds were believed to be entrances, doorways, to the undersea palace kingdoms (Ryūgū-iri)
of dragons. The Chronicles of
the Great Peace (Taiheiki) contains a relevant illustration of
Ryūgū-iri by way of Emperor
Daigo's restoration of the Garden of Divine Waters (Park of
the Sacred Spring, Shinsen-en)
within the Imperial Palace in the
capital city of Purple Mountains
and Crystal Streams. Shubin,
a monk, became jealous of the
relationship between the emperor and the Shingon monk
Kōbō Daishi (Kūkai, 774–835);
"capturing the dragon-gods
who dwell in the vast universe
of the three kinds of thousands
of worlds, he shut them up in
a tiny water jar, wherefore no
rain fell for three months, even
from the beginning of summer"
(McCullough 1990:376). Some
rain dragons were small enough
to be captured, and Shubin apparently was able to control rain
through the control of rain dragons. In response, "Kōbō Daishi
composed his mind in a trance
for seven days, looking clearly
into the three kinds of thousands
of worlds. . . . But there was one
Dragon King called Zennyo,
dwelling in Heatless Lake [the
fabled Anavatapta pond], north-
ward from the Great Snowy

Mountains on the border of northern India. Because he was a higher Bodhisattva than Shubin, he alone had not responded to Shubin's summons, but had stayed in Heatless Lake" (McCullough, 376–77). Meditation enabled Kobo Daishi to "see" across time and space, to see even into the depths of vast bodies of water. Interestingly, Dragon Kings as well as people were Bodhisattvas electing to aid the salvation of human beings. "When Kōbō Daishi awoke from his trance, he told these things to the Emperor, who at once caused a lake to be dug in front of his palace enclosure, filled it with fresh cool water, and prayed the Dragon King to come there" (McCullough, 377). The pond in the Garden of Divine Waters became a potential abode for a Dragon King. The *Chronicles of the Great Peace* continues, noting that "the Dragon King Zennyo indeed came to the lake in the guise of a golden dragon ten inches long, riding on a nine-foot snake" (McCullough, 377). Snakes were linked to dragons, and both the dragon and the snake were linked to water (the turtle also was linked to both the snake and the dragon). The narrative from the *Chronicles of the Great Peace* concludes by emphasizing that a Dragon King from India continued to dwell in the pond of the Garden of Divine Waters. The seasonal rising and falling of the water of the pond signaled the periodic departure and return of the Dragon King;

rain signaled the arrival of the Dragon King, and high water levels in the pond were signs of a residing Dragon King. During periods of prolonged drought and accompanying low levels of water, Buddhist monks often were called upon by emperors to recite "rain-making sūtra" to induce the Dragon King back into ponds.

14 A version of the legend, in the *Chronicles of Japan*, says that "a man of Tsutsukaha in the district of Yosa in the province of Tamba, the child of Urashima of Mizunoye, went fishing in a boat" (Aston 1972, 1:368). See also Blacker (1975:75–78) and Senda (1988:136).

15 McCullough (1990:368). *Yorishiro* are architectured spaces and places inviting the descent of *kami*. Pine trees, in particular, long have been favored for the descent of *kami*. Blacker (1975:38–39) notes that "tall pine trees are found constantly in the neighborhood of a shrine, and innumerable place-names survive which associate trees with a numinous presence." On the creation of trees by Iso-Takeru no Kami, see Aston (1972,1:58).

16 Carroll (1972:21).

17 Loewe and Blacker (1981:46). Several species of turtle within the taxonomic category *Chinemys* remain prevalent in China and Japan. The popular Chinese and Japanese pond turtle, the so-called "coin" turtle, is a member of *Chinemys reevesii* and conventionally is named Reeve's Turtle. Turtles from the taxon *Maure-*

mys also frequent the myths of China and Japan, and this taxonomic group includes *Mauremys japonica*, common in southern Kyūshū, and *Mauremys nigricans*, terrapins including the Yellow Turtle common to China as well as Japan. A turtle on the island of Mauritius lived for a hundred and fifty years. Leatherback turtles (*Dermochelys*) attain weights of fifteen hundred pounds and Testudos (*Macrochelys*) attain weights of five hundred pounds. Galapagos Island tortoises (*Geochelone elephantopus*) routinely grow to lengths of four feet and to weights of five hundred pounds.

18 Vedic India, for instance, fashioned a correspondence between the shape and construction of the shell of a turtle, the human body, and the believed shape of the universe. The shell of a turtle, a microcosmic universe, was the dome of the sky as the macrocosmic universe. The outer portion of a turtle's shell is bony plates, but the inside of the shell is a smoothly arched bowl. Both the dome of the sky and the inside of a turtle's shell were likened to a protective umbrella. Ordinarily there are two small holes, passages for the spinal cord, at the rear of a turtle's shell. The spinal column is fused to the shell, and runs along the arc of the shell like the ridgepole of a house. Faint lines etched in the shell, channels for nerves emanating from the spine, suggest human endoskeletal ribs. The channel in the shell for the fused spinal

column was interpreted as a Cosmic Axis (*Axis Mundi*), and nodes along the channel in the shell were believed analogous to the *chakra* nodes of the human body as an *axis mundi* (see Eliade 1986). The (physical) spinal holes in the rear of the turtle's shell corresponded to the (metaphysical) hole through which one must pass to experience the center of the universe (and, metaphysically, where "ordinary" consciousness yields to "enlightened" consciousness).

19 Zoologists have identified fragments of shells used in divination as belonging to the extinct turtle *Pseudocadia anyangensis*. The *Chronicles of Japan* and the *Record of Ancient Matters* tell us that "ancient Japanese divination was by roasting deer's shoulder blades and observing the cracks thus caused, not by the shell of a tortoise, which is the Chinese practice." The *Chronicles of Japan* (Aston 1972,1:152), though, notes that emperors "commit the matter to the Sacred Tortoise," through which *kami* declare their presence.

20 Aston, 1:152.

21 Taiji Maeda (1960:26) notes that "in addition to the importation of tortoise shell for combs and such, during the 1980s Indonesia exported about 28,000 hawksbill turtles to Japan, especially for use as stuffed wall decorations." Lehrer (1990:110–11) adds that "in 1980, according to one estimate, raw tortoise shell was selling for $45 a pound in Japan, and 45,000 pounds were be-

ing imported annually for that
country's crafts industry. Other
sources estimate the amount
imported annually into Japan at
closer to 100,000 pounds."

22 Merwin and Shigematsu
(1989:28).

CHAPTER 7: BRIDGE TO
BUDDHA-NATURE

1 See Shigemori (1936–39:2,2:61).
2 Access without permission to,
and thus direct experience of, the
temple gardens of Japan increasingly is limited and/or restricted
(cf. Scott and Scott 1982).
3 Nishimura, Satō, and Smith
(1973:1).
4 Masami (1942:89).
5 Teiji Itoh (1985:40) acknowledges the convention of conceptualizing the bridge as a
tripartite structure but, without
citing the source of his interpretation, writes that the bridge
"represents the three faiths of
Buddhism, Confucianism, and
Taoism that must be mastered
and then transcended to reach
enlightenment."
6 Unsui names monks in training
that "gather around a great Zen
Master as water or clouds gather
in certain places" (Nishimura,
Satō, and Smith 1973:1). In addition to referring to novices,
note that the word unsui at once
also assumes a teacher, a place
of teaching and learning, and an
assembly (such as the assembly
gathered around Shākyamuni
in the Heart Sūtra). On the
traditional temple training of
monks see Kapleau (1980:3–68),

Nishimura, Satō, and Smith
(1973), Suzuki (1959, 1962:62–
70), Suzuki (1970), and Yoshioka
(1984).
7 See Nishimura, Satō, and Smith
(1973).
8 Pilgrim (1981:32).
9 Suzuki (1962:153–247).
10 Suzuki (1970:72).
11 Sato (1984:150).
12 Images of Shākyamuni and Bodhisattvas invariably include a
lotus, yet another illustration
of the influence of nature on
religion in general and, here,
on Buddhism in particular (cf.
Coomaraswamy 1972, Irie and
Aoyama 1982, and Rowland
1963).
13 Suzuki (1970:17).
14 McRae (1986:113).
15 McRae, 112.
16 McRae, 113.
17 Nishimura, Satō, and Smith
(1973:10).
18 Enomiya-Lassalle (1990:20). See
Miura and Sasaki (1966, 1965)
on the history of kōan study in
Rinzai Zen Buddhism.
19 Enomiya-Lassalle, 21. See also
Nishimura, Satō, and Smith
(1973:8).
20 Enomiya-Lassalle, 22.
21 Bukkyo Dendo Kyokai (Society
for the Promotion of Buddhism)
(1966:168).
22 Sekida (1975:98).
23 Kohn (1991:118).
24 Suzuki (1959:25).
25 See Murphy and Murphy
(1968:192–216).

CHAPTER 8: SITTING IN THE
GARDEN

1   As presented in the literature
    of a number of cultures, stones
    are believed to be embodiments
    of spirit and often are animated,
    recalling the Shintō embodiment
    and personification of features of
    nature as *kami*. In T. S. Eliot's
    (1972:72–79) poem "Choruses
    from the Rock," for instance, an
    animistic stone serves as narra-
    tor and leads the reader through
    an assessment of human history.
    Priest Ogotemmêli's narrative
    account of the origin of the Do-
    gon people of Mali, West Africa,
    speaks of deities giving sacred
    covenant stones to the ances-
    tors of humans through which
    creator ancestors subsequently
    maintain relationship with hu-
    man beings (Griaule 1965:58).
    In Daoist China certain stones
    were regarded as earthly pieces
    of heaven, bits of the legend-
    ary Islands of the Immortals
    (see Graham 1938:27–32). To be
    near rocks, to touch stones, by
    contagious association is to par-
    ticipate in their nature, invari-
    ably thought of as immutability
    and stability (see also Hay 1985;
    Neruda 1970; Sallis 1994).
2   Davidson (1982:14).
3   Kohn (1991:260); see also Fuji-
    moto (1961).
4   Sato (1984:143).
5   Suzuki (1970:25).
6   Nishimura, Satō, and Smith
    (1973:144).
7   Enomiya-Lassalle (1990:23) and
    Bancroft (1979:53).
8   Merwin and Shigematsu

(1989:63).
9   Collcutt (1981:183).
10 Davidson (2007:41).
11 Tsunoda et al. (1958:254).
12 Johnson (1999a, 1999b, 1991b).
13 On the cave-in-the-mountain
    design of temples, see Kramrisch
    (1976) and Wu (1963).
14 Fergusson and Burgess
    (1969:175).
15 Volwahsen (1969:103). Eihō-ji
    (1313, Gifu Prefecture) is the
    first temple the design of which
    is firmly attributed to Musō.
    Interestingly, within Eihō-ji,
    Davidson (2007:202) notes that
    "a path crosses the stream . . .
    the Tsusho-ro, or 'night medita-
    tion path.' . . . On top of the cliff
    . . . tradition has it that a large
    flat stone, thought to be Soseki's
    zazen-seki, was located in this
    garden."
16 Matsunosuke Tatsui (1942:139)
    refers to the cave chamber as
    Tennyokutsu (天女窟, Cave of
    the Heavenly Nymphs). Though
    referring specifically to Aspa-
    ras, female celestial beings, the
    connection of Tennyo to a cave
    evokes the legend of Amaterasu-
    ō-mi-Kami emerging from the
    cave within which she had been
    imprisoned; *ipso facto*, light and
    generativity re-emerged into exis-
    tence. The cave of Amaterasu-ō-
    mi-Kami, and the Floating Bridge
    of Heaven, is believed to be
    an actual place—the Heavenly
    Rock Dwelling Cave at Takachi-
    ho, on the island of Kyūshū (see
    also Chamberlain 1981:63–69
    and Aston 1972,1:39–50). The
    names associated with both
    caves of Shintō legend connote

transformation and en-'lighten'-ment, qualities also associated with *zazen* in Rinzai Zen Buddhism. On the cave as a feature of nature important in various religions, see Weinberg (1986).

17 Dumoulin (1963:292).

CHAPTER 9: ANCHORS ALONG THE JOURNEY

1   Kuck (1940:93).
2   See Kuitert (1988:10).
3   Kuck (1968:107).
4   Kuck (1968:131). See also Shigemori (1957:8).
5   Slawson (1987:132) adds that "spatially, the Boat-Concealing Rocks are to be set by twos or threes, in a string or as a horizontal triad."
6   Kuitert (1988:10).
7   Takakuwa and Asano (1973:126).
8   The Seven Deities of Good Fortune are Benzaiten (art and beauty, usually depicted seated on a dragon), Bishamonten (a guardian of Buddha and Buddhism), Daikokuten (wealth), Ebisu (fecundity), Fukurokuju (a deity associated with turtles and longevity, whom we met previously), Hotei (Happiness), and Jurōjin (carrying *makimono*, scrolls of wisdom).
9   Morris (1964:29).
10 Chamberlain (1981:20).
11 Shigemori (1957:8). *Origuchi Shinobu* refers to the legend of Tokoyo, a fabled land inhabited by benevolent spirits of the dead (*marebito*) (Blacker 1975:72–74). *Marebito* were believed to travel by boat from Tokoyo to the land of the living, especially at the

beginning of the New Year and, traditionally, during periods of harvest. The garden-caretaker with whom Claire E. Sawyers (1985:67) studied also told her that the "low stones in a line . . . are ships tied in a harbor protected from the vast ocean." The context within which the caretaker places the line of stones is congruent with that of the priest as well as garden scholars. All of these interpretations include boat imagery, pond stones, and movement across the water as a motif corresponding to the aforementioned reference to the *Heart Sūtra*.

12 Kuck (1968:126).
13 Harada (1956:9).
14 Eliade (1954).
15 There is an explicitly boat-shaped stone in the *karesansui* garden within Daisen-in, a subtemple of Daitoku-ji (大徳寺). Daisen-in dates to 1509, and the design of this garden has been attributed either to the Zen priest Kogaku Sōtan or to Sōami, a descendent of *kawaramono senzui*. Interestingly, the distinctive boat-shaped stone is named "Heavenly Ship" (see Cave 1993:17).
16 Merwin and Shigematsu (1989:77).
17 Neruda (1970:23).
18 Minakami (1976:69).
19 Kuck (1940:93).
20 Merwin and Shigematsu (1989:63).
21 Merwin and Shigematsu, 112.
22 Saito and Wada (1964:86).
23 Myokyo-ni (1987:vii).
24 Tsunoda et al. (1958:253).

25 Pilgrim (1981:30). The Bodhisattva Mañjuśrī, again, is believed embodied as the wisdom and compassion of such behavior.

26 Interestingly, a variant meaning of *sekkyō*, as a noun, is "stone bridge" (石橋). This meaning of *sekkyō* thus links the Night-Mooring Stones to the Bridge of Stones, and to the motif of novice priests being exposed (the bridge) to the Dharma (the pond) of Shākyamuni.

27 Horiguchi (1977:123).

CHAPTER 10: THE DRAGON GATE

1 Kino Kazuyoshi (1978:65) claims that "this [the waterfall, as well as other compositions of stone in the pond and around the garden] was done by the Chinese priest Rankei Doryū, who resided in Kyōto three years [1261–64]."

2 Matsunosuke Tatsui (1942:142) says that "at some point in history water was funneled by a pipe and fell from the waterfall. There are indications of damage on the upper areas of the [upright] stones, which I regret. This waterfall is the most magnificent of dry waterfalls and expresses, through stones, a mass of falling water."

3 Newsom and Shigemori (1988:230).

4 Mirei Shigemori (1936–39:2,2:56) says that "water was led from the mountain [Turtle Mountain] by a water pipe made of bamboo. But there was little water flowing from Mount Kameyama as there were spells of dry weather, and water from Mount Kameyama would stop." To my knowledge, there are no records indicating with certainty whether or not water actually flowed over the stones immediately after they were set.

5 Newsom and Shigemori (1988:7).

6 Merwin and Shigematsu (1989:32).

7 Eliot (1972:39–40).

8 Neruda (1970:13).

9 Sinclair (1987:16). Specifically, the legend is that "several thousands of big fishes assemble under the Dragon Gate without being able to ascend it [to swim against the current]. Those which succeed in ascending it become dragons; those which fail remain fishes" (de Visser 1913:86).

10 Yang (1982:113). De Visser (1913:128) adds that "fishes were believed to become dragons when they succeed in ascending the Dragon Gate." Most likely, the "fish" in question were sturgeon rather than carp. "None of the other 270 or so species of fish [other than carp and sturgeon] in the [river] is strong enough to battle the powerful currents in the gorges . . . they never migrated to the upper part of the river" (Graves 1982:270–71).

11 Little (1988:6).

12 Schafer (1973:16).

13 Williams (1989:185).

14 Shigemori (1936–39:2,2:50).

15 Minakami (1976:70).

16 Merwin and Shigematsu (1989:115).

17 Samuel Newsom (Newsom and Shigemori 1988:231) interprets

the Dragon Gate Waterfall in terms of formal principles of composition. "The principal stone is the Tall Vertical, with a projection suggesting the Reclining form. To the rear, only partly seen, is a Low Vertical. Slightly detached, and to the left rear, is an Arching stone, while in the immediate foreground is the fifth shape, the Flat stone." Wybe Kuitert (1988:86–94) offers a lucid description and interpretation of the waterfall, emphasizing its relative importance not only to the pond garden but to the historiography of the gardens of Japan. See also Harada (1956.15–18).

18 Keir Davidson's (2007:185) perceptive vision is that "the waterfall itself consists of seven main rocks: a lower group of three, in which the large vertical rock of the fall is flanked by two 'guest peaks'; a central group of three, halfway up the slope and marking the course of the water down from the peak above; which, in turn, is marked by a triangular shaped rock that sits on the crest of the slope." Davidson also sees the asymmetry in the composition, and his vision also includes the embankment of earth as an aspect of the composition by emphasizing the dragon-stone on top of the embankment of earth.

19 Minakami (1976:70).

20 de Visser (1913:60).

21 Merwin and Shigematsu (1989:62).

22 Minakami (1976:70).

23 Saito (1969:15).

24 Shigemori (1936–39:2,2:55).

25 Shigemori, 52.

26 Mori (1988) summarizes contrasting views of dragons in the so-called "East" and "West," but it is erroneous to stereotype "Asian" dragons as beneficent and Anglo-European dragons as harmful. On non-"Asian" conceptions of and behaviors toward dragons, especially the slaying of dragons, see Day (1985), DePaola (1980), Hodges (1984), Newman (1979), and Tripp (1983).

27 *Koi* have been domesticated and bred in Japan since the second century A.D. *Koi* (and cranes) were raised for food during World War II. During this period, carp almost met with extinction. The efforts of a few breeders, though, kept the species alive (the village of Yamakoshi in Niigata Prefecture, in particular, continues to be known for the breeding of carp). Carp have been known to grow to more than three feet in length, to weigh over thirty pounds, and to live to more than fifty years. Prize carp have been purchased for as much as $200,000 (cf. Tamaki 1977 and Zuritsky 1985).

28 A monk or priest "would become a dragon and have a very long life in order to . . . thoroughly study Buddha's doctrine" (de Visser 1913:193). See also Huxley (1979:26–30).

29 Spirals are cross-culture archetypal images of generativity and creativity, as "a spiral is a figure which retains its shape, its proportions, as it grows in one dimension by addition at an open

end" (Bateson 1978:10). Spirals
are archaic images of life itself;
DNA is a double-helix spiral,
and our image of infinity is a
figure-eight spiral, laid horizontally. See Cook (1979), Johnson
(2004), and Purce (1975:26) on
archaic and cross-cultural conceptions of spirals.

30 Bruyere and Farrens (1989:34).
See also Motoyama (1981). Traditionally, there are seven (Sanskrit) *chakra*: Mūlādhāra, at base
of spine; Svādhiṣthāna, above
the spleen; Manipūra, at the
navel; Anāhata, above the heart;
Vishuddha, at the front of the
throat; Ājñā, between the eye-
brows; Sahasrāra, on top of the
head.

31 See Krishna (1971).

32 Rawson and Legeza (1979:27–28).

33 The Caduceus, two snakes inter-
twined around an *axis mundi*,
was the Egyptian winged staff
associated with healers and continues to be associated with resurrection and with an ascending
movement of death to life.

34 Transformation of consciousness
also has been envisioned as "the
lonely mountain of essential Being, which is one with the world
mountain, around which the
heavens circle, through which
the polar axis runs, and round
which glide the dragons of the
cosmic powers" (Burckhardt
1967:174). This passage is from
an Anglo-European alchemy
text, dated 1330 A.D., contemporaneous with construction of the
Temple of the Heavenly Dragon.
Anglo-European alchemists concluded that "the occurrence of

spiritual transmutation is already
a miracle, and is certainly no
smaller a miracle than the sudden production of gold from a
base metal" (Burckhardt, 204).
Chinese Daoist alchemists acknowledged "transformational
process as the core of physical
existence" (Burckhardt, 204).
The metaphoric language of
these passages paraphrases the
priest's evocative language about
his experiences with the Dragon-
Gate Waterfall. Alchemists no
doubt would have recognized
the metaphysics of the design
and physical form of the Dragon-
Gate Waterfall, as well as the
priest's drawings, as evoking an
ascent through what Christians
then would have termed Heavenly Spheres. Dante Alighieri's
Paradiso, Book III of the *Divine
Comedy*, for instance, depicts
the ascent of the soul to the Em-
pyrean to participate directly
in Christ consciousness, corresponding to the priest's images
of ascent of ordinary awareness
up the waterfall of stones analogous to initial experience of Buddha-Nature. The ascent through
Dante's Heavenly Spheres was
"an ascent through a hierarchy
of spiritual degrees, by means
of which the soul, which successively realizes these, gradually turns from a discursive
knowledge bound to forms to
an undifferentiated and immediate vision in which subject and
object, knower and known, are
one" (Burckhardt, 47). Imme-
diacy of experience; the mutabil-
ity of awareness; a dissolving of

physical forms as the final resting place for an awareness of "reality"—these concerns correspond to descriptions of awareness of Buddha-Nature in Rinzai Zen Buddhism (see Sekida 1975:207–22). In addition to the pervasive image of spatial ascent, in each instance, as well, transformation of awareness is likened to a physical transformation, a literal metamorphosis bringing into being a latency already present.

35 Portman (1964) gives thoughtful consideration to the philosophical and religious issues raised by the fact of biological metamorphosis.

36 Cross-cultural images of human transformation invariably are associated with amphibious beings such as the snake and the dragon. "If he desires to become small," it was said of the dragon, "he assumes a shape resembling that of a silkworm, and if he desires to become big, he lies hidden in the world" (de Visser 1913:63). Physical metamorphosis is a defining characteristic of dragons and snakes. Snakes shed their skins and in Vedic India "having cast off their old skins—which means that they acquired immortality ('they have conquered Death'), they [snakes] became gods, Devas" (Eliade 1978:204). Extended into the cultural realm of humans, metamorphosis often is looked upon as escape from death. Chinese Daoist images of transformation-as-metamorphosis often depict snakes shedding their skin as akin to opening a grave to find . . . nothing, except

perhaps grave-cloths. It then was assumed that either the spirit awaited transformation to paradise or already had been "transported to paradise in a Heavenly chariot, or ascended on high riding a phoenix, a crane, or a dragon" (Yetts 1919:37). Metamorphosis was imaged as movement from death to life, immortality, synonymous with movement from the earth to the sky. For further conceptions of dragons in 'Asia' (or, more accurately, the relatively eastern areas of the Eurasian continent), see especially Allen and Griffiths (1979:34–45), Hino (1979:189–209), Smith (1919), and Mori (1988). Note that there were female dragons, as well as dragon images associated with females (see de Visser 1913:70–71, 172, and Schafer 1973:147–85).

37 Burckhardt, 161.

38 See Johnson (1991a). Along with gardening, drawing and painting are so-called "meditation arts" in Zen Buddhism and drawing and painting, as well as gardening, have been influential in the lives of priests (cf. Hasumi 1962, and Pilgrim 1981). On the relationship of Zen Buddhism to painting and drawing, see Franck (1973), Hisamatsu (1971), Holmes and Horioka (1973), Ishida (1963).

39 The Chinese square-of-three, for instance, was considered "magical" as dots and numbers within each cell could be manipulated in any combination yet result in the number fifteen, a number of mythic significance. As early as the tenth century in China,

nine black (*yang*; primarily male) dots and white (*yin*; primarily female) dots, and later numbers, adding to fifteen were manipulated in various combinations within nine cubes arranged into a square—the "magic" square-of-three (*lo shu*, in Chinese) (cf. Cammann 1961, 1960).

40 Fletcher (1988:46). See Doczi (1981), Ghyka (1977), and Guthrie (1987), for neo-Pythagorean discussions of geometry relevant to interpretations of the form and shape of pond gardens.

41 Schaarschmidt-Richter and Mori (1979:41). Jiro Harada (1956:9–10) adds that "they are the lucky odd numbers. Seven is used in 'seven rare treasures,' 'seven wise men of the bamboo thicket,' and 'seven lucky gods' while five is the number associated with *gogyo* (the ancient conception of the five elementary forces, wood, fire, earth, metal, and water, believed to be ever-producing, and the same time ever-destroying each other) and with *gojo* (five cardinal virtues—humanity, justice, politeness, wisdom, and fidelity). Three is used in *sanyu* (three friends in a cold winter) or refers to the plum-tree, daffodil and bamboo, but this is a rather Chinese usage. These numbers are also those of the tufts of rice straw or paper which are twisted at fixed intervals in shrines in order to sanctify the place within . . . seven is unchangeable and appropriate to *yo*, five in combination of *in* and *yo*, and three signifies heaven, earth, and man."

42 Kurt Singer (1973) discusses the interrelationship of aesthetics, design, and geometry.

43 On music history and theory relevant to the study of gardens, see especially Harich-Schneider (1973:295–339), Kishibe (1984:14–24), and Tokumaru (1990:1).

44 Ueda (1967:70).

45 Singer, 110. See Asano and Takauwa (1973:62–68) on the compelling "Sounds of Waterfalls and Streams," Cave (1993:102), and Lai (1979).

46 Newsom and Shigemori (1988:7).

47 See Saito and Wada (1964:94).

48 Newsom and Shigemori (1988:7).

49 Merwin and Shigematsu (1989:115).

50 Nitschke (1993:76).

51 The present-day *karesansui* within the Temple of the Peaceful Dragon (竜安寺, Ryōan-ji) highlights fifteen stones arranged in subtle proportional interrelationship in a bed of sand. This well-known Rinzai Zen Buddhist temple garden has been experienced as "frozen music" (cf. Johnson 2001, Kuck 1968:163–171, and Schaarschmidt-Richter and Mori 1979:71–73, 101–3). Irmtraud Schaarschmidt-Richter (Schaarschmidt-Richter and Mori 1979:43) underscores "how immensely important are the relationships of individual groups [of stones, in the garden within the Temple of the Peaceful Dragon] to one another, particularly in their position on the surface and in the variety of their forms, their height, volume and edges, which produce something like a musical sequence." Music is un-

derutilized in the experience and interpretation of gardens.

52 Doczi (1981:8–13), Kandinsky (1977), Leonard (1978), Levin (1994), and Rudhyar (1982) informed this discussion of the metaphysics of music applicable to the study of gardens.

53 Johnson (2001).

54 Merwin and Shigematsu (1989:109).

PART III: GARDEN AS LIFE AND SPIRIT

1 Kitao (1985:6).

2 Itoh (1985:87).

3 See in particular Eliade (1959), Nasr (1981), and Smith (2001). Orsi (2005) influenced the conception of religion here. Orsi (74) concludes that "religion is the practice of making the invisible visible . . ." in order to "render them [spirit] . . . tangible, present to the senses in the circumstances of everyday life." This conception of religion acknowledges the reality of the pan-human vision of existence as composed of animistic realms seen and unseen, where human action rather than ideology functions to enable people to be present fully to existence-as-it-is (真如, shinnyo), in Buddhist language.

4 Garden scholars have generated a category of gardens termed "paradise gardens." The category itself, though, privileges the adjective "paradise" as a *type* of garden thus delimiting a conception of garden itself as a religious phenomenon.

5 This conception of "life" was informed by Margulis and Sagan (1995).

6 Berthier and Parkes (2000:117, 119, 121).

7 Keane (2002:122, 127). Orsi (2005:73) coins the phrase "real presence" as a characteristic of religious experience, congruent with all of these instances of encounters with stones deemed animistic.

8 Harvey (2006:xiv). In *The Unknown Craftsman*, his profound meditation on the interrelationship of the spirit of the creative process and things created, Sōetsu Yanagi (1972:96) tells us that "work done with heart and hand is ultimately worship of Life itself."

9 Houston and Houston (1972:89).

10 See Johnson (2010); Naumann (2000:36–38).

11 See Aikens and Higuchi (1982:175–77).

12 On stone tools from Ethopia see Lewin (1981), Semaw et al. (1977), and Kibunjia (1994).

13 Wolkstein and Kramer (1983:xvi). Narratives on Inanna and *The Huluppu Tree* are on Tablet XII (cf. Kramer 1963:197–205; Shaffer 1974).

14 Wolkstein and Kramer (1983:37). See also Wiseman (1983).

15 Wolkstein and Kramer, 47;101.

16 Wolkstein and Kramer, 4–5. See Frayne (2001:129–43) on "Gilgamesh, Enkidu, and the Netherworld."

17 The manner in which Inanna behaves toward nature as she "rescues" then tends the Huluppu Tree is in contra-distinction

to the behavior of Gilgamesh as he ravishes the extensive forest of cedars guarded by the deity Humbaba (Huwawa'). Gilgamesh's telling belief is that "Because of the evil that is in the land, we will go to the forest and destroy the evil" (Sandars 1960:69). Enkidu and Gilgamesh slay Humbaba, then also destroy the life guarded by the deity. Robert Pogue Harrison, in his masterful work *Forests: The Shadow of Civilization*, details the enduring consequences of the act, quite rightly interpreted as tragedy, for humanity as a whole (see also Johnson 2010). This conception of the earth/nature as "evil" of course remains deeply embedded within the formative narratives of world-influencing religious traditions.

18 Marie-Luise Gothein (1928:29) also noted the significance of *The Epic of Gilgamesh*, with respect to the genesis of the idea of garden. Yet, Ms. Gothein stopped her journey with Gilgamesh amid the dense cedar woods guarded by Humbaba. For Ms. Gothein, the idea of garden began as a clearing-in-the-woods, a meadow, perhaps, like early Saga. Her stopping-points and ideas of garden are coterminous with our conventional horticulture-based conception of "garden."

19 Sandars (1960:98).

20 Sandars, 99.

21 Sandars, 100.

22 Neruda (1970:35).

23 Wolkstein and Kramer (1983:49;53).

24 Wolkstein and Kramer, 115.

25 Shigemori (1936–39, 2–2:46).

"JUST AS BEFORE"

1 In *Angels Fear: Toward an Epistemology of the Sacred*, Gregory Bateson reconceptualized *Creatura*, previously characterized by Jung as the domain of immutable distinction and difference, in order to frame his "necessary unity" of mind/consciousness and nature (Johnson 1989). The idea of appearance here also is informed by Owen Barfield's *Saving the Appearances: A Study of Idolatry* where phenomena become idols when experienced "without substance," what Barfield terms "alpha thinking." Barfield's useful notion of phenomena experienced as appearances depends upon awareness not stopping at material form or image to experience that in which form and image participate, what he terms "beta thinking." Appearance is not exclusively materiality, or form. Barfield's vision is animistic, a vision enabling experience of person and garden as distinct yet mutually participating in the Buddhist absolute ground of being (寸矢他, *sūnyatā*).

2 As well as the past, we ought to be aware of the implications of humanity extending the phenomenon of the garden into the future and into realms extraterrestrial (see Johnson 2010). A garden presently is orbiting approximately 350 kilometers above the surface of Terra Fir-

ma. The garden is a suitcase-size arena of water and light, earth, and foliage, within the Zvezda Service Module of the International Space Station. The garden has been named Lada. Lada is a Slavic deity associated with Sol, with growth and fecundity, beauty and harmony—with life. Even in extra-terrestrial space there are vital links between religion, gardens, and people independent of instrumental concerns with garden-as-food. The garden of Leda, alive in the microgravity of the International Space Station, expands our thinking as to possibilities for future conceptions of gardens and gardening.

To date, some 700 extra-solar-system planets have been inferred to exist, though not directly observed (using ground- and space-based telescopes with methods such as high-resolution spectroscopy, polarimetry, and gravitational microlensing). Analysis of data reveals that virtually all of the extra-solar-system planets inferred to exist, to date, exhibit masses up to fourteen times that of the outer (past the main asteroid belt between Mars and Jupiter) "gas giant" planets (Jupiter, Saturn, Uranus, Neptune) of the Sol system. None of the extra-solar-system planets detected, to date, in vital respects are similar to Terra Firma—none are relatively small telluric *rocky* planets with comparable planet-to-star distances, iron/nickel cores with silicate crusts, and approximately

78% nitrogen/20% oxygen atmospheres enabling aerobic life, as we presently understand "life," to exist. To date, Terra Firma appears to be the "garden spot" of the Milky Way Galaxy. In our postmodern, globalizing world, Terra Firma therefore perhaps ought to be considered a garden for humanity. Recall Candide's famous declaration "Il faut cultiver notre jardin." Candide's admonition that "we must cultivate our garden" becomes a declaration of our responsibility to Terra Firma. Interestingly, the primordial idea of garden as stones and rocks corresponds with the primordial nature of Terra Firma itself. With respect to its core/mantle, Terra Firma basically is a fertile island of rock and stone in space.

The idea of garden is being carried still farther into extra-terrestrial space. The Pathfinder Rover *Sojourner* at this writing is exploring a particularly rocky, hilly area on Mars aptly named "The Rock Garden." An archetypal notion of garden-as-stones must have been alive to those generating this named correspondence, on Mars, between rocks and garden. Stereoscopic images from both the Pathfinder Lander IMP camera and the Rover forward cameras reveal that dense concentrations of rocks make up this garden area and that rocks here differ distinctly in roundness, angularity, and density, most likely as a result of eolian abrasion and micrometeorite impact cratering. The conception of garden here, the Mars "Rock Garden," corresponds to the Garden of the Sun experienced by Gilgamesh as well as to cross-cultural conceptions of garden as compositions of rocks and stones.

Ideas of garden, and religion, increasingly are being extended into the cosmos. The idea and phenomenon of garden now are extra-terrestrial. Gardens are deemed important enough, apart from function or aesthetics, to accompany humans venturing forth from the home planet.

The idea of garden in associa-tion with conceptions of deity and, synonymous with life itself, with spirit, remains alive within the infinite vacuum of space.

3   Merwin and Shigematsu (1989:25).

CAPTION NOTES

f29 Newsom (1960:33).
f51 Newsom (1988:7).
f54 Warner (1952:108).
f85 Takakuwa (1962:2).
f87 Takakuwa, 2.

BIBLIOGRAPHY

Adams, Robert. M., translator and editor. 1966. *Candide, or Optimism*. New York: W. W. Norton and Company.

Aikens, C. Melvin, and Takayasu Higuchi. 1982. *Prehistory of Japan*. New York: Academic Press.

Akamatsu, Toshihide, and Philip Yamplonsky. 1977. "Muromachi Zen and the Gozan System." In *Japan and the Muromachi Age*. John W. Hall and Toyoda Takeshi, editors. Pp. 313–29. Berkeley: University of California Press.

Allen, Judy, and Jeanne Griffiths. 1979. *The Book of the Dragon*. Secaucus, NJ: Chartwell Books.

Anesaki, Masaharu. 1963. *History of Japanese Religion, with Special Reference to the Social and Moral Life of the Nation*. Rutland, VT, and Tōkyō: Charles E. Tuttle.

———. 1933. *Art, Life, and Nature in Japan*. Boston: Marshall Jones.

Argüelles, José and Miriam. 1972. *Mandala*. Boulder, CO, and London: Shambhala.

Armstrong, Robert Plant. 1971. *The Affecting Presence: An Essay in Humanistic Anthropology*. Urbana: University of Illinois Press.

Asano, Kiichi, and Gisei Takakuwa. 1973. *Japanese Gardens Revisited*. Rutland, VT, and Tōkyō: Charles E. Tuttle.

Aston, W. G., translator. 1972. *Nihongi: Chronicles of Japan from the Earliest Times to A.D. 697*. Volumes 1 and 2. Rutland, VT, and Tōkyō: Charles. E. Tuttle.

Autret, Jean; William Burford; and Phillip J. Wolfe, translators and editors. 1987. *On Reading Ruskin*. New Haven: Yale University Press.

Bachelard, Gaston. 1958. *The Poetics of Space*. Maria Jolas, translator. Boston: Beacon Press.

Bakhtin, Mikhail M. 1981. *The Dialogic Imagination: Four Essays*. Austin: University of Texas Press.

Ball, Philip. 1999. *The Self-Made Tapestry: Pattern Formation in Nature*. Oxford: Oxford University Press.

Bancroft, Anne. 1979. *Zen. Direct Pointing to Reality*. London: Thames and Hudson.

Barfield, Owen. 1988. *Saving the Appearances: A Study in Idolatry*. Middletown, CT: Wesleyan University Press.

Basso, Keith H. 1996. "Wisdom Sits in Places: Notes on a Western Apache Landscape." In *Senses of Place*. Steven Feld and Keith H. Basso, editors. Pp. 53–90. Santa Fe: School of American Research Press.

Bateson, Gregory. 1978. "The Pattern Which Connects." *Co-Evolution Quarterly* 9:5–15.

Beck, B. E. F. 1976. "The Symbolic Merger of Body, Space, and Cosmos in Hindu Tamil Nadu." *Contributions in Indian Sociology* 10:213–43.

Berque, Augustin. 1986. *Le Sauvage et L'Artifice: Les Japonais devant La Nature* [The Wild and the Human-Made: The Japanese before Nature]. Paris: Gallimard.

Berthier, François, and Graham Parkes. 2000. *Reading Zen in the Rocks: The Japanese Dry Landscape Garden*. Chicago and London: University of Chicago Press.

Black, Walter J., compiler. 1929. *The Works of Anton Chekov*. New York: Walter J. Black.

Blacker, Carmen. 1975. *The Catalpa Bow: A Study of Shamanistic Practice in Japan*. London: G. Allen.

Bring, Mitchell, and Josse Wayembergh. 1981. *Japanese Gardens: Design and Meaning*. New York: McGraw-Hill.

Britton, Dorothy, and Tsuneo Hayashida. 1986. *The Japanese Crane: Bird of Happiness*. Tōkyō, New York, and San Francisco: Kodansha International.

Bruun, Ole, and Arne Kalland. 1992. *Asian Perceptions of Nature*. Copenhagen: Nordic Institute of Asian Studies.

Bruyere, Rosalyn L., and Jeanne Farrens, 1989. *Wheels of Light: A Study of the Chakras*. Sierre Madre: Bon Productions.

Bukkyo Dendo Kyokai [Society for the Promotion of Buddhism]. 1966. *The Teaching of Buddha*. Tōkyō: Kosaido Printing Company.

Burckhardt, Titus. 1967. *Sacred Art in East and West: Its Principles and Methods*. London: Perennial Books.

Cammann, Schuyler. 1961. "The Magic Square of Three in Old Chinese Philosophy and Religion." *History of Religions* 1:37–80.

———. 1960. "Evolution of Magic Squares in China." *Journal of the American Oriental Society* 80:116–24.

Carroll, David M. 1972. "Japanese Coin Turtle." *International Turtle and Tortoise Society Journal* 6(2):20–22, 36.

Carver, Norman H. 1955. *Form and Space in Japanese Architecture*. Tōkyō: Shokokusha.

Casalis, Matthieu. 1983. "Semiotics of the Visible in Japanese Rock Gardens." *Semiotica* 44:349–62.

Cave, Philip. 1993. *Creating Japanese Gardens*. Boston: Charles E. Tuttle.

Chamberlain, Basil Hall, translator. 1981. *The Kojiki: Records of Ancient Matters*. Rutland, VT, and Tōkyō: Charles E. Tuttle.

Chambers, E. K., editor. 1896. *Poems of John Donne*. Volume I. London: Lawrence and Bullen.

Chan, Wing-Tsit. 1963. *The Way of Lao Tsu (Tao-Te Ching)*. New York: Bobbs-Merrill.

Cirlot, J. E. 1984. *A Dictionary of Symbols*. London and Henley: Routledge and Kegan Paul.

Cleary, Thomas, translator and editor. 1996. *Dream Conversations on Buddhism and Zen/Musō Kokushi [Muchū Mondōshū]*. Boston: Shambhala.

———. 1978. *The Original Face: An Anthology of Rinzai Zen*. New York: Grove Press.

Collcutt, Martin. 1982. "The Zen Monastery in Kamakura Society." In *Court and Bakufu in Japan: Essays in Kamakura History*. Pp.191–220. New Haven and London: Yale University Press.

———. 1981. *Five Mountains: The Rinzai Zen Monastic Institution in Medieval Japan*. Cambridge and London: Council on East Asian Studies, Harvard University and the Harvard University Press.

———. 1977. "Musō Soseki." In *The Origins of Japan's Medieval World*. Jeffrey P. Mass, editor. Pp. 261–94. Stanford: Stanford University Press.

Conan, Michel, editor. 2003. *Landscape Design and the Experience of Motion*. Washington, DC: Dumbarton Oaks.

Conder, Josiah. 1964. *Landscape Gardening in Japan*. New York: Dover.

Conze, Edward, translator. 2001. *Buddhist Wisdom: The Diamond Sutra and the Heart Sutra*. New York: Vintage Books, Random House.

———. 1982. *A Short History of Buddhism*. London: Unwin.

Cook, Theodore Andrea. 1979. *The Curves of Life: Being an Account of Spiral Formations and their Application to Growth in Nature, to Science and to Art. With Special Reference to the Manuscripts of Leonardo da Vinci*. New York: Dover.

Coomaraswamy, Ananda K. 1972. *The Origin of the Buddha Image*. New Delhi: Munshiram Manoharial.

Corless, Roger J. 1989. *The Vision of Buddhism. The Space under the Tree*. New York: Paragon House.

Covell, Jon, and Abbot Sobin Yamada. 1974. *Zen at Daitoku-ji*. Tōkyō and New York: Kodansha International.

Covello, Vincent, and Yuji Yoshimura. 1984. *The Japanese Art of Stone Appreciation: Suiseki,*

and Its Use with Bonsai. Rutland, VT, and Tōkyō: Charles E. Tuttle.

Critchlow, Keith. 1980. "Nikke: The Siting of a Rural Japanese House." In *Shelter, Sign, and Symbol*. Paul Oliver, editor. Pp. 219–26. Woodstock: Overlook Press.

Davidson, Andrew Keir. 2007. *A Zen Life in Nature: Musō Soseki in his Gardens*. Michigan Monograph Series in Japanese Studies #56. Ann Arbor: Center for Japanese Studies, University of Michigan.

———. 1982. *Zen Gardening*. London: Rider.

Day, John. 1985. *God's Conflict with the Dragon and the Sea: Echoes of a Canaanite Myth in the Old Testament*. New York: Cambridge University Press.

de Lubicz, R. A. S. 1977. *The Temple in Man: The Secrets of Ancient Egypt*. Brookline, MA: Autumn Press.

dePaola, Tomie. 1980. *The Knight and the Dragon*. New York: Putnam.

de Visser, Marinus William. 1913. *The Dragon in China and Japan*. Amsterdam: Johannes Muller.

Doczi, György. 1981. *The Power of Limits: Proportional Harmonies in Nature, Art, and Architecture*. Boulder, CO: Shambhala.

Dorson, Richard M. 1962. *Folk Legends of Japan*. Rutland, VT, and Tōkyō: Charles E. Tuttle.

Dumoulin, Heinrich. 1990. *Zen Buddhism, A History*. Volume 2: *Japan*. New York and London: Macmillan/Collier.

———. 1963. *A History of Zen*

Buddhism. New York: Pantheon Books, Random House.

Dunn, Charles J. 1972. *Everyday Life in Traditional Japan*. Rutland, VT, and Tōkyō: Charles E. Tuttle.

Dupre, Alain; Berbard Devaux; and Franck Bonin. 2006. *Turtles of the World*. Peter C. H. Pritchard, translator. Baltimore: Johns Hopkins University Press.

Eco, Umberto. 1986. *Art and Beauty in the Middle Ages*. New Haven and London: Yale University Press.

Eliade, Mircea. 1986. "Sacred Architecture and Symbolism." In *Symbolism, the Sacred, and the Arts*. Diane Apostolos-Cappadona, editor. Pp. 105–129. New York: Crossroad.

———. 1978. *A History of Religious Ideas*. Volume 1: *From the Stone Age to the Eleusinian Mysteries*. Willard R. Trask, translator. Chicago: University of Chicago Press.

———. 1959. *The Sacred and the Profane: The Nature of Religion*. New York: Harcourt Brace.

———. 1954. *The Myth of the Eternal Return, or Cosmos and History*. Willard R. Trask, translator. Princeton: Princeton University Press.

Eliade, Mircea, and Joan P. Couliano. 1991. *The Eliade Guide to World Religions*. San Francisco: Harper Collins.

Eliot, Thomas Stearns. 1972. *The Wasteland and Other Poems*. London: Faber and Faber.

Enomiya-Lassalle, Hugo M. 1990. *The Practice of Zen Meditation*. Roland Ropers and Bogdan

Snela, compilers and editors. Michelle Bromley, translator. Hammersmith and San Francisco: Harper Collins.

Evans-Pritchard, E. E. 1956. *Nuer Religion*. Oxford: Clarendon Press.

Eyama, Masami. 1942 "Teien Keitai no Kyūmei [A Study of Styles of Gardens]." *Teien* 24:88–98.

Fergusson, James, and James Burgess. 1969. *The Cave Temples of India*. Delhi: Oriental Books.

Feuchtwang, Stephen D. R. 1974. *An Anthropological Analysis of Chinese Geomancy*. Laos: Editions Vithagna.

Fischer-Schreiber, Ingrid; Franz-Karl Ehrhard; and Michael S. Diener, editors. 1991. *The Shambhala Dictionary of Buddhism and Zen*. Boston: Shambhala.

Fletcher, Rachael. 1988. "Proportion and the Living World." *Parabola* 13:29–66.

Foster, Nelson; Jack Shoemaker; and Robert Aitken, editors. 1996. *The Roaring Stream: A New Zen Reader*. New York: Harper Collins.

Fox, Michael V., editor. 1988. *Temple in Society*. Winona Lake: Eisenbrauns.

Franck, Frederick. 1973. *The Zen of Seeing: Seeing/Drawing as Meditation*. New York: Vintage Books.

Frayne, Douglas, editor. 2001. *The Epic of Gilgamesh*. Benjamin R. Foster, translator. New York: Norton.

Frederic, Louis, 1972. *Daily Life in Japan at the Time of the Samurai, 1187-1603*. Eileen M. Lowe, translator. Tōkyō: Charles E. Tuttle.

Fujimori, Terunobu. 1990. "Traditional Houses and the Japanese Way of Life." *Japan Foundation Newsletter* 18(1):10–15.

Fujimoto, Rindo. 1961. *The Way of Zazen*. Cambridge: Cambridge Buddhist Association.

Ghyka, Matila. 1977. *The Geometry of Art and Life*. New York: Dover.

Gothein, Marie-Luise. 1928. *A History of Garden Art*. Laura Archer-Hind, translator. London and Toronto: J. M. Dent.

Graham, Dorothy. 1938. *Chinese Gardens; Gardens of the Contemporary Scene, an Account of their Design and Symbolism*. New York: Dodd Mead.

Grapard, Allan G. 1981. "Flying Mountains and Walkers of Emptiness: Toward a Definition of Sacred Space in Japanese Religion." *History of Religions* 20(3):195–221.

Graves, William. 1982. "Yangtze River: Torrent of Life." In *Journey Into China*. Pp. 263–308. Washington, DC: National Geographic Society.

Griaule, Marcel. 1965. *Conversations with Ogotemmêli: An Introduction to Dogon Religious Ideas*. London: Oxford University Press.

Grube, G. M. A., translator. 1992. *Plato, Republic*. Indianapolis and Cambridge: Hackett Publishing Company.

Guest, Harry. 1995. *Traveller's Literary Companion: Japan*. Lincolnwood: Passport Books.

Guthrie, Kenneth Sylvan, translator. 1987. *The Pythagorean Sourcebook and Library*. Grand Rapids, MI: Phanes Press.

Haldar, Jnanranjan. 1977. *Early Buddhist Mythology*. New Delhi: Manohar Book Service.

Hall, John Whitney. 1983. "Terms and Concepts in Japanese Medieval History: An Inquiry into the Problems of Translation." *Journal of Japanese Studies* 9:1–32.

Hall, John Whitney, and Toyoda Takeshi. 1977. *Japan in the Muromachi Age*. Berkeley: University of California Press.

Harada, Jiro. 2002. *The Gardens of Japan*. London: Kegan Paul. 1956. *Japanese Gardens*. London: The Studio Limited.

———. 1936. *The Lesson of Japanese Architecture*. London: The Studio Limited (New York: Dover, 1985).

Harich-Schneider, Eta. 1973. *A History of Japanese Music*. London: Oxford University Press.

Harrison, Robert Pogue. 2008. *Gardens: An Essay on the Human Condition*. Chicago and London: The University of Chicago Press.

———. 1992. *Forests: The Shadow of Civilization*. Chicago: The University of Chicago Press.

Harvey, Graham. 2006. *Animism: Respecting the Living World*. New York: Columbia University Press.

Hasumi, Toshimitsu. 1962. *Zen in Japanese Art: A Way of Spiritual Experience*. New York: Philosophical Library.

Hay, John. 1985. *Kernels of Energy, Bones of Earth: The Rock in Chinese Art*. New York: China House Gallery, China House Institute of America.

———. 1983. "Arterial Art." *Stone Lion Review* 11:71–84.

Hayakawa, Masao. 1984. *The Garden Art of Japan*. New York and Tōkyō: Weatherhill/Heibonsha.

Hayashiya, Tatsusaburo, with George Nelson. 1977. "Kyōto in the Muromachi Age." In *Japan in the Muromachi Age*. Pp. 15–36. John Whitney Hall and Toyoda Takeshi, editors. Berkeley and London: University of California Press.

Higuchi, Tadahiko. 1988. *The Visual and Spatial Structure of Landscapes*. Charles Terry, translator. Cambridge and London: MIT Press.

Hino, Awao. 1979. *Dōbutsu Yokaiden* [Stories of Fabulous Animals]. Tōkyō: Matsuo Kinjino, Ariake Shobo.

Hirakawa, Akira. 1990. *A History of Indian Buddhism: From Sakyamuni to Early Mahayana*. Paul Groner, translator and editor. Honolulu: University of Hawaii Press.

Hisamatsu, Shin'ichi. 1982. "On the Record of Rinzai: Part III." *Eastern Buddhist* 25:74–87.

———. 1971. *Zen and the Fine Arts*. New York and Tōkyō: Kodansha International.

Hodges, Margaret. 1984. *Saint George and the Dragon: A Golden Legend*. Boston: Little Brown.

Hogan, Linda. 1995a *Dwellings: A Spiritual History of the Living World*. New York: Touchstone.

———. 1995b *Solar Storms*. New York: Scribner.

Holmes, Stewart W. and Chimyo Horioka. 1973. *Zen Art for Meditation*. Rutland, VT, and Tōkyō: Charles E. Tuttle.

Holtom, Daniel Clarence. 1940. "The Meaning of Kami." *Monumenta Nipponica* 3: 2–27, 32–53.

Hori, Ichiro. 1975. "Shamanism in Japan." *Japanese Journal of Religious Studies* 2: 231–87.

———. 1969. "Hitotsu-Mono: A Human Symbol of the Shintō Kami." In *Myths and Symbols: Studies in Honor of Mircea Eliade*. Joseph M. Kitagawa and Charles H. Long, editors. Pp. 291–308. Chicago and London: University of Chicago Press.

Horiguchi, Sutemi. 1977. "Tenryū-ji no Niwa [The Tenryū-ji Garden]." In *Niwa to Kūkan Kōsei no Dentō* [Tradition of Garden Design and Spatial Structure]. Pp. 121–23. Tōkyō: Zenjirō Kawasho, Kajima Kenkyūsho.

———. 1963. "Nihon Teien no Oitachi [The Early Days of Japanese Gardens]." *Bunkazai* 2:16–24.

Houston, Jeanne Wakatsuki, and James D. Houston.1972. *Farewell to Manzanar*. New York: Houghton Mifflin.

Hunt, John Dixon. 1975. *The Genius of the Place: The English Landscape Garden, 1620-1820*. London: Elek.

Hürlimann, Martin, and Francis King. 1970. *Japan*. D. J. S. Thomson, translator. Tōkyō: Charles E. Tuttle.

Huxley, Francis. 1979. *The Dragon: Nature of Spirit; Spirit of Nature*. New York and London: Themes and Hudson.

Ienaga, Saburo. 1973. *Painting in the Yamato Style*. New York: Weatherhill/Heibonsha.

Ikeda, Daisaku. 1976. *The Living Buddha: An Interpretative Biog-*

raphy. New York and Tōkyō: Weatherhill.

Inoue, Mitsuo. 1985. *Space in Japanese Architecture*. New York and Tōkyō: Weatherhill.

Irie, Taikichi, and Shigeru Aoyama. 1982. *Buddhist Images*. Ōsaka: Hoikusha.

Ishida, Ichiro. 1963. "Zen Buddhism and Muromachi Art." *Journal of Asian Studies* 22: 417-32.

Itoh, Teiji. 1985. *The Gardens of Japan*. Tōkyō, New York, San Francisco: Kodansha International.

———. 1983. *Space and Illusion in the Japanese Garden*. Ralph Friedrich and Masajiro Shimamura, translators. New York, Tokyo, and Kyōto: Weatherhill/Tankosha.

———. 1972. *The Japanese Garden: An Approach to Nature*. New Haven: Yale University Press.

Itoh, Teiji; Tanaka Ikko; and Sesoko Tsune, editors. 1993. *Wabi, Sabi, Suki: The Essence of Japanese Beauty*. Tōkyō: Cosmo Public Relations Corporation, Mazda Motor Corporation.

Johnson, Charles. 2003. *Turning the Wheel: Essays on Buddhism and Writing*. New York: Scribner.

Johnson, Norris Brock. 2010. "Religion, Spirit, and the Idea of Garden." *Religious Studies Review* 36(1):1-13.

———. 2004. "The Spiral Designs of Nature, and Craft." In *The Nature of Craft and the Penland Experience*. Jean W. McLaughlin, editor. Pp. 74-82. New York: Lark Books.

———. 2003. "Mountain, Temple, and the Design of Movement: 13th Century Japanese Zen Buddhist Landscapes." In *Landscape Design and the Experience of Motion*. Michel Conan, editor. Pp. 157-85. Washington, DC: Dumbarton Oaks.

———. 2001. "Gardens of the Heart." *Parabola* 26(1):29-35.

———. 1999a "A Song of Secret Places." *Pilgrimage* 25 (3, 4):4-10.

———. 1999b "Temple of the Abundant Flowing Spring." *Kyōto Diary* 5(2):1-6.

———. 1993a "Buddhist Ethics, Environment, and Behavior: Musō Kokushi and the Cave in Zuisen Temple, Kamakura, Japan." *The National Geographic Journal of India* 39.161 78.

———. 1993b "Musō Kokushi and the Cave in Zuisen Temple, Kamakura, Japan: Buddhist Ethics, Environment, and Behavior." In *Environmental Ethics: Discourses and Cultural Traditions*. Rana P. B. Singh, editor. Pp. 123-40. Varanasi: The National Geographical Society of India.

———. 1991a "Garden as Sacred Space." In *The Power of Place*. James Swan, editor. Pp. 167-87. Wheaton, IL: Quest Books.

———. 1991b "Zuisen Temple and Garden, Kamakura, Japan: Design Form and Phylogenetic Meaning." *Journal of Garden History* 10:214-36.

———. 1989. "Geomancy, Sacred Geometry, and the Idea of a Garden: Tenryū Temple, Kyōto, Japan." *Journal of Garden History* 9:1-19.

———. 1988. "Temple Architecture as Construction of Consciousness." *Architecture and Behavior*

4:229–49.

Jung, Carl G. 1980. *The Archetypes of the Collective Unconscious*. R. F. C. Hull, translator. Princeton: Bollingen Series XX, Princeton University Press.

Kandinsky, Wassily. 1977. *Concerning the Spiritual in Art*. New York: Dover.

Kapleau, Roshi Philip. 1980. *The Three Pillars of Zen: Teaching, Practice, and Enlightenment*. Garden City: Anchor Books, Anchor Press, Doubleday.

Kato, Genchi, and Shoyu Hanayama. 1988. *A Historical Study of the Religious Development of Shintō*. New York, Westport, and London: Greenwood Press.

Kawase, Kazuma. 1968. *Zen to Teien* [Zen and Gardens]. Tōkyō: Kōdansha.

Keane, Marc Peter. 2002. *The Art of Setting Stones and Other Writings from the Japanese Garden*. Berkeley: Stone Bridge Press.

Keane, Marc P., and Jiro Takei. 2001. *Sakuteiki: Visions of the Japanese Garden*. Boston: Charles E. Tuttle.

———. 1996. *Japanese Garden Design*. Photographs by Ōhashi Hazurō, drawings by the author. Rutland, VT, and Tōkyō: Charles E. Tuttle.

Kibunjia, Mzalendo. 1994. "Pliocene archaeological occurrences in the Lake Turkana basin." *Human Evolution* 27:159–171.

Kidder Jr., Edward J. 1985. *The Art of Japan*. New York: Park Lane.

Kino, Kazuyoshi. 1978. "Meisō to Sansui no Bi [The High-Ranked Priest and the Beauty of Nature]." In *Tanbo Nippon no Niwa* [Research on Japanese Gardens] 7:65–74. Kyōto: Shōgakukan.

Kishibe, Shigeo. 1984. *The Traditional Music of Japan*. Tōkyō: Ongaku no Tomosha.

Kitagawa, Joseph M. 1980. "A Past of Things Present: Notes on Major Motifs of Early Japanese Religions." *History of Religions*: 27–42.

Kitao, T. Kaori. 1985. "Rocks, Islands, Mountains and the Japanese Garden." *Brooklyn Botanic Garden Record* 41(3):5–8.

Knight, Michael. 1992. *East Asian Lacquers in the Collection of the Seattle Art Museum*. Seattle: Seattle Art Museum.

Kohn, Michael H. 1991. *The Shambhala Dictionary of Buddhism and Zen*. Boston: Shambhala Publications.

Koren, Leonard. 1994. *Wabi, Sabi, for Artists, Designers, Poets, and Philosophers*. Berkeley: Stone Bridge Press.

Kraft, Kenneth. 1981. "Musō Kokushi's 'Dialogues in a Dream': Selections." *The Eastern Buddhist* (1)14:75–93.

Kramer, Samuel Noah. 1963. *The Sumerians: Their History, Culture, and Character*. Chicago: University of Chicago Press.

Kramrisch, Stella. 1976. *The Hindu Temple*. Delhi: Motilal Banarsidass.

Krishna, Gopi. 1971. *Kundalini: The Evolutionary Energy in Man*. Berkeley: Shambhala.

Kuck, Loraine. 1968. *The World of the Japanese Garden: From Chinese Origins to Modern Landscape Art*. New York and Tōkyō:

Walker and Weatherhill.

———. 1940. *The Art of Japanese Gardens*. New York: John Day.

Kuitert, Wybe. 1988. *Themes, Scenes, and Taste in the History of Japanese Garden Art*. Amsterdam: J. C. Gieben.

Kuroda, Toshio. 1981. "Shintō in the History of Japanese Religion." *Journal of Japanese Studies* 7(1):1–21.

Ladner, Gerhart B. 1953. "The Concept of the Image in the Greek Fathers and the Byzantine Iconoclastic Controversy." *Dumbarton Oaks Papers* (Number 7). Washington, DC: Committee on Publications, Dumbarton Oaks Research Library and Collections, Harvard University.

Lai, Whalen. 1979. "Ch'an Metaphors: Waves, Waters, Mirror, Lamp." *Philosophy East and West* 29(3):243–54.

Lawlor, Robert. 1982. *Sacred Geometry*. London and New York: Thames and Hudson.

——— . 1980. "Ancient Temple Architecture." *Lindisfarne Letter #10, Geometry and Architecture*. Pp. 33–99. Grand Rapids: Phanes Press.

Lehrer, John. 1990. *Turtles and Tortoises*. New York: Mallard Press.

Leonard, George. 1978. *The Silent Pulse: A Search for the Perfect Rhythm That Exists in Each of Us*. New York: E. P. Dutton.

Lessa, William A. 1968. *Chinese Body Divination: Its Forms, Affinities, and Functions*. Los Angeles: United World.

Levin, Flora R. 1994. *The Manual of Harmonics of Nicomachus the Pythagorean*. Grand Rapids:

Phanes Press.

Lewin, Roger. 1981. "Ethiopian Stone Tools are World's Oldest Authors." *Science*. Volume 211 (4484): 806–7.

Little, Stephen. 1988. *Realm of the Immortals: Daoism in the Arts of China*. Cleveland: Cleveland Museum of Art and Bloomington: Indiana University Press.

Loewe, Michael, and Carmen Blacker, editors. 1981. *Oracles and Divination*. Boulder, CO: Shambhala.

Lyons, Elizabeth, and Heather Peters. 1985. *Buddhism: History and Diversity of a Great Tradition*. Philadelphia: University Museum, University of Pennsylvania.

Mabbett, I. W. 1981. "The Symbolism of Mount Meru." *History of Religions* 23: 64–83.

Maeda, Taiji. 1960. *Japanese Decorative Design*. Tōkyō: Japan Travel Bureau.

Maquet, Jacques. 1986. *The Aesthetic Experience: An Anthropologist Looks at the Visual Arts*. New Haven: Yale University Press.

Marc, Oliver. 1977. *The Psychology of the House*. London: Thames and Hudson.

Margulis, Lynn, and Dorian Sagan. 1995. *What Is Life?* Berkeley: University of California Press.

Masami, Eyama. 1942. "Teien Keitai no Kyūmei [A Study of Styles of Gardens]." *Teien* 24:88–98.

Mason, Penelope. 1993. *History of Japanese Art*. New York: Harry N. Abrams.

Mass, Jeffrey P. 1982. *Court and Bakufu in Japan: Essays in Kamakura History*. New York and

London: Yale University Press.
———. 1979. *The Development of Kamakura Rule, 1180–1250: A History with Documents*. Stanford: Stanford University Press.
———, editor. 1997. *The Origins of Japan's Medieval World: Courtiers, Clerics, Warriors, and Peasants in the Fourteenth Century*. Stanford: Stanford University Press.

Matsubayashi, Kazuo. 1992. "Spirit of Place: The Modern Relevance of an Ancient Idea." In *The Power of Place: Sacred Ground in Natural and Human Environments*. James A. Swan, editor. Pp. 334–46. Wheaton: Quest Books.

McAlpine, Helen, and William McAlpine. 1958. *Japanese Tales and Legends*. London: Oxford University Press.

McCullough, Helen Craig, translator. 1990. *The Taiheiki: A Chronicle of Medieval Japan*. New York: Columbia University Press.

McDougall, William. 1961. *Body and Mind: A History and Defense of Animism*. Boston: Beacon Press.

McRae, John R. 1986. *The Northern School and the Formation of Early Ch'an Buddhism*. Honolulu: University of Hawaii Press.

Merwin, W. S., and Soiku Shigematsu. 1989. *Sun at Midnight, by Musō Soseki: Poems and Sermons*. San Francisco: North Point Press.
———. 1987. "The Poems of Zen Master Musō." *The American Poetry Review* (March/April): 25–32.

Minakami, Tsutomu. 1976. "Tenryū-ji Gen'ei 〖Tenryū-ji, an Illusion〗." In *Koji Junrei Kyōto* 〖Pilgrimage to Old Temples of Kyōto〗: *Tenryū-ji*. Tsutomu Minakami and Bokuō Seki, editors. Pp. 68–77. Kyōto: Tankōsha.

Minakami, Tsutomu, and Bokuō Seki, editors. 1976. *Koji Junrei Kyōto* 〖Pilgrimage to Old Temples of Kyōto〗: *Tenryū-ji*. Kyōto: Tankōsha.

Miura, Isshu, and Ruth Fuller Sasaki. 1966. *Zen Dust: The History of the Koan Study in Rinzai (Lin chi) Zen*. New York: Harcourt Brace.
———. 1965. *The Zen Koan: Its History and Use in Rinzai Zen*. New York: Harcourt, Brace and World.

Moir, Julie, and Renny Merritt. 1977. "Kinsaku Nakane: Interviewing a Teacher and Garden Designer/Builder." *Landscape Architecture* (March):140–48.

Mori, Osamu. 1960. *Nippon no Niwa* 〖Japanese Gardens〗. Tōkyō: Asahi Shinbun.

Mori, Yutaka. 1988. "A Magnificence of Dragons." *Japan Quarterly* (April–June):163–70

Morris, Ivan T. 1964. *The World of the Shining Prince: Court Life in Ancient Japan*. New York: Knopf.

Morse, Edward. 1972. *Japanese Homes and their Surroundings*. Rutland, VT, and Tōkyō: Charles E. Tuttle.

Mosher, Gouverneur. 1964. *Kyōto: A Contemplative Guide*. Rutland, VT, and Tōkyō: Charles E. Tuttle.

Motoyama, Hiroshi. 1981. *Theories of the Chakras: Bridge to Higher*

Consciousness. Wheaton: Theo-
sophical Publishing House.

Mountain, Marian. 1982. *The Zen
Environment: The Impact on Zen
Meditation*. New York: William
Morrow.

Munsterburg, Hugo. 1971. *Dragons
in Chinese Art*. New York: China House Gallery.

Muraoka, Tsunetsugu. 1988. *Studies in Shinto Thought*. Westport,
CT: Greenwood Press.

Murphy, Gardner, and Lois B. Murphy, editors. 1968. *Asian Psychology*. New York: Basic Books.

Myokyo-ni (the Venerable Irmgard
Schloegl). 1987. *The Zen Way*.
London: The Zen Center and
Boston: Charles E. Tuttle.

Nakane, Kinsaku. 1970a "Character
of Japanese Gardens." *Chanoyu
Quarterly* I (3):16–27.

———. 1970b "Zen and Japanese
Gardens." *Chanoyu Quarterly* I
(4):43–47.

Naramoto, Tatsuya. 1978. *Tenryū-ji*
[Temple of the Heavenly Drag-
on]. Kyōto: Nakanishi Toshio,
Tōyō Bunka-Sha.

———. 1976. "Watashi o to,
Tenryū-ji [Tenryū-ji, and Me]."
In *Koji Junrei Kyōto* [Pilgrimage
to Old Temples of Kyōto]. Tsutomu Minakami and Bokuō Seki,
editors. Volume 4: *Tenryū-ji*. Pp.
26–31 Kyōto: Tankōsha.

Nasr, Seyyed Hossein. 1981. *Knowledge and the Sacred*. New York:
Crossroads.

Naumann, Nelly. 2000. *Japanese
Prehistory: The Material and
Spiritual Culture of the Jōmon
Period*. Harrassowitz Verlag:
Wiesbaden.

Neruda, Pablo. 1970. *Stones of the
Sky* [Las Piedras del Cielo].
James Nolan, translator. Port
Townsend, WA: Copper Canyon
Press.

Newcomb, Franc J., and Gladys A.
Reichard. 1975. *Sandpaintings
of the Navaho Shooting Chant*.
New York: Dover Publications.

Newman, Paul. 1979. *The Hill of
the Dragon: An Inquiry into the
Nature of Dragon Legends*. Bath:
Pitman Press.

Newsom, Samuel, and Kanto Shi-
gemori. 1988. *Japanese Garden
Construction*. Poughkeepsie,
NY: Apollo.

———. 1960. *Japanese Gardens: A
Guide to Form and Serenity in
Contemporary Living*. Tōkyō:
Tōkyō News Service.

Nishimura, Eshin; Giei Satō; and
Bardwell L. Smith. 1973. *Unsui:
A Diary of Zen Monastic Life*.
Honolulu: University Press of
Hawaii.

Nitschke, Günter. 1993. *Japanese
Gardens: Right Angle and Natu-
ral Form*. Cologne: Benedikt
Taschen.

———. 1987. "Space Tunnels:
Routes of Passage to Places of
Stillness." *Kyōto Journal* (Spring):
31–33.

Okamoto, Toyo, and Gisei Taka-
kuwa . 1962. *Zen no Niwa* [Zen
Gardens], Volume 2. Pp.11–18.
Tōkyō: Mitsumura Suiko Shoin.

Ono, Sokyo. 1962. *The Kami Way*.
Rutland, VT, and Tōkyō:
Charles E. Tuttle.

Orsi, Robert A. 2005. *Between Heav-
en and Earth: The Religious
Worlds People Make and the
Scholars Who Study Them*. Princeton: Princeton University Press.

Ōta, Hirotarō, Takaaki Matsushita, and Masao Tanaka. 1967. *Zendera to Sekitei* [*Zen Temples and Rock Gardens*]. Tōkyō: Soka Tetsuo, Shōgakukan.

Ōta, Yōko. 1991. *Japanese Women Writers*. Noriko Mizuta Lippit and Kyoko Iriye Selden, translators and editors. Armonk, NY: M. E. Sharpe.

Paine, Robert Treat, and Alexander Soper. 1955. *The Art and Architecture of Japan*. Middlesex: Penguin Books.

Paul, Diana Y. 1985. *Women in Buddhism: Images of the Feminine in Mahāyāna Tradition*. Berkeley: Asian Humanities Press.

Paul, Robert A. 1976. "The Sherpa Temple as a Model of the Psyche." *American Ethnologist* 3:131–46.

Picken, Stuart D. B. 1994. *Essentials of Shintō: An Analytical Guide to Principal Teachings*. Westport, CT, and London: Greenwood Press.

———. 1980. *Shintō: Japan's Spiritual Roots*. Tōkyō, New York, and San Francisco: Kodansha International.

Piggott, Juliet. 1983. *Japanese Mythology*. New York: Peter Bedrick.

Pilgrim, Richard B. 1986. "Intervals (*Ma*) in Space and Time: Foundations for a Religio-Aesthetic Paradigm in Japan." *History of Religions* 25:255–77.

———. 1981. *Buddhism and the Arts of Japan*. Chambersburg: Anima Books.

Ponsonby-Fane, R. A. B. 1956. *Kyōto: The Old Capitol of Japan (794-1869)*. Kyōto: Ponsonby Memorial Society.

Portman, Adolf. 1964. "Metamorphosis in Animals: The Transformation of the Individual and the Type." In *Man and Transformation*. Joseph Campbell, editor. Pp. 297–325. Princeton: Princeton University Press.

Potter, Jack M. 1970. "Wind, Water, Bones and Souls: The Religious World of the Cantonese Peasant." *Journal of Oriental Studies* 8:139–53.

Preston, David. 1988. *The Social Organization of Zen Practice*. New York: Cambridge University Press.

Purce, Jill. 1975. *The Mystic Spiral*. London: Thames and Hudson.

Raine, Kathleen. 1967. *Defending Ancient Springs*. London and New York: Oxford University Press.

Rawson, Philip, and Laszlo Legeza. 1979. *Tao: The Chinese Philosophy of Time and Change*. New York: Thames and Hudson.

Rickman, H. P., editor. 1976. *Wilhelm Dilthey: Selected Writings*. Cambridge: Cambridge University Press.

Rowland, Jr., Benjamin. 1963. *The Evolution of the Buddha Image*. New York: The Asia Society, Harry N. Abrams.

Rowley, George. 1959. *Principles of Chinese Painting*. Princeton: Princeton University Press.

Rudhyar, Dane. 1982. *The Magic of Tone and the Art of Music*. Boulder, CO: Shambhala.

Sadler, A. L. 1962. *A Short History of Japan*. London: Angus and Robertson.

Saito, Katsuo. 1969. *Japanese Gar-*

dening Hints. Tōkyō: Japan Publications Trading Company.

Saito, Katsuo, and Sadaji Wada. 1964. *Magic of Trees and Stones: Secrets of Japanese Gardening.* New York: JPT Book Company.

Sallis, John. 1994. *Stone.* Bloomington and Indianapolis: Indiana University Press.

Sandars, N. K., translator. 1960. *The Epic of Gilgamesh.* Middlesex and New York: Penguin Books.

Sansom, George. 1961. *A History of Japan, 1334–1615.* Stanford: Stanford University Press.

———. 1958. *A History of Japan to 1334.* Stanford: Stanford University Press.

Sato, Koji. 1984. *The Zen Life.* Photographs by Sosei Kuzunishi. New York, Kyōto, and Tōkyō: Weatherhill/Tankosha.

Sawyers, Claire E. 1985. "Working for Sone-san at Tenryū-ji." *Brooklyn Botanic Garden Record* 41:67–71.

Schaarschmidt-Richter, Irmtraud, and Osamu Mori. 1979. *Japanese Gardens.* Janet Seligman, translator. New York: William Morrow.

Schafer, Edward H. 1973. *The Divine Woman: Dragon Ladies and Rain Maidens in T'ang Literature.* Berkeley: University of California Press.

Schloegl, Irmgard (the Venerable Myokyo-ni). 1976. *The Zen Teaching of Rinzai* [*The Record of Rinzai*]. Berkeley: Shambhala.

———. 1975. *The Record of Rinzai.* London: The Buddhist Society.

Schwartzberg, Joseph E. 1992. "Cosmographical Mapping." In *The History of Cartography,* Volume 2, Book 1: *Cartography in the Traditional Islamic and South Asian Societies.* J. B. Harley and David Woodward, editors. Pp. 332–83. Chicago and London: University of Chicago Press.

Scott, Geraldine Knight, and Mel Scott. 1982. "By Invitation Only: Limiting Access to Japan's Gardens." *Landscape Architecture* 72:80–82.

Seki, Bokuō. 1976. "Tenryū-ji no Rekishi to Zen [History of Tenryū-ji and Zen]." In *Koji Junrei Kyōto* [Pilgrimage to Old Temples of Kyōto]: *Tenryū-ji.* Tsutomu Minakami and Bokuo Seki, editors. Pp. 78–113. Kyōto: Tankōsha.

Sekida, Katsuki. 1975. *Zen Training: Methods and Philosophy.* New York and Tōkyō: Weatherhill.

Semaw, S.; P. Renne; J. W. K. Harris; C. S. Feibel; R. L. Bernor; N. Fesseha; and K. Mowbray. 1997. "2.5-million-year-old Stone Tools from Gona, Ethiopia." *Nature,* Volume 385 (6614):333–36.

Senda, Minoru. 1988. "Taoist Roots in Japanese Culture." *Japan Quarterly* 35(2):133–38.

Shaffer, Aaron. 1974. *Sumerian Sources of Tablet XII of the Epic of Gilgamesh.* Ann Arbor: University Microfilms.

Shaner, David Edward. 1989. "The Japanese Experience of Nature." In *Nature in Asian Traditions of Thought: Essays in Environmental Philosophy.* J. Baird Callicott and Roger T. Ames, editors. Pp. 163–82. Albany: State University of New York Press.

———. 1985. *The Bodymind Experience in Japanese Buddhism: A*

Phenomenological Approach. Albany: State University of New York Press.

Shigemori, Kanto. 1957. *The Artistic Gardens of Japan: History of Japanese Gardens.* Thomas Hatashita, translator. Tōkyō: Rikōtosho.

Shigemori, Mirei. 1936–39. *Nihon Teienshi Zukan* [Illustrated History of Japanese Gardens]. Volume 2, Part 2: *Kamakura and Yoshino Periods.* Tōkyō: Yūkōsha.

Shimizu, S. 1981. "Seasons and Places in Yamato Landscape and Poetry." *Ars Orientalis* XII:1–14.

Sinclair, Kevin. 1987. *The Yellow River: A 5000 Year Journey through China.* Los Angeles: Knapp Press.

Singer, Kurt. 1973. *Mirror, Sword, and Jewel: The Geometry of Japanese Life.* Tōkyō, New York, and San Francisco: Kodansha International.

Skinner, Stephen. 1982. *The Living Earth Manual of Feng Shui, Chinese Geomancy.* London: Routledge and Kegan Paul.

Slawson, David. 1987. *Secret Teachings in the Art of Japanese Gardens: Design Principles / Aesthetic Values.* Tōkyō and New York: Kodansha International.

———. 1985. *Secret Teachings in the Art of Japanese Gardens: Illustrations for Designing Mountain, Water, and Hillside Field Landscapes.*" Ann Arbor: University Microfilms International.

Smith, G. Elliot. 1919. *The Evolution of the Dragon.* Manchester: Manchester University Press.

Smith, Huston. 2001. *Why Religion Matters: The Fate of the Human Spirit in an Age of Disbelief.* San Francisco: Harper Collins.

Snodgrass, Adrian. 1988. *The Symbolism of the Stupa.* Ithaca, NY: Cornell University, Studies on Southeastern Asia.

Soper, Alexander C. 1942. "The Rise of Yamato-e." *Art Bulletin* 24:351–79.

Suzuki, Daisetz Teitaro. 1962. *The Essentials of Zen Buddhism.* New York: E. P. Dutton.

———. 1959. *The Training of the Zen Buddhist Monk.* New York: University Books.

Suzuki, Shunryu. 1970. *Zen Mind: Beginner's Mind; Informal Talks on Zen Meditation and Practice.* New York and Tōkyō: Weatherhill.

Tachibana, Toshitsuna. 1976. *Sakuteiki* [Book of the Garden]. Shigemaru Shimoyama, translator. Tōkyō: Town and City Planners.

Takakuwa, Gisei. 1962. *The Zen Gardens,* II. Kyōto: Mitsumura Suiko Shoin.

Takakuwa, Gisei, and Kiichi Asano. 1973. *Japanese Gardens Revisited.* Rutland, VT, and Tōkyō: Charles E. Tuttle.

Takeda, Yoshifumi. 1993. "Falling Flowers Rising to the Threshold of the Eye." *Kyōto Journal* 25:27.

Takei, Jiro, and Marc Peter Keane. 2001. *Sakuteiki: Visions of the Japanese Garden.* Rutland, VT, and Tōkyō: Charles E. Tuttle Co.

Tamaki, Takehiko. 1977. *Nishikigoi* [Fancy Koi]. Shimonoseki City: Shunposha Photo Printing Company.

Tamamura, Takeji. 1958. *Musō Kokushi* [Musō, National Teacher]. Kyōto: Heirakuji Shoten.

Tange, Kenzo, and Noboru Kawazoe. 1965. *Ise: Prototype of Japanese Architecture*. Cambridge: MIT Press.

Tanizaki, Jun'ichirō. 1993. *The Makioka Sisters*. New York: Alfred A. Knopf.

Tatsui, Matsunosuke. 1942. "Musō Kokushi to Zōen [Musō Kokushi and Garden Making]." *Teien* 24: 138–42.

———. 1939. "Tenryū-ji no Teien [The Garden of Tenryu Temple]." *Teien* 21:350–52.

Tellenbach, Hubertus, and Bin Kimura. 1989. "The Japanese Concept of Nature." In J. Baird Callicott and Roger T. Ames, editors. *Nature in Asian Traditions of Thought: Essays in Environmental Philosophy*. Pp. 153–62. Albany: State University of New York Press.

ten Grotenhuis, Elizabeth. 1999. *Japanese Mandalas: Representations of Sacred Geography*. Honolulu: University of Hawai'i Press.

Tenryū-ji Daihonzan [Tenryū-ji, Head Temple of the Tenryū-ji School of Buddhism]. 1992. *Tenryū-ji*. Kyōto: Saiko.

———. 1980. *Tenryū-ji*. Kyōto: Tenryū-ji Teaching Department.

Thompson, D'Arcy Wentworth. 1961. *On Growth and Form*. Cambridge: Cambridge University Press.

Tokumaru, Yoshihiko. 1990. "Japanese Music As World Music." *The Japan Foundation Newsletter* 18(2)1–6.

Tonomura, Hitomi. 1997. "Revisioning Women in the Post-Kamakura Age." In *The Origins of Japan's Medieval World: Courtiers, Warriors, and Peasants in the Fourteenth Century*. Jeffrey P. Mass, editor. Pp. 138–70. Stanford: Stanford University Press.

Tripp, Raymond Paul. 1983. *More About the Fight with the Dragon*. Lanham, MD: University Press of America.

Tschumi, Christian, and Markuz Wernli Saito. 2005. *Mirei Shigemori, Modernizing the Japanese Garden*. Berkeley: Stone Bridge Press.

Tsunoda, Ryūsaku; William Theodore deBarry, and Donald Keene, compilers. 1958. *Sources of Japanese Tradition*. Volume 1. New York: Columbia University Press.

Tuan, Yi-fu. 1979. *Landscapes of Fear*. New York: Pantheon Books.

———. 1977. *Space and Place: The Perspective of Experience*. Minneapolis: University of Minnesota Press.

Turner, Harold W. 1979. *From Temple to Meeting House: The Phenomenology of Places of Worship*. The Hague: Mouton.

Turner, Victor W., and Edward M. Bruner, editors. 1986. *The Anthropology of Experience*. Urbana and Chicago: University of Illinois Press.

Ueda, Makoto. 1967. *Literary and Art Theories on Japan*. Cleveland: The Press of Western Reserve University.

van de Wetering, Janwillem. 1974. *The Empty Mirror: Experiences in a Japanese Zen Monastery*. Boston: Houghton Mifflin.

Vatsyayan, Kapila. 1991. *Concepts*

of Space, Ancient and Modern.
New Delhi: Abhinav Publica-
tions, Indira Gandhi National
Centre for the Arts.

Victoria, Brian. 1997. Zen at
War. New York and Tōkyō:
Weatherhill.

Volwahsen, Andreas. 1969. Living
Architecture: Indian. New York:
Grosset and Dunlap.

Wales, H. G. Quaritch. 1953. "The
Sacred Mountain in Old Asiatic
Religion." Journal of the Royal
Asiatic Society of Great Britain
and London:23–30.

Waley, Arthur, translator. 1960. The
Tale of Genji, A Novel in Six
Parts. New York: The Modern
Library.

———. 1925. The Tale of Genji by
Lady Murasaki. London: George
Allen and Unwin.

Walker, Alice. 1989. Temple of My
Familiar. San Diego: Harcourt
Brace Jovanovich.

Warner, Langdon. 1952. The Enduring Art of Japan. Cambridge:
Harvard University Press.

Watanabe, Yasutada. 1974. Shintō
Art: Ise and Izumo Shrines. New
York and Tōkyō: Weatherhill/
Heibonsha.

Weinberg, Francis M. 1986. The
Cave: The Evolution of a Metaphoric Field from Homer to Aris-
to. New York: Peter Lang.

Wheatley, Paul. 1971. The Pivot of
the Four Quarters: A Prelimi-
nary Inquiry Into the Origin and
Character of the Ancient Chinese
City. Chicago: Aldine.

Williams, Paul. 1989. Mahayana
Buddhism: The Doctrinal Foun-
dation. London and New York:
Routledge.

Wiseman, Donald J. 1983. "Meso-
potamian Gardens." Anatolian
Studies 33:137–44.

Wolkstein, Diane, and Samuel Noah
Kramer. 1983. Inanna, Queen
of Heaven and Earth: Her Sto-
ries and Hymns from Sumer.
New York: Harper and Row,
Publishers.

Wu, Nelson I. 1963. Chinese and
Indian Architecture: The City
of Man, the Mountain of God,
and the Realm of the Immortals.
New York: George Braziller.

Yanagi, Sōetsu. 1972. The Unknown
Craftsman: A Japanese Insight
into Beauty. Tōkyō and New
York: Kodansha International.

Yang, Hongxun. 1982. The Classi-
cal Gardens of China: History
and Design Techniques. Wang
Zheng Gui, translator. New
York and London: Van Nostrand
Reinhold.

Yetts, Major W. Perceval. 1919.
"The Chinese Isles of the Blest."
Folklore 30:35–62.

Yoshikawa, Isao. 1971. "Karesansui no Niwa [Waterless
Gardens/'DryLandscape'
Gardens]." Nihon no Bijutsu
61:1–98.

Yoshioka, Toichi. 1984. Zen. Ōsaka:
Hoikusha.

Young, David E., and Jean-Guy Goulet, editors. 1994. Being Changed:
The Anthropology of Extraordinary Experience. Peterborough,
ON: Broadview Press.

Zuritsky, Joseph S. 1986. The World
of the Dragon and Tiger. Tōkyō:
Nara Institute of Fine Arts.

———. 1985. "Koi: The Colorful
Carp of Japan." Brooklyn Botanic
Garden Record 41(3):72–74.

INDEX

IMAGE CREDITS

The following photographs and illustrations are used with grateful acknowledgment of permission to reprint. All other photographs are by the author.

Figure 2: From *A History of Japan, 1334-1615*, by George Sansom (1961:42). Reprinted with the permission of Stanford University Press, Board of Trustees of the Leland Stanford Junior University.

Figures 6, 36, 41: From *Koji Junrei Kyōto* [Pilgrimage to Old Temples of Kyōto]: *Tenryū-ji*. Tsutomo Minakami and Bokuō Seki, editors (1976:flycover; Plate 14; flyleaf with superimposition of Figure 40 by the author). Reprinted with the permission of Tankōsha.

Figure 30: From *Japanese Gardens: Design and Meaning*, by Mitchell Bring and Josse Wayembergh (1981:2, with added line and shading). Reprinted with the permission of McGraw-Hill Education, McGraw-Hill Companies.

Figure 33: From *Buddhism: History and Diversity of a Great Tradition*, by Elizabeth Lyons and Heather Peters (1985:6). Reprinted with the permission of the University of Pennsylvania Museum of Archaeology and Anthropology.

Figure 34: From *The Lesson of Japanese Architecture*, by Jiro Harada (1936:56).

Figure 37: From *The Dragon: Nature of Spirit; Spirit of Nature*, by Francis Huxley (1979:59). Reprinted with the permission of Freer Gallery of Art and Arthur M. Sackler Gallery, Smithsonian Institution. Gift of Charles Lang Freer, F1905.230.

Figure 38: From *The Book of the Dragon*, by Judy Allen and Jeanne Griffiths (1979:45). Photograph by Thierry Ollivier. Reprinted with the permission of Art Resource, MG18127.

Figure 40: From *Five Mountains: The Rinzai Zen Monastic Institution in Medieval Japan*, by Martin Collcutt (1981:185, with lettering added by the author). Reprinted with the permission of the Harvard University East Asia Center.

Figures 52, 56, 64, 74, 97, 108, 118, 129: From *The Artistic Gardens of Japan*, by Kanto Shigemori (1957:38 with line definition, shading, annotation, dots, and numbers added by the author). Reprinted with the permission of Rikōtosho.

Figures 57, 58: From *The Aesthetic Experience: An Anthropologist Looks at the Visual Arts*, by Jacques Maquet (1986:114). Reprinted with the permission of Yale University Press.

Figures 75, 84: From "Cosmographical Mapping," by Joseph E. Schwartzberg (1992: 370, 342), in *The History of Cartography*, Volume 2, Book 1: *Cartography in the Traditional Islamic and South Asian Societies*, edited by J. B. Harley and David Woodward. Reprinted with the permission of University of Chicago Press.

Figure 78: From *Realm of the Immortals: Daoism in the Arts of China*, by Stephen Little (1988:48). Photograph by Robert Newcombe. Reprinted with the permission of Nelson-Atkins Museum of Art, Kansas City. Purchase acquired through the Fortieth Anniversary Fund, F75-43.

Figures 81, 103, 145, 148: By a priest within the temple, with shading for emphasis added by the author.

Figure 82: From *The Art of Japan*, by Edward J. Kidder Jr. (1985:42). Reprinted with the permission of Shōgakukan Publishing Company.

Figures 92-94: From *East Asian Lacquers in the Collection of the Seattle Art Museum*, by Michael Knight (1992:19). Photograph by Paul Macapia. Reprinted with the permission of Seattle Art Museum. Gift of Mrs. Donald E. Frederick.

Figure 114: From *Tenryū-ji*, by Tenryū-ji Teaching Department (1980:11). Photograph by Katsutoshi Okada. Reprinted with the permission of Reverend Masataka Toga, Tenryū-ji.

Figures 124, 135: From *Tao: The Chinese Philosophy of Time and Change*, by Philip Rawson and Laszlo Legeza (1979:Figure 58; Figure 7). Reprinted with the permission of Thames and Hudson.

Figures 136, 139, 146: Drawing by Wybe Kuitert (1988:88). Reprinted with the permission of Professor Kuitert.

Figure 143: From *Japan*, by Martin Hürlimann and Francis King (1970:63). Reprinted with the permission of Thames and Hudson.